What Your Colleagues A

James Nottingham and Bosse Larsson offer an important and useful new addition to the ongoing conversation about mindset first introduced by Carol Dweck. Too often, theories such as mindset get reduced down to the simplest dichotomies and ideologies. Here, Nottingham and Larsson challenge our own mindset about the very idea of mindset theory itself, showing us what is possible if we really understand the theory and use it to challenge ourselves and our students.

–Jim Burke
Teacher, Burlingame High School
Author, Common Core Companion Series

James Nottingham's work on Challenging Learning is a critical element of creating Visible Learners. This new series will help teachers hone the necessary pedagogical skills of dialogue, feedback, questioning, and mindset. There's no better resource to encourage all learners to know and maximize their impact!

–John Hattie
Professor and Director
Melbourne Education Research Institute
University of Melbourne

Mindset is a word that has been thrown around a great deal over the years. Unfortunately, most educators who use the word didn't understand the real context behind it. Nottingham and Larsson not only focus on the nuances of mindset, but offer practical strategies on how to use the research correctly so students can succeed! Challenging Mindset will be an important read for a very long time.

–Peter DeWitt, Ed.D
Author, Collaborative Leadership
Blogger, Finding Common Ground
Facilitator of Learning

James Nottingham and Bosse Larsson have the unique ability to activate the thinking of their readers by bridging the divide between research and practice. The 'Now Try This' sections encourage readers to engage with heart, head, and hand to relate what they are learning to their current practices and to share those ides with colleagues. They have masterfully deepened our understanding of Carol Dweck's work and aligned her thinking to their work around The Learning Challenge.

–Julie Smith
Author, Evaluating Instructional Leadership
Pacific City, OR

Nottingham and Larsson provide a much needed clarification of growth mindset, grounded in research and illustrated through relevant classroom examples. The authors provide practical tools and strategies to support educators in the correct application of mindset to impact student learning. A must read for all educators!

–Cathy Lassiter
Author, Everyday Courage for School Leaders
Virginia Beach, VA

CHALLENGING
MINDSET

Challenging Learning Series

The Learning Challenge: How to Guide Your Students Through the Learning Pit to Achieve Deeper Understanding

by James Nottingham

Challenging Mindset: Examining Why a Growth Mindset Makes a Difference to Learning—and What to Do When It Doesn't

by James Nottingham and Bosse Larsson

Challenging Learning Through Dialogue: Strategies to Engage Your Students and Develop Their Language of Learning

by James Nottingham, Jill Nottingham and Martin Renton

Challenging Learning Through Feedback: How to Get the Type, Tone and Quality of Feedback Right Every Time

by James Nottingham and Jill Nottingham

Challenging Learning Through Questioning

by Martin Renton

Learning Challenge Lessons, Elementary: 20 Lessons to Guide Young Learners Through the Learning Pit

by Jill Nottingham, James Nottingham, Mark Bollom, Joanne Nugent and Lorna Pringle

Learning Challenge Lessons, Secondary English Language Arts

by Jill Nottingham, James Nottingham, Mark Bollom, Joanne Nugent and Lorna Pringle

Learning Challenge Lessons, Secondary Mathematics

by Jill Nottingham, James Nottingham, Mark Bollom, Joanne Nugent and Lorna Pringle

Learning Challenge Lessons, Secondary STEM

by Jill Nottingham, James Nottingham, Mark Bollom, Joanne Nugent and Lorna Pringle

CHALLENGING MINDSET

*Why a Growth Mindset Makes a Difference in Learning –
and What to Do When It Doesn't*

JAMES NOTTINGHAM • BOSSE LARSSON

CORWIN
A SAGE Publishing Company

FOR INFORMATION:

Corwin
A SAGE Company
2455 Teller Road
Thousand Oaks, California 91320
(800) 233-9936
www.corwin.com

SAGE Publications Ltd.
1 Oliver's Yard
55 City Road
London EC1Y 1SP
United Kingdom

SAGE Publications India Pvt. Ltd.
B 1/I 1 Mohan Cooperative Industrial Area
Mathura Road, New Delhi 110 044
India

SAGE Publications Asia-Pacific Pte. Ltd.
3 Church Street
#10-04 Samsung Hub
Singapore 049483

Acquisitions Editor: Ariel Bartlett
Editorial Assistant: Jessica Vidal
Production Editor: Victoria Nicholas
Typesetter: C&M Digitals (P) Ltd.
Proofreader: Sharon Cawood
Cover Designer: Janet Kiesel
Marketing Manager: Margaret O'Connor

Printed in the United States of America

ISBN 978-1-5063-7662-2

This book is printed on acid-free paper.

Certified Chain of Custody
Promoting Sustainable Forestry
www.sfiprogram.org
SFI-01268

SFI label applies to text stock

18 19 20 21 22 10 9 8 7 6 5 4 3 2 1

CONTENTS

PART VI WHAT NEXT? 167

Chapter 11: Growth Mindset Lessons 169

References 191

Index 195

LIST OF FIGURES

THE CHALLENGING LEARNING STORY

By James Nottingham

Challenging Learning was the title I used for my first book back in 2010. I chose the title because it brought together two key themes of my work and it gave a relevant double meaning – challenging the way in which learning takes place *and* showing how to make learning more challenging (and therefore more compelling).

More recently, 'Challenging Learning' is the name my co-founder Jill Nottingham and I have given to a group of organisations set up in seven countries across Europe and Australasia. These educational companies bring together some of the very best teachers and leaders we know. Together we transform the most up-to-date and impressive research into best pedagogical practices for schools, kindergartens and colleges.

This book continues in the same tradition: challenging learning and making learning more challenging. The main difference between this book and the original Challenging Learning title is that this one focuses deeply on one topic – mindset – rather than summarising many of the ideas connected with feedback, attitudes, challenge, thinking skills and self-efficacy.

As you read this book, you will notice that Bosse and I have made many references to 'teachers' and 'teaching'. When we have done so, it is *not* our intention to exclude other staff working in education, nor indeed anybody else involved in the education of others. We have simply used the terms 'teacher' and 'teaching' as shorthand for the role and pedagogy of someone engaged in helping others to learn.

Throughout the book, there are some 'Now Try This' sections. We have written these to encourage you to think about current practice and to share those ideas with your colleagues. Chatting with someone else about what you think works well (and how you know it does), what you would like to change, and, in an ideal world, what you would like your pedagogy to be like, will definitely help you to use this book as the reflective journal it is intended to be.

There are also margin notes at the side of many of the pages. These serve two purposes: the first is to help you identify key points even if you don't have time to read the full book just yet. The second reason is to encourage you to add your own margin notes. If these focus on repertoire and judgement, then this should serve you well with the professional learning this book is written to support.

A broad repertoire – or tool kit of teaching strategies as some authors call it – is crucial to improving pedagogy. Yet repertoire alone is not sufficient; good judgement is also needed. So, whereas the strategies in this book should be sufficient to broaden your repertoire, your good judgement will come from reflections on your own experiences, from trying out the new strategies with your students and from dialogue with your colleagues. Our suggestions for review are there to help you with your reflections.

If you are a member of staff in an educational setting, then you are amongst the most powerful influences on student learning. Back when you were a secondary student and went from teacher to teacher, you knew exactly which member of staff had high expectations and which had low; which had a good sense of humour and which you suspected had not laughed since childhood. It is the same today. Your students know what your expectations and ethos are. So, it is not the government, students' parents nor the curriculum that sets the culture (though they all have influence). It is *you* who sets the culture and so it is *your* actions that count most.

With this book we aim to inspire you to ever more expert actions.

PREFACE

The purpose of this book is to answer questions about Carol Dweck's theory of mindset:

> What is 'mindset' and where does it come from?
>
> What difference does mindset make?
>
> Why are growth mindset interventions *not* working very well (yet)?
>
> When is a growth mindset most effective and how can you influence those conditions?
>
> How can you get yourself, students, your colleagues and your family into a growth mindset?

The term 'mindset' comes from the work of Carol S. Dweck, the Lewis and Virginia Eaton Professor of Psychology at Stanford University. Her bestselling book, *Mindset: The New Psychology of Success* (2006b) has sold over a million copies. In 2009, she received the E. L. Thorndike Award for Career Achievement in Educational Psychology. Previous winners include B. F. Skinner, Benjamin Bloom and Jean Piaget, so she is in good company.

From her decades of research, Professor Dweck has described two contrasting self-theories that she now calls 'fixed mindset' and 'growth mindset'.

People in a fixed mindset think of talents and intelligence as relatively stable and innate. People in a growth mindset think of talents and intelligence as highly responsive to nurture. They don't deny the role that genetics play but they see nature as the starting point rather than as the defining quality. Dweck examines the reasons why people get into these different mindsets and the impact that has on personality, motivation and development.

The popularity of Dweck's work is undeniable and yet the theory has been subjected to growing disquiet. Some commentators have complained that mindset equates success with effort; that Dweck overlooks the effects of genetics; and that her work is simply 'positive thinking' dressed up for the 21st century, wilfully ignoring the complex causes of accomplishment. The fact that Dweck has never put forward *any* of these over-simplifications doesn't seem to stop people asserting that she has. As is so often the case, too many people won't let facts spoil a great headline!

Some of the critics, having had their fill of sugar-coated renditions of life in a growth mindset, claim mindset is all based on a lie. It isn't. It is based on decades of precise, peer-reviewed, academic research. The problem is more to do with the *implementation* of a growth mindset: something seems to get lost in translation from research into practice. This book addresses why this is and what we can all do about it.

We have included the pros *and* the cons of mindset. We have examined what is great about mindset and looked at the problems of implementation and over-simplification. We show you why mindset does *not* matter so much when things are easy; that it is only when faced with challenges that your mindset really matters. We demonstrate that a parent's response to failure is arguably more important than their mindset when it comes to influencing their children's mindset. We show that you already hold a mindset, whether or not you like it. So, if you want to examine it and adjust it then this book should help you with that.

Most of the situations we examine are from the educational world. We make no apologies for that: we are both teachers at heart, with almost 60 years' teaching experience between us. However, parenting, business, sport and music also feature. We are both parents and one of us is a granddad; Bosse plays bass guitar to a level that his teachers would never have predicted; James has created a group of companies that now employs 30 people in six countries; both of us love our sport, although if we're honest only the elder of the two of us is any good at it. So, throughout this book, you will find examples from a whole range of contexts. We have also included observations from our travels with Carol Dweck, during three week-long tours together across Scandinavia and the UK, which have given us a rare depth of insight into the nuances and importance of her work.

We are absolutely delighted to say that Carol has also generously and thoughtfully given us feedback on the draft of this book so that what you have in front of you is the much-improved version of *Challenging Mindset*. Indeed, at some points in the text, you will find comments directly from Professor Dweck.

So, thank you for taking the time to join us on this journey. We hope you enjoy the ride!

James Nottingham and Bosse Larsson

January 2018

ACKNOWLEDGEMENTS

The authors owe a debt of gratitude to the following people for their critiques, contributions and encouragement:

Carol Dweck

Jill Nottingham

John Hattie

Ariel Curry

Mark Bollom

Marianne Miles

Lorna Pringle

Beccy Morley

George Telford

Marianne Skogvoll

Gerda Lundberg

The examples of progress shown in Chapter 6 came from:

Ava Nottingham, eldest daughter of James

Bente Bahrt, at Dronninggårdskolen in Rudersdal, DK

Jennie Carter at Highweek School in Newton Abbot, UK

Jill Harland at Brudenell Primary School in Leeds, UK

Marianne Skogvoll, Challenging Learning, Norway

Nana Roger Thunø at University College, Copenhagen, DK

Tom Savill at Dulwich Prep, London, UK

A big thank you for their support with design, layout and proofreading goes to:

Andrew Parsons

Åse Ranfelt

Astrid Holtz Yates

Dan Henderson

Deb Ions

Elaine Davies

Helen Richards

Lesley Roberts

Lisa Barrett

Marilyn Keenan

Martin Renton

Michael Dassa

Phil Thompson

Tom Burston

Be careful of your thoughts, for your thoughts become your words.

Be careful of your words, for your words become your actions.

Be careful of your actions, for your actions become your habits.

Be careful of your habits, for your habits become your character.

Be careful of your character, for your character becomes your destiny.

Chinese proverb, author unknown

ABOUT THE AUTHORS

James Nottingham is co-founder and director of Challenging Learning, a group of companies with 30 employees in six countries. His passion is in transforming the most up-to-date research into strategies that really work in the classroom. He is regarded by many as one of the most engaging, thought-provoking and inspirational speakers in education.

His first book, *Challenging Learning*, was published in 2010 and has received widespread critical acclaim. Since then, he has written six books for teachers, leaders, support staff and parents. These books share the best research and practice connected with learning, dialogue, feedback, the learning pit, early years education and growth mindset.

Before training to be a teacher, James worked on a pig farm, in the chemical industry, for the American Red Cross, and as a teaching assistant in a school for deaf children. At university, he gained a first-class honours degree in education (a major turnaround after having failed miserably at school). He then worked as a teacher and leader in primary and secondary schools in the UK before co-founding an award-winning, multi-million-pound regeneration project supporting education, public and voluntary organisations across north-east England.

Skolvärlden (Swedish Teaching Union) describes James as 'one of the most talked about names in the world of school development' and the *Observer* newspaper in the UK listed him amongst the Future 500 – a 'definitive list of the UK's most forward-thinking and brightest innovators'.

Bosse Larsson is a Swedish teacher, trainer and concept developer. He has extensive experience developing creative thinking and learning with primary and secondary students, and is a sought-after keynote speaker and workshop leader.

He started working as a science teacher more than 30 years ago and has, for over a decade, been supporting secondary school dropouts and students with special educational needs.

Responding to many requests to share his ideas, Bosse began his own educational consultancy in 2007 (www.tankvidare.nu). He is also a long-time consultant for Challenging Learning. Through this work, he aims to broaden, break and change thought patterns about education, organisation and leadership. He still works part-time in local schools where he collaborates with teams in action learning cycles and individual teachers through lesson planning and giving feedback after lesson observations.

Bosse has given presentations, keynotes and led workshops both nationally and internationally, and has worked with staff training from pre-school to further education. The main themes of his work focus on creativity, future skills, thinking habits, thinking tools, Dweck's mindset, metacognition, motivation and feedback.

This book is for Agnes

www.instagram.com/heja-agnes

WHAT IS MINDSET?

It was the best of times, it was the worst of times, it was the age of wisdom, it was the age of foolishness, it was the epoch of belief, it was the epoch of incredulity, it was the season of Light, it was the season of Darkness, it was the spring of hope, it was the winter of despair, we had everything before us, we had nothing before us, we were all going direct to Heaven, we were all going direct the other way – in short, the period was so far like the present period, that some of its noisiest authorities insisted on its being received, for good or for evil, in the superlative degree of comparison only.

Introduction to *A Tale of Two Cities*
by Charles Dickens (1859: 5)

A TALE OF
TWO MINDSETS

The terms 'fixed mindset' and 'growth mindset' come from the work of Carol S. Dweck, the Lewis and Virginia Eaton Professor of Psychology at Stanford University. They are based on decades of precise research into how people think about talents and success.

▶ **Figure 1: Carol Dweck at a Challenging Learning Conference, 2017**

Everyone has a mindset that shapes their personality, motivation and development.

After decades of careful and precise research, Carol Dweck has identified two main mindsets: a fixed mindset and a growth mindset.

Photograph by andrewbillingtonphotography.com

1.0 • DEFINITION OF MINDSET

> When someone is in a fixed mindset, they believe intelligence and abilities are innate.

A mindset is a self-perception or 'self-theory' that people hold about themselves.

Fixed Mindset: A fixed mindset refers to a belief that intelligence and abilities are relatively innate, changing very little over time. Someone in a fixed mindset is likely to think that they have 'always' been good at something (for example, 'I have always been good at art') or that they will 'never' be proficient at other things (for example, 'I don't have a mind for languages').

When responding to behaviour, someone in a fixed mindset would be likely to use generalisations that suggest a pattern of behaviour. For example, 'why do I *always* do that?'. Or when observing someone else, they might think, 'they always do that,' 'or that's just how they are'.

Growth Mindset: A growth mindset refers to a belief that intelligence and abilities can be 'grown' through experience, effort, strategy, and instruction and support from others. Genetics are seen as the starting point rather than the defining quality. When someone is in a growth mindset, they are likely to think that they have 'developed' their ability for some things (for example, 'I have developed my talent for public speaking') and that other talents are possible to develop or improve (for example, 'this is the year that I will learn to play the piano'). Similarly, when someone is in a growth mindset, they are more likely to think, 'I can help children learn to manage their impulsivity' rather than to think, 'that is *typical* of those children to overreact'.

Someone in a growth mindset would be less inclined to ascribe behaviour to personality, preferring instead to identify what can be done next to alter or reinforce the outcome. So, instead of saying, 'why are you such an inconsiderate person?' as they might when in a fixed mindset, they would be more inclined to ask, 'why did you do that just now?'

1.1 • A COMPARISON OF FIXED AND GROWTH MINDSETS

> When someone is in a growth mindset, they believe intelligence and abilities have been developed over time.

It is important to note how unlikely it is that a person will always be in one mindset or the other; we all tend to be a mix of both. Indeed, as Carol Dweck said at a conference we were presenting at together in Copenhagen in August 2017: 'Claiming that you are always in a growth mindset might be one of the surest signs of a fixed mindset!'

This powerful statement will be explored later but for now, we will give examples of the things people might think when they are in a fixed mindset compared with what they think when they are in a growth mindset. As you read through them, think of the times when you might lean towards one or other – or both – of the circumstances described.

▶ Figure 2: Examples of Fixed and Growth Mindset Thinking

Fixed Mindset	Growth Mindset
Abilities are FIXED	Abilities are GROWN
The belief that abilities and intelligence are fixed by nature and are relatively innate.	The belief that abilities and intelligence are grown through nurture and are relatively malleable.
'I have always been good at this'. 'I don't have the mind for that'.	'I have developed a talent for this'. 'I have never tried learning that'.

Fixed Mindset	Growth Mindset
Saying Usain Bolt, Marie Curie, Leonardo da Vinci, Albert Einstein, Whitney Houston, Steve Jobs, Hedy Lamarr and Wolfgang Mozart were all successful only because of the gifts they were born with.	Saying the people mentioned in the left-hand column turned their 'natural advantage' into world-beating excellence through extraordinary drive, ambition, effort, opportunity, culture and resilience.

Fixed Mindset	Growth Mindset
KNOW Your Limitations	TEST Your Limitations
The belief that our limitations tell us how far we can go before we can expect to fail.	The belief that our limitations are there to be tested, stretched and overcome.
'I know and accept my limitations'.	'I want to test my limitations to the maximum to see if I can break past them'.
Quickly concluding others can't do something because they are female, disabled, poor, have ADHD, are from the wrong side of the tracks, have a bad attitude and so on.	Thinking of athletes at the Paralympics, and people like Dame Evelyn Glennie, Stephen Hawking, Rosa Parks, Oprah Winfrey.

Fixed Mindset	Growth Mindset
PROVE Your Ability	IMPROVE Your Ability
Abilities and intelligence are relatively fixed. Therefore, it is important to prove one's talents.	Abilities and intelligence are relatively malleable. Therefore, it is important to grow and improve.
'I have always been really good at that'. 'I can't do this but that's OK because I'm better at other things'.	'I would love to have a go at improving that'. 'I have never had much success with this so I'm trying to improve it now'.
Choosing activities that are likely to end in success.	Choosing activities that are likely to take you out of your comfort zone.

Fixed Mindset	Growth Mindset
I CAN'T do that	I can't do that YET
Earlier failures or anticipated failure indicate that we can't do it.	Earlier failures or lack of familiarity indicate that we can't do it yet.
'I know I can't do that'. 'I've tried it before and proved I'm hopeless at it'.	'I know I can't do it yet but I'm willing to have a go'. 'I'm hopeful I can do it better next time'.
Saying 'I can't do it' as an excuse for not joining in.	Saying 'I can't do it yet' to reflect the possibilities of future success, and to signal a willingness to try.

Most people experience both fixed and growth mindset thinking in their lives. For example, some people will say they could become athletic if they train hard enough (growth mindset thinking), but at the same time think they will *never* be able to speak a foreign language (fixed mindset thinking).

This comparison of fixed and growth mindsets shows some of the more common differences in attitudes and beliefs according to the mindset you are in at any given time.

(Continued)

(Continued)

Fixed Mindset	Growth Mindset
AVOID Challenges	SEEK Challenges
Challenges are uncomfortable so they should be avoided unless absolutely necessary.	Challenges are stimulating so it is good to seek them out whenever appropriate.
'Why would I want to try that and make a fool of myself?' 'That looks far too difficult'.	'I would love to have a go at that to see how I get on with it'. 'That looks really exciting'.
Using excuses and diversionary tactics to avoid challenges.	Looking for opportunities to have a go at different challenges.

Fixed Mindset	Growth Mindset
Struggling indicates INADEQUACY	Struggling indicates LEARNING
Talented people can do things with ease. So, if we are struggling then that means we are inadequate.	Talented people have been through many struggles to get where they are today. So, if we are struggling then *maybe* we are on our way too.
'I hate struggling. It shows I can't do it and that's embarrassing'. 'I get frustrated when I struggle and feel like giving up'.	'Struggling means I am trying to learn'. 'When I'm struggling, I reassure myself that the outcome is going to be worth it'.
Trying not to show anyone that you are struggling; asking to be rescued or giving up too quickly.	Persevering through the struggle; even growing to find joy in the knowledge that it leads to growth and personal development.

Fixed Mindset	Growth Mindset
HIDE Mistakes	EXAMINE Mistakes
Mistakes are embarrassing because they indicate a lack of talent, understanding or attention.	Mistakes can lead to a better understanding of what might be needed for increased success.
'I hate making mistakes; they show I'm not concentrating or, even worse, that I can't do it'.	'Mistakes are not great but I can turn them into something positive if I learn from them'.
Hiding mistakes from other people; pretending (sometimes even to yourself) that they never happened; blaming circumstances.	Examining what went wrong, lessons learned and possible solutions. Deciding cause and effect rather than blame and punishment.

Fixed Mindset	Growth Mindset
Feedback is CRITICISM	Feedback is INFORMATION
Feedback is a euphemism for criticism. It leaves the receiver feeling inadequate and crestfallen.	Feedback is not personal; it is information that could be used to improve future performance.

Fixed Mindset	Growth Mindset
'Please be gentle when giving me feedback'. 'So basically, what you're telling me is that I'm not good enough?'	'Feedback helps me to understand how well I am doing and what I could do next to improve'.
Thinking feedback is directed towards the person and their inadequacy. Preferring feedback to be praise-based rather than critique-based.	Thinking feedback is directed towards process and improving future performance. Wanting clarity and purpose rather than flattery or false praise.

Fixed Mindset MOTTOS	Growth Mindset MOTTOS
Fortune favours the strong.	Fortune favours the brave.
If you're really good at something, you shouldn't need to try.	No matter how good you are at something, you can always improve.
If you have to try, you must be stupid; effort is for losers.	If you have to try, you must be learning something; effort is how people succeed.
Don't try too hard; that way you've got an excuse if things go wrong.	Always try hard; that way you've more chance of success and making progress.
No pain, no pain.	No pain, no gain.

At particular moments in our lives and in different situations, everybody will have acted in fixed mindset ways at times, and in growth mindset ways at other times. Figure 2 gives examples of what these behaviours might look like. Remember: the purpose of Figure 2 – and indeed of the book as a whole – is *not* to state that 'fixed is bad' and 'growth is good'. Rather, it is to examine the differences between the two and to identify the triggers, behaviours and responses to each one.

NOW TRY THIS

Divide the nine sections in Figure 2 between your colleagues or your students. Invite everyone to consider the section they have been given whilst responding to the following prompts:

1. Describe an occasion when you acted according to the fixed mindset examples given.

2. Describe an occasion when you acted according to the growth mindset examples given.

3. What were the main differences between these occasions?

4. What were the differences in outcomes?

5. Can you think of times in which it might be an advantage to act according to the fixed mindset examples given?

6. How much control do you think you have over the mindset you are in?

7. Is there anyone you know who seems to almost always be in one of the mindsets?

This is the first 'Now Try This' section. You will find many others throughout the book. They are here to support your professional and personal learning.

1.2 • WHAT DIFFERENCE DOES MINDSET MAKE?

Carol Dweck's research shows that people subconsciously (implicitly) have ideas about their own intelligence and abilities, and about the intelligence and abilities of others. This is now known in social and developmental psychology as a person's 'implicit theory of intelligence' or 'mindset'.

In practice, this means that when a person observes talent or intelligence, they can view that quality to be either fixed or malleable. If they hold an 'entity theory of intelligence' (a fixed mindset), they infer that talent to be a fixed trait, one that has not and will not change much over time. Whereas, if they hold an 'incremental theory of intelligence' (a growth mindset) then they will view the perceived talent as something that can be developed over time. In Chapter 4, we explore how this plays itself out by asking you to consider the terms used for students at either end of the ability scale. For example, are students in your school with top grades referred to as the bright or gifted students whilst those with the lowest scores are referred to as the slow, special needs or less intelligent students? If so, then this suggests the fixed mindset or entity theory of intelligence is very much at play in your school. Similarly, if it is the obvious physical qualities of the top performers in your sporting teams that are used to explain success then a fixed mindset could be at play; whereas, if the emphasis is on the players' commitment to training, their development and mastery of skills, then a growth mindset or incremental theory is more likely to be influencing actions.

These assessments are referred to as 'implicit theories' because they are present even though we are often unaware of them. In some ways, they are similar to our prejudices: making snap judgements in response to circumstances, based on beliefs that we may be unaware of.

These judgements can influence our goals, motivations and behaviour. They can also affect how we interact with other people. They might even influence how the people we connect with then perceive their world, particularly if those people are generally guided by us (our students or our own children, for example).

A good illustration of this last point can be drawn from an article Carol Dweck wrote with Claudia Mueller for the *Journal of Personality and Social Psychology* in 1998. In it they describe six tests they did to discover the effect of praise on children's performance.

The first test involved 128 fifth graders (70 girls and 58 boys, aged 10–12 years). Each student was seen individually. After being escorted from their usual classroom to an empty one, they were introduced to the task. They were given a brief guide to problem solving and then asked to solve 10 moderately difficult questions in four minutes.

As soon as the time was up, the adult marked their tests and told the child he/she had done well:

> Wow, you did very well on these problems. You got [number of problems] right. That's a really high score.

Each child then received one of three types of praise, as follows:

> Approximately one-third of the students were given **intelligence praise** – they were told they had done well 'because they were clever'.

Approximately one-third of the students were given **process praise** – they were told they had done well 'because they had tried hard'.

Approximately one-third of the students were the **control group** – they were told they had done well but given no further explanation as to why.

Each student was then given another test, this time far more difficult. Every child struggled. They were then told they had performed 'a lot worse' on the second test than on the first test (before worrying unduly about this message, please see the note about test conditions at the end of Section 1.4).

After receiving this negative feedback, each student was asked to work on the third and final set of problems. These were of the same standard as the first set (moderate difficulty) so it could be reasonably expected that each child would have got the same score as they had on the first test. Except they didn't.

Figure 3 shows how the students' scores changed from the first set of problems to the third set of problems, after receiving the different types of praise.

► Figure 3: Change in Students' Scores After Receiving Different Messages About the Causes of Success

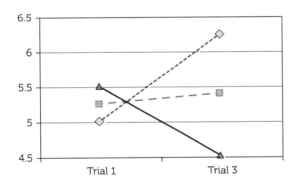

The numbers down the left show the average score out of 10 achieved by the groups of children.

Solid Line – children who received intelligence praise

Dotted Line – children who received process praise

Dashed Line – children in the control group

Figure 3 shows:

> The students who were praised for being clever did worse on the third test than they had on the first test.

> The students who were praised for having tried hard did better on the third test than they had on the first test.

> The students in the control group did slightly better over time, probably because they were getting used to taking the tests.

Caution: although the Mueller and Dweck study praised effort, that is not always a good thing to do – particularly if effort has been applied to the wrong strategy. So be careful not to reduce growth mindset down to simply praising effort alone.

1.2.1 • Notes About Process Praise

The term 'process praise' is used in this study – and throughout this book – to refer to comments used to commend the *processes* people use. These include, but are not limited to, effort. In addition to effort, process praise would *also* be used to commend engagement, perseverance, strategy, determination, willingness to have a go and so on.

We mention this at this point to emphasise that process praise is *not just* about praising effort, even though the Mueller and Dweck (1998) study used that as their example. Too many teachers – indeed, too many people – have reduced the complexities of mindset down to a simple, 'praise effort' mantra. That is so simple as to be misleading. Of course, effort can be – and often is – a good thing. But there is little to be gained in putting effort into the wrong thing! So, please be careful to distinguish between effort and process: praising effort is indeed process praise but not all process praise focuses on effort.

The problems of reducing mindset down to a 'praise effort' mantra are explored in more depth in Sections 2.6 and 6.4.

> **NOW TRY THIS**
>
> Looking back at the outcomes of the Mueller and Dweck study, talk with one of your colleagues about the results shown in Figure 3. Think of reasons why students who were praised for being clever after doing well on the first test subsequently performed worse in the third test; whereas those students who were praised for trying hard after doing well on the first test, then performed even better in the third test.

1.2.2 • Explaining the Change in Students' Scores

In the 'Now Try This' section above, we have asked you to think about why the students responded so differently in the third test depending on the type of praise they received after the first test. Our own explanations are in Section 1.4. We have placed them there so that we don't give the game away too soon! Therefore, we recommend that you complete the 'Now Try This' section first and then turn to Section 1.4 before returning to this page to continue reading.

1.3 • MINDSET IS NOT BLACK AND WHITE

Reading through Sections 1.1 and 1.2, you might wonder if there are *any* redeeming features of a fixed mindset, which in turn might lead you to question why anyone would ever choose anything other than a growth mindset, but it is not as simple as that. The question about choice will be explored in a moment. For now, let's look at a few of the complexities of mindset because it is not as straightforward as saying growth mindset will win every time.

1.3.1 • What Is Your Motivation for Learning?

- Do you believe learning is a normal and necessary part of life, not only in school but throughout adulthood?

Though it may seem that fixed mindset thinking is bad and growth mindset thinking is good, the truth is more complex than that. If, for example, you find yourself in a fixed mindset environment (one that praises performance and grades, and punishes mistakes) then a growth mindset might be more of a hindrance than a help.

- In the last few years, we have seen app developers, web designers, social media managers, drone operators and so on, added to the jobs market. Do you think this increase in the type of jobs required will continue to grow?

- Do you think adults are less likely than previous generations to have a job for life and more likely to enter a number of different sectors throughout their working life?

- Do you think the next generation will need to be able to understand, analyse and solve problems that are, as yet, unknown?

If you have answered yes to each of these questions then you will no doubt agree that 'learning *how* to learn' should be one of the key functions of education. This means not only learning but also learning *how* to improve the effectiveness[1] of that learning – for example, students thinking about how best to analyse and respond to a text as well as reading the text; or reflecting on recent successes to identify the strategy that helped them most *as well as* enjoying their triumph.

The approach a person takes to 'learning how to learn' would be influenced by mindset. When in a growth mindset, the motivation might be to do with personal development, fulfilment and a love of learning. Whereas, in a fixed mindset, the motivation might be more to do with competing against others, and doing whatever is needed to secure the top grades or best results. Of course, the outcome might be the same: that is, improved performance. So, some might argue that in this circumstance, mindset doesn't matter much. So long as you have achieved what you wanted to achieve then why worry about the path you took to get there. Of course, others would argue that process and reason *are* just as important as outcome. We explore this a bit more in Sections 3.0 and 3.1.

This then leads to the connected topic of grades and outperforming your peers.

1.3.2 • What About Grades and Mindset?

Some people dismiss the efficacy of mindset by pointing to examples of those who have succeeded despite being in a fixed mindset much of the time. For example, most of us can think of peers who are driven towards high performance not by the love of what they do but by an anxiousness to prove they are the best. These same people appear to take their setbacks particularly badly and are often enraged by defeat.

Think, for example, of students with top grades at school. Some of them have achieved these top grades by believing they have a natural talent for the subjects they score well in; others by a competitive drive to beat everyone else. This compares with those who do brilliantly because they have an insatiable desire for learning or are always seeking ways to improve their own performance because they take great delight in mastery. Again, as with the previous section on 'learning how to learn', some might argue that it matters not which mindset a person was in in order to achieve top grades, just so long as they did. Others, of course, would say that they would much rather students achieved top grades through a love of learning than through an anxiety to prove themselves or fear of failure.

The real conversation-starter might come from the question, would you rather someone scored very highly but suffered anxiety along the way or didn't score so well but weren't so anxious?

That said, the question assumes that high performance and anxiety go hand in hand. Though we could probably think of examples in which this was true, probably many of

---

1. In this section, we would define 'effectiveness' as efficient, ethical and sustainable but we would also add the caveat that context and culture would influence the actual definition in any given circumstance.

> This book is focused primarily on learning, so it is worth considering your motivation for learning. If you are motivated by beating your peers and 'proving' yourself, then a fixed mindset shouldn't be a hindrance; whereas if your motivation is to grow your talents and 'improve' yourself irrespective of others, then a growth mindset will definitely be more advantageous.

> Both mindsets might lead to success, but the journey and motivation are likely to be different. Fixed mindset success often comes from a fear of failure, whereas growth mindset success generally comes from determination and a willingness to be challenged.

> Giving students choice is often assumed to lead to increased motivation. However, it can also reveal the mindset your students are in, so pay attention to their choices and encourage them to choose options that will stretch and challenge them.

which would come from a school situation, it isn't perhaps a generalised picture. Think, for example, of the greatest innovations in technology, sport, art, music and so on: they seem to have come from a deep passion and love of exploration rather than from the anxiety or fear of failure that we associate with too many of our 'brightest' students. Thus, excellence and passion can – and perhaps more often than not do – go hand in hand. At least in the fields of innovation and human endeavour they do, if not in the exam halls of many of our schools.

1.3.3 • What About Mindset and Choice?

When students are offered a choice between which activities they would like to try, who they would like to work with, how they would want to present their findings, or what subjects they would prefer to study during their teenage years, too many of them choose the one they think they are best at. Though this might not seem like such a bad idea, the problem is that choosing familiarity and comfort tends to reduce the amount of learning that subsequently ensues.

John Hattie touched upon this topic in his seminal book, *Visible Learning* (2009):

> The effect of student choice and control over learning is somewhat higher on motivation outcomes (d = 0.30) than on subsequent student learning (d = 0.04; Niemiiec, Sikorski, & Walberg, 1996; Patall, Cooper, & Robinson, 2008). (Hattie, 2009: 193)

Bear in mind that the typical effect of all 250+ influences on learning that Hattie has identified is an effect size of 0.4. This shows how poorly the effect size of 0.04 when giving students control over their learning compares to the average effect. Indeed, in Hattie's most recent analysis, available online at VisibleLearningPlus.com (Hattie, 2017), the effect of giving students control over their learning has dropped to 0.02. Whichever effect size you rely on, it appears that giving students control over their learning does *not* lead to the gains most people suppose it does.

That is not to say that giving students choice is necessarily a bad thing. What it does suggest, though, is that we should be aware of the choices we are offering our students and the choices they are making. If the options we offer are too easy and we subsequently praise our students for succeeding at those easy tasks, then we are in danger of promoting fixed mindset thinking. Similarly, if our students are choosing the easiest option for them in the expectation that adults are most likely to praise them when they get things right, then, again, there is a risk of promoting fixed mindset thinking.

This is explored in more depth in Chapter 8.

NOW TRY THIS

As you can see from Section 1.3, it is too simplistic to say, 'growth mindset: good; fixed mindset: bad' or even to say that 'growth mindset will always make the difference' because the chances are it won't. Instead, it is likely to make a significant difference in some circumstances for some people some of the time. Before exploring some of these conditions in more depth, we recommend that you pause for a moment to consider the following questions with your colleagues:

1. When might a fixed mindset be advantageous, if at all?

2. When might a growth mindset be disadvantageous, if at all?

3. In an ideal situation, excellence would come from a love of learning but, for some, high performance is driven by high anxiety. If the choice was to reduce anxiety and thereby reduce performance (not that one necessarily leads to the other but go with it for the sake of argument) then would you accept that? Would you rather go for lower anxiety/lower performance or higher anxiety/higher performance? For your own students? For your own children/grandchildren? For yourself?

4. Think of people in the public eye who have achieved great things. Though mindset is less than obvious to the spectator, do you suppose that mindset had anything to do with their public successes? If so, then in what way? If not, then why not?

1.4 • MUELLER AND DWECK RESULTS

As promised, we will now return to the research results shown in Section 1.2. To remind you, the students who received intelligence praise after the first test performed worse in the third test. Whereas those who received process praise after the first test performed better in the third test. We then asked you why you think this happened.

Here are some of our thoughts about it.

1.4.1 • Equal and Opposite

The key to the effects is the second test in which all students failed. They were not given reasons why they failed; that was left to their own imagination.

So, those students who had been told they had done well in the first test because they are smart, began to imagine that they had failed at the second test because they were not smart enough. So, they went into the third test with a crisis of confidence, thinking 'I'm just not smart enough'.

By comparison, the students who had been told they had done well in the first test because they had tried hard, began to imagine that they had failed at the second test because they had not tried hard enough. So, they went into the third test thinking, 'I need to try harder'. That is a very different and far less negative thought than 'I'm not smart at this'. Thinking they need to try harder also tends to steel their resolve to do better.

Lesson: When recognising factors that influence success and failure, it is better to focus on the ones that are process-related rather than those that are entity-related. In other words, use verbs to describe actions (e.g. trying, applying, focusing) rather than nouns to label individuals (e.g. clever person, natural performer, genius individual).

1.4.2 • Influence

The students who began imagining they were 'not smart enough' after the second test may well also have thought, 'What can I do about it? I can't make myself smarter'. This, in turn, may have led to a feeling of powerlessness or enervation – or, in other words, a lower sense of self-efficacy (see Sections 1.5, 5.0 and 9.3).

Whereas, the students who began imagining they 'needed to try harder' after the second test may well have also thought, 'So that is what I will do: I will try harder!' In turn, this

> The Mueller and Dweck study showed the effects of different types of praise on student achievement. This section explains some of the reasons for those differences.

> Telling someone they are 'smart' when they succeed seems positive, but it risks them thinking they are the opposite of smart (i.e. 'stupid') when they fail.

may have led to them feeling in control of their own destiny or, at the very least, having the sense of being able to influence their performance – in other words, a higher sense of self-efficacy.

Lesson: It is not over-stating the situation to say that focusing on entity-related factors (e.g. smart child) may well disempower that person when they hit difficulty, whereas focusing on process-related factors (e.g. effort, strategies, concentration, actions) should empower them and add to their feelings of self-efficacy.

1.4.3 • False Sense of Security

People who are told they are smart, clever or naturally talented sometimes develop a false sense of security in which they think that all they have to do is turn up for everything to go well. So prevalent is the idea that smart people don't have to try that the students receiving the 'intelligence praise' in the Mueller and Dweck (1998) study may well have assumed similar beliefs. That is, until they did badly in the second test. After which, they might have felt despondent or even lied to by the adults praising them earlier.

Lesson: A much safer, as well as more accurate, message to give is that success comes from talent *and* effort, determination, strategy, timing and so on. It is not enough simply to turn up with your superior brain or brawn and expect everything to go your way every time. There has never been an influential or celebrated inventor, artist or sports star who has triumphed through talent alone. Every single one of them has grafted, overcome adversity, been in the right place at the right time, and made the most of personal drive and ambition.

1.4.4 • Defence Mechanisms

The students who received the 'intelligence praise' after the first test and then went on to do badly on the second test, may well have resorted to defence mechanisms to reduce the threat of being thought of as 'not smart'. These could have included such thoughts as:

- These tests don't matter.
- These tests are too hard.
- The researchers are trying to trick me.
- I don't need to do well at these silly tests.
- I am never going to try these again.

Compare these opinions to the ones that the students receiving process praise are more likely to have thought of:

- These tests don't matter (but I still want to do well on them).
- I didn't do well on that second test (but I did on the first. So, let's try to finish on a high).
- The researchers are trying to trick me (but I won't let them get the better of me).
- I don't need to do well on these tests (but I want to anyway).
- I need to try harder next time (because effort served me well first time around).

As you can see, the first set of 'defences' is much more defeatist whereas the second set, though similar in structure, is much more tenacious and galvanising.

Note about the test conditions:

> During the debriefing given at the end of the experimental session, all children were informed that the second problem set contained problems of increased difficulty, which were considered to be appropriate for older, seventh-grade students. In fact, they were told that answering even one of these difficult problems was quite an achievement for students in their grade level. Thus, they were assured of the overall high quality of their task performance. Extensive precautions were taken to ensure that all children left the experimental setting proud of their performance. (Mueller & Dweck, 1998: 36)

1.5 • WE ARE ALL A MIX OF MINDSETS

It is rare for anyone to be in the same mindset in every part of their life. More common is to be in one mindset for some things and another mindset for others. For example, you might be in a growth mindset in contexts in which you have already overcome difficulties and made good progress, whereas you might be in a fixed mindset when it comes to those things you have never tried or feel particularly helpless with.

(Authors): At primary school, my eldest daughter tended to be in a growth mindset when swimming but in a fixed mindset when doing maths. This meant that whenever she came up against a problem that she couldn't immediately solve, in swimming she would tell herself, 'There is a way to do this; I just need to find the solution'. In maths, however, she would tell herself, 'Here is yet more proof that I can't do maths'. Happily, when she moved schools, she started to make palpable progress in maths and so along with it, her confidence grew and her patterns of thinking began to change. That is not to say she is always in a growth mindset with maths yet, but she is on her way.

It is better to think about being 'in' a mindset instead of 'having' a mindset, as this helps recognise that we are all a mix of both mindsets.

Other examples include being in a growth mindset when trying something that you are familiar with and enjoy, compared to being in a fixed mindset with something that you don't want to do or that you feel threatened by the circumstance (for example, being observed by hostile or suspicious onlookers).

Sometimes it helps to make some comparisons with connected theories. Take, for example, the idea of introversion and extraversion: it used to be commonplace to describe someone as either an introvert or an extrovert. Yet, it is much more likely that behaviour and attitude are context-dependent. For example, someone might act very extraverted when they are the host of their own party but much more introverted when dragged along to a party where they know no one. Or they might be willing to play a larger-than-life role on stage but shy away from presenting their 'true' face to a room full of strangers. Indeed, some of our best-loved performers are very often intensely private and shy individuals offstage.

It can be helpful to compare mindset with the related theory of 'self-efficacy'. Created by Bandura in the 1970s, self-efficacy refers to the extent to which a person believes they can influence (or 'effect') outcomes.

So it is with mindset: whereas some people might be very much growth-orientated when it comes to familiar or 'safe' contexts, those same people could be much more fixed in their outlook when it comes to unfamiliar or 'threatening' situations.

It can also be useful to think about the 'self-efficacy' dimension of mindset. Proposed by Stanford psychologist Albert Bandura in the 1970s, self-efficacy is the belief someone has about their abilities to 'effect' a new outcome; not just 'affect' it but actually *create a new* result. Useful synonyms for efficacy include potency and influence.

> When a person is in a growth mindset, they believe they have more influence on outcomes than if they are in a fixed mindset. So, in a sense, a person has more self-efficacy when in a growth mindset.

Those people in a growth mindset believe they are efficacious, even outside of their comfort zone; that is, they believe they can significantly influence outcomes. Mean-while, people in a fixed mindset believe their influence is limited other than with things they believe they are already good at.

One reason to draw out the 'self-efficacy' part of mindset is that too many people ascribe fixed mindset to negativity, whereas a growth mindset is thought by many to be optimistic, noble even. That makes questions about which mindset you are in a particularly value-laden inquiry. However, if we think about the differing degrees of self-efficacy within each mindset, then it might be easier to admit to feeling relatively powerless to influence a new outcome than it is to admit being in a fixed mindset about the same thing. For example, to say, 'I don't feel I can influence the outcome of this' might feel less revelatory than to say, 'I am in a fixed mindset about this'.

This distinction is particularly pertinent when it concerns something that matters. It is one thing to laughingly say, 'I'm always in a fixed mindset when it comes to remembering my friends' partners' names', but another thing to admit being in a fixed mindset with something that counts towards your performance-related pay (unless, of course, the culture of your whole organisation is entirely growth-related).

Thus, the question, 'Which activities do you feel less efficacious about?' might result in less guarded and perhaps more honest answers than, 'Which activities do you tend to be in a fixed mindset about?'

> In many quarters, a growth mindset had become the right thing to have, the right way to think. It was as though educators were faced with a choice: Are you an enlightened person who fosters students' well-being? Or are you an unenlightened person, with a fixed mindset, who undermines them? So, of course, many claimed the growth-mindset identity. But the path to a growth mindset is a journey, not a proclamation. (Dweck, 2015a)

NOW TRY THIS

Many people find it uncomfortable to say when they are in a fixed mindset because of the value judgement attached to such a revelation (growth mindset: good; fixed mindset: bad). If this is the case amongst your colleagues then it could be advantageous to think about efficacy instead.

Think of something that you would love to be able to do but have a low sense of self-efficacy about. Choose something that is humanly possible (so nothing like living forever or being invisible for a day!) that you wish you could develop but that you think is beyond your own influence. Examples might come from one or more of the following categories:

- Skill-related actions such as carpentry or using technology (e.g. I wish I was good at DIY).
- Health-related actions such as diet or exercise (e.g. I wish I was fitter).
- Temperament-related actions such as the ways in which you respond to your children, your students, your partner (e.g. If only I could stop losing my temper).
- Perfectionist-related actions such as not being able to switch off or worrying that you're not good enough (e.g. I sometimes wish I could lower my own expectations).

- Memory-related actions such as forgetting birthdays, shopping require-ments or instructions (e.g. I never seem to be able to remember the things my partner thinks are important).

- Behaviour management-related actions such as being quicker to chastise the naughty children and more forgiving of the 'nicer' ones (e.g. I don't know what it is about that person but I am less patient with them than with others).

Once you have thought of one or two examples, talk to a colleague about them. As you describe your thoughts, answer the following questions:

1. Have you always had a sense of low self-efficacy about this?

2. What has your response been so far (for example, accept it, avoid it or ignore it)?

3. Why do think you have particularly low self-efficacy about it?

4. Looking at the comparison of fixed and growth mindset attitudes in Figure 2, which descriptions in that table help explain how you feel about your chosen example?

1.6 • A FIXED MINDSET MIGHT BE MORE COMMON THAN WE CARE TO ADMIT

Very few people like to think of themselves as being prone to fixed mindset thinking. After all, that is just for the glass-half-empty people, isn't it?

Actually, no, it's not just for the pessimists, despite what the over-simplistic posters and soundbites would have us believe. As the previous section described, it is more likely that we are a mix of both fixed and growth mindsets.

So, in the spirit of showing just how common fixed mindset thinking is, this section shares some connected ideas that might help to reveal how prone we all are to it! We do this not to admonish or criticise but to illuminate and raise awareness of it.

It seems to us there are a number of conditions that, although certainly not unique to the teaching profession, seem to be particularly prevalent in school staff rooms. So, beware the following attitudes that might mean you are more susceptible to fixed mindset thinking:

> Since we are all a mix of mindsets, it can be useful to consider which actions promote a fixed mindset and which promote a growth mindset.

1.6.1 • The Superhero

Are you the sort of teacher or leader who is on a mission to save all students? If so, do any of the following seem familiar?

- You swoop in to 'save' your students (or your colleagues) from struggles. This inadvertently gives the impression that struggling is a bad thing rather than a learning opportunity.

- You will be the first to volunteer for something that is outside everyone else's comfort zone. Though this might seem noble, it could also be seen as a way of denying others their opportunity to experience learning 'wobble' (see Section 8.1).

> These 'roles' that are commonplace in schools could be indicators of fixed mindset thinking.

- By being the superhero, you have created a dependency culture in which everyone else will look to you to solve problems, deal with uncomfortable situations and generally take charge. This in turn gives the impression that some people (in this case, you) are born to be great whereas others (in this case, those who follow you) are 'naturally' not so competent.

1.6.2 • The Perfectionist

Do you set extremely high goals for yourself and then experience self-doubt or worry when you don't reach those dizzying heights? Do any of these seem familiar to you?

- You find it difficult to delegate to others because you think the only person capable of doing it properly is you. This causes many people to infer that you believe there is no time or, worse still, no place for learning: that either someone can do it or they can't do it – and the person who can do it is you!
- When you try to delegate tasks, you end up micro-managing. This can lead to the same implication as above.
- When you fall short of your own uncompromising standards, you worry that maybe you're not cut out for the job or task.

These beliefs are based on very good intentions. They are also in alignment with high expectations, which is what we should all have in teaching (shouldn't we?). However, a perfectionist is quick to beat themselves up for not being perfect right away. Instead of focusing on the progress they have made so far and the possibilities they have for improvement, a perfectionist can be too quick to criticise themselves; after all, they are their own worst critics!

1.6.3 • The Natural

'See that teacher through there' (pointing through the classroom window), 'she was born to teach; she's an absolute natural'. That observation, or one very similar, has been made many times to both authors of this book during our time working with schools.

It would be interesting to note the reasons for these assertions. Is it because that teacher is so comfortable in the company of kids? Is it that they are able to motivate and engage the harder-to-reach students? Is it that they love their job? Put in more effort than anyone else? Or maybe, is it because they waste no opportunity to tell you how talented they are?

The problem with being 'a natural' is that the following might be harder to handle:

- Other staff just not 'getting it'; they don't understand what you understand. Why do they have to try so hard? After all, it all comes so easy to you.
- The leaders or inspectors not recognising just how gifted you are. In fact, on occasion they have even suggested new actions which, in your opinion, are pointless because every situation is different so generalisations don't work.
- Data showing that students are not doing any better in your class than in other classes (the data is obviously inaccurate or counting the wrong thing).

- Being mentored by a more experienced teacher who, in your mind, is more interested in processes and rubrics than in encouraging free-spirited inspiration to lead the kids where they want to go.

- Being asked to teach a group or a subject that is so far out of your comfort zone that you won't be able to put your talents to good effect.

Again, none of these notions come from malicious intent but perhaps they are misguided at times. They are also likely to lead to some fixed mindset thinking along the lines of, 'I've always been good at this (so I'd better not risk losing face)', or 'naturally talented people don't have to try (so why do I need any professional development or mentoring?)'.

1.6.4 • The Expert

Some people are regarded as experts simply in reference to their longevity in the profession. This makes them susceptible to the following ideas:

- The expert should always have the best ideas.

- You can't teach an old dog new tricks.

- Professional development is unnecessary or, worse still, wasted on someone so expert.

- If the expert receives a poor grading then the whole system must be suspect (which, in turn, diminishes the achievements of others within the same system).

We are not for a moment suggesting there is no such thing as an expert. Instead, we are suggesting that not only might the status of 'expert' be conferred imprecisely but that attitudes towards and from experts might lean towards fixed mindset thinking – for example, 'once the best, always the best' or 'experts don't need to improve'.

NOW TRY THIS

1. Which of the four types described (superhero, perfectionist, the natural or the expert) are you most prone to? Share your thoughts with a colleague, identifying the connections with the differing types of mindset thinking described in Figure 2.

2. Consider how the attitudes you've described in response to question 1 might affect how your students think about talents and performance.

3. Fill in as much of the mindset self-reflection in Figure 4 as you can now, then return to it as and when appropriate to help you with your reflections.

Words, thoughts or deeds	Trigger	Impact	Amplify, mute or change	Next steps
What do you do that reveals fixed or growth mindset attitudes?	*What prompts these actions to surface?*	*What impact do these actions have on others?*	*Are the actions (and the impact of those actions) best amplified, muted or changed?*	*What could you or someone else do next to help amplify, mute or change future actions?*
e.g. I find it difficult to delegate important tasks to others.	e.g. I believe that if a job is worth doing, it's worth doing well so when someone doesn't do it right, I take over and do it for them.	e.g. I lose patience and too often give others the impression that I don't think they're capable enough.	e.g. I need to mute these tendencies in the first instance and then work out a way to change things in the future.	e.g. I'm going to agree clearer success criteria with my students so that they can more accurately assess their own performance so that I don't need to be the judge all the time. And I'm going to take a chill pill!

WHAT IS THE IMPACT OF MINDSET?

Students who endorse an incremental theory of intelligence are more likely to make plans to improve their performance after a setback, due in part to their holding learning goals in academic situations and to their focus on the positive role that effort can play in achievement. In comparison, students who hold ability goals are more likely to withdraw from challenges, due in part to their focus on lack of ability as the reason for failure and their tendency to experience deactivating loss of interest/excitement after a setback.

Smiley, Buttitta, Chung, Dubon & Chang, 2016: 890

GROWTH MINDSET IMPLEMENTATION IS NOT THERE (YET)

Chapter 1 introduced mindset and explained some of the reasons why it is not a simple choice between being in a fixed mindset or in a growth mindset. Most people are a complex mix of both mindsets, and this mix is determined in part by context. That said, the underlying message of the chapter (and indeed of this book) is that being in a growth mindset *is* better than being in a fixed mindset. When in a growth mindset, you are more willing to try; you approach challenges with a sense of determination rather than foreboding; and you are more open to learning from your own mistakes and from the feedback of others.

So being in a growth mindset will make a significant difference to achievement at school then. Right? Actually no. Not yet anyway. Early indications are that growth mindset interventions in schools are not influencing achievement anything like as much as you might suppose. Of course, many of these interventions are very short 'lessons', many of which are self-administered online. So, the fact that they do anything for anybody, much less low-achieving adolescents, is surprising.

That said, this chapter explores some of the reasons why mindset interventions are not working as effectively as they could. It also tackles head on some of the connected criticisms of mindset.

> Having explored the meanings of fixed and growth mindsets, our mission now is to find out when mindset matters most and when it doesn't.

2.0 • GROWTH MINDSET EFFECT SIZE

In 2013, Jeni Burnette, Ernest O'Boyle, Eric VanEpps, Jeffrey Pollack and Eli Finkel published a meta-analytic review of implicit theories and self-regulation. It is the only meta-analysis to date of studies comparing incremental and entity thinking, though there are others on connected topics such as mindfulness and grit.

Burnette et al.'s meta-analysis reviewed 85 studies that between them included 113 effects and involved 28,217 people ranging from 5 to 42 years old. In their introduction, they stated:

> With a random effects approach used, meta-analytic results across diverse achievement domains (68% academic) . . . demonstrated that implicit theories predict distinct self-regulatory processes, which, in turn, predict goal achievement. Incremental theories, which, in contrast to entity theories, are characterized by the belief that human attributes are malleable rather than fixed, significantly predicted goal setting (performance goals vs. learning goals), goal operating (helpless-oriented strategies vs. mastery oriented strategies), and goal monitoring (negative emotions vs. expectations). (2013: 655)

Figure 5 shows a copy of one of the tables they shared in their paper. As you can see, the effect of each dimension mentioned above differs according to the perceived threat to the ego of the people involved.

▶ **Figure 5: Comparison of Effects from Burnette et al.'s Meta-Analysis**

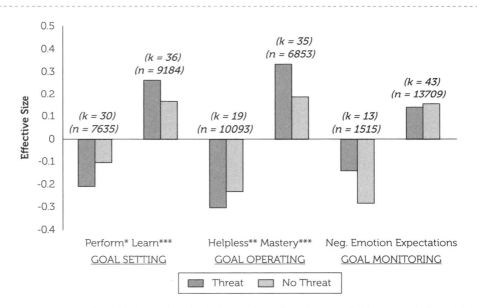

Source: Burnette et al., 2013: 671, where (*k*) is the number of studies included in the analysis and (*n*) is the number of participants.

A first glance at Figure 5 gives the impression that attitudes associated with a growth mindset make a difference to learning outcomes. Engaging with activities for the sake of learning (Learn) rather than to beat others (Perform) makes a difference. Believing in your ability to learn new skills (Mastery) is much better than adopting a stance of learned helplessness (Helpless). And having higher expectations of success (Expectations) is, unsurprisingly, more effective than having negative emotions towards the task (Neg. Emotion).

Towards the end of the report, the authors went on to state:

> In summary, the present meta-analysis suggests that mind-sets matter. That is, implicit theories are indeed consequential for self-regulatory processes and goal achievement. (2013: 680)

So, things are looking good! Being in a growth mindset is better than being in a fixed mindset. Just as we thought.

However, here is the downside: the effect is not *that* great. Sure, it makes a difference but the overall effect of these 85 studies of incremental vs. entity thinking gives an effect size of 0.19. That compares unfavourably with the typical effect of the 80,000 studies in education Hattie (2017) has analysed that have an effect size of 0.40. So yes, the differences are there to be seen but the magnitude is relatively small. How very disappointing.

That said, perhaps it is not so surprising. After all, when promising ideas from research are transformed into workable solutions for educators, they generally face the risk of being over-simplified. Take, for example, *Visible Learning*, *Assessment for Learning* and *Building Learning Power*: all particularly well-known terms that have gone from research into practice. Yet, all of them have suffered similar fates. For example, Visible Learning has been reduced by many to a Top Ten Rank of things to do or simply dismissed because 'John Hattie says class size does not matter' (even though he doesn't say that); Assessment for Learning has been over-simplified to 'Two Stars and a Wish' or to Dylan Wiliam using lollipop sticks to choose kids at random; and Building Learning Power has suffered from Guy Claxton's comment, taken completely out of context, about erasers being 'an instrument of the devil'!

It is perhaps, as some commentators describe, research that is lost in translation!

A new meta-analysis is coming out with a much smaller effect size (than Burnette et al.'s 0.19). This is partly because so many people are doing very superficial things and calling it growth mindset. It is also because it's really hard to do a short intervention (as school timetables often demand) and change grades months later. That's just how it is.

We have a new nationwide study that we're writing up – again, the overall effect is small but we're asking, where does mindset work and where doesn't it, and how can we learn to make it better? It should also be noted that this particular programme cost less than 50c per student to implement and yet the effect sizes are equal to many more costly programmes. So, this has to be factored in too.

In the end, short interventions won't reflect the potential of growth mindset; to see that, we will have to learn how to help school staff infuse it into classroom learning.

The next section explores some of the possible reasons why mindset is currently suffering a similar fate. Later in the book, we will show exactly what you can do to make it so much more powerful in practice.

> ## NOW TRY THIS
>
> It is good practice to look at the impact of our teaching so as to make decisions about what is worth doing and what is not. On the face of it, growth mindset interventions are not showing a particularly big impact.
>
> 1. Do you think growth mindset interventions are still worthwhile even with a low effect size?
> 2. If yes, then why? And how do you know it's not just another bandwagon that over-promises and under-delivers?

(Continued)

The effect size of all 85 studies is just 0.19. This compares unfavourably with the average effect of 0.40 across the 80,000 studies analysed by John Hattie.

That said, many of the studies Burnette et al. included in their meta-analysis examine mindset interventions lasting just a few hours, administered online. So, the fact that they have made some difference to student achievement is impressive. Furthermore, mindset interventions tend to be less focused on grade improvement and more on student motivation. So, although there might not have been much change in grades, the motivation for those grades (avoiding failure or seeking learning) might have changed significantly.

(Continued)

> 3. If no, then what other reasons would you add for not doing it? After all, there are many factors that show a similarly low effect (for example, lack of stress, extra-curricula programmes, pre-school programmes, co-/team-teaching, one-on-one laptops), which many people still want for their students despite the low effect scores. So why not add growth mindset to that list?

2.1 • REDUCED EFFICACY 1: THIRD-HAND KNOWLEDGE

> The impact of growth mindset interventions is reduced when those leading the approach in school have yet to develop a deep understanding of mindset theory.

In our work with Carol Dweck and our own experience helping teachers implement growth mindset, we've come across five significant problems that are diluting its effectiveness. These are covered in the next five sections.

1. Huge numbers of people have heard about Carol Dweck's mindset research; far fewer have actually read original texts penned by the professor herself. There may be many reasons for this.

2. Almost every week, there is an article or a blog published referencing, criticising or extolling mindset. This leads many to think they are reading about mindset, which in turn leads them to believe they 'know' mindset. Without having read the research themselves, many teachers cannot identify when these articles may be based upon inaccuracies and falsehoods (see Section 2.6 for examples).

3. Coming across so many articles about mindset leads many people to think they don't need to hear about it from Carol Dweck herself. The summary they've just read by someone else is good enough; there's no need to read a longer version penned by Dweck a few years earlier.

4. You know that person you've been making small talk with for years but don't actually know their name? It just feels far too late in the day to ask them their name now, doesn't it! We suspect it is the same with mindset. So many people give affirmative nods when the topic of growth mindset comes up that it seems shameful to admit we don't really know what it's all about. So, better to pretend than to admit (incidentally, that's a pretty fixed mindset thing to do!).

5. Many people have bought one of Dweck's books; in fact, more than a million copies of *Mindset* (2006b) have been sold worldwide. But how many people have actually read those books? As the 19th century philosopher Arthur Schopenhauer once said, 'Buying books would be a good thing if one could also buy the time to read them in: but as a rule, the purchase of books is mistaken for the appropriation of their contents' (Schopenhauer, [1891] 2009: 17).

These comments are *not* intended to be holier-than-thou. Nor do they apply uniquely to mindset. As well as presenting alongside Carol Dweck, we (the authors of this book) also present alongside John Hattie and could be writing equivalent comments about the misinterpretation and misrepresentation of Visible Learning. Indeed, there are probably more falsehoods about Hattie's work than of anyone else's we know right now.

Perhaps it is the human condition or a sign of the times to rely on commentary rather than to check original sources. Nonetheless, we anticipate that, as a reader of this book, you are far less interested in hearsay and much more determined to identify the best ways forward in understanding and applying mindset properly. We hope this book can help

you with that, as a supplement to Dweck's own words about research that she herself has conducted and had peer-reviewed before publication.

2.2 • REDUCED EFFICACY 2:
MINDSET IS MADE TO SOUND TOO EASY

Maybe we made the development of a growth mindset sound too easy. (Dweck, 2015a)

Do a search online for 'fixed mindset' or 'growth mindset' and you will find tens of thousands of results. Most of them will quote summaries of the research, such as:

People with a fixed mindset . . .

- believe talents and abilities can be relatively innate
- focus on showing that they are more intelligent or able than others
- choose to do things that are easy for them so that they look clever.

People with a growth mindset . . .

- believe talents and abilities can be grown
- focus on learning and improving
- choose things that will stretch and challenge them.

> Infographics and summaries of mindset theory have a place in helping busy teachers gain a quick overview of an important theory, but they also risk overlooking important nuances.

Though these summaries might in themselves seem accurate enough, there is a danger that such summaries and their associated pretty posters might overlook too much of the context and nuance. The list above, for example, is likely to lead to the idea that people are either one or the other, rather than a mix of both (which, as we've described in Chapter 1, is much more likely).

This, in turn, can lead to people wondering why on earth anyone would 'choose' to be in a fixed mindset. Very obviously, a growth mindset is better. This common assumption has led to many 'quick fixes' and 'silver bullet' strategies to attempt to change students' mindsets. Tell our children, tell our students, tell our team mates, tell our colleagues, tell our bosses (perhaps in a slightly smug, tables are reversed kind of way) that 'growth mindset' is the way forward. Wave our magic wand, utter the words 'expelliarmus' to release the fixed mindset thoughts, and delight at the results!

Or not, as the case may be.

In Section 1.2, we drew comparisons between implicit theories of intelligence and prejudices. We noted that responding to a person because of 'who they are' has parallels with an entity theory, whereas responding to a person because of 'how they are behaving' has closer ties with an incremental theory. We are not saying mindset is the same as prejudice but we are saying there are similarities because they both involve assessments made by a person at a subconscious level.

So, if we then consider that the most common forms of prejudice such as racism, sexism, elitism and so on have had decades of interventions without solving the problems, then it stands to reason that getting a whole school community into a growth mindset will not be easy either.

2.3 • REDUCED EFFICACY 3: TOO MUCH PERFORMANCE-FOCUS, NOT ENOUGH TIME

> Sadly, some school environments are currently incompatible with a growth mindset, especially when there is an emphasis on separating the clever and talented from those who are less able.

Perhaps the most significant reason why the effectiveness of growth mindset strategies is reduced comes from an emphasis in too many schools on performance rather than progress.

Across the world, there are classrooms, schools and whole systems focused more on the success of individuals relative to other people rather than on learning for the sake of learning. League tables and within-school rankings emphasise the difference between one student (or one school) and another. Prizes and praise are offered to those who perform best. Recognition is given to the most impressive talents within any given cohort. Everyone knows who is the best and who is the worst in each subject. Ability grouping is used to separate out those who do well and those who don't. In these kinds of environments, a growth mindset will still help but its effectiveness (as measured by achievement data) will be reduced. We share the evidence for this bold claim in Section 3.1. We also examine the situations in which a growth mindset is most effective as well as least effective.

Time, or rather the lack of it, also has an impact on the quality of growth mindset interventions. You don't need to be a teacher to know that schools are demanding, complex places. Staff make hundreds of decisions on how to act and respond in situations that frequently occur. Some situations are expected; others are not.

Students come to school with different starting points. These differing circumstances include how well they've been cared for by their family (assuming they have a functional family); what cognitive resources they have by then; how well they've been eating and sleeping and so on. As staff, we try to welcome them with effective pedagogy and an encouraging environment; all the time trying to bridge the gap between prescribed curricula and personal interests.

Now added to all that is the desire (need?) to get all of our students into a growth mindset! Being the complex places schools are, some students will already be there most of the time, some of them some of the time, some of them now and then, and then some of them not at all. It is the same for the school staff. And for the students' parents. Not to mention the policy makers and district leaders.

> Quick fixes have their appeal but rarely work for long. So, although it might be tempting to put up motivational posters and utter the words, 'growth mindset', the impact is likely to be limited without a more complex narrative supporting the journey.

Most teachers are not academic researchers; we are not normally fascinated by contradictory data, sets and subsets, or the difference between causation and correlation. We are more concerned with meeting the needs of each and every student we are responsible for. We know that one size does not fit all but it's difficult to create a different 'size' for every individual when there are so many in each class. So, no wonder we look for quick fixes or general theories that will help most students most of the time.

> If a doctor, lawyer, or dentist had 40 people in his office at one time, all of whom had different needs, and some of whom didn't want to be there and were causing trouble, and the doctor, lawyer, or dentist, without assistance, had to treat them all with professional excellence for nine months, then he might have some conception of the classroom teacher's job. (Donald Quinn (n.d.), Professor of Mechanical Engineering, University of Akron, Ohio)

That is not to say teachers aren't interested in research; we wouldn't be writing this book if we thought that. It is just that time is so limited when there are so many lessons to teach, so many students to support, so many meetings to attend, reports to write, hoops to jump through. Is it little wonder then, that something as complex as changing someone's implicit theories of intelligence is so difficult to achieve with great quality?

Dweck explains in a podcast shared by the *Times Educational Supplement* in the UK (October 2017) that she and her colleagues have never claimed growth mindset to be a fully-formed concept, or an answer to the golden rule of education. It is a work in progress. She reminds the listeners that the process of research includes sharing findings with others and being open to feedback and critiques. The quest is to learn more.

That's all well and good but we teachers want the answer now! Our current students can't wait another decade until we figure it out. They will have left school by then! If we don't get going with promising strategies then our students might just miss out on something great. There is no time to wait (even though quality takes time).

2.4 • REDUCED EFFICACY 4: INFLUENCES ARE COMPLEX

It turns out that growth mindset is in good company, appearing as it does down the lower end of John Hattie's Visible Learning list of influences on student achievement. Figure 6 shows some of the factors that, like growth mindset, also have a surprising low effect.

We share these as a way to say that a low effect size does not necessarily mean the influence should be dismissed. Instead, if you consider the influence to be an important one then at least two questions should be asked:

1. Why is it not having the impact we would expect?
2. What can we do to make it a more significantly positive effect?

For each influence, we have offered suggestions as to why the effects might be low. Taken together, these examples give more weight to the notion that classrooms – and indeed education as a whole – are complex places with multiple stories.

Despite the low effect sizes of the interventions shown in Figure 6, we would still want these factors to be part of our students' lives, wouldn't we? Of course, if it came down to a *choice* between some of the high-impact factors and the low-impact ones, then we ought to give preference to the more powerful ones. However, some of the lower-impact factors are still desirable. For example, we would still want our kids to have a certain degree of control over their learning; for their teachers to have good subject matter knowledge and to be trained well before they enter the profession; and if the budget was available, we would want to reduce the average number of students in each class. Similarly, if you're like us, you would also want the traditional summer vacation to remain intact, and for everyone in a school community to get into a growth mindset. Even if all of these have lower-than-expected effect sizes!

At this point, it is probably worth mentioning, in the spirit of full disclosure, that we (the authors) are fans of John Hattie's work. Indeed, we are lucky enough to call him our friend, having toured with him many times. This gives us a good insight into his thinking and it is fair to say that Hattie does not present his findings as a set of instructions for everyone to follow. Instead, he says: 'Here is what I have found from inspecting more than 1,400 meta-analyses in education; now it is up to you, the educators and decision-makers, to decide what to do next'.

Hattie doesn't just talk the talk, he also walks the talk. Look at the low effect of teacher education: ES = 0.12, then think about his role: teacher education! As we write this book, Hattie is Deputy Dean of the Melbourne Graduate School of Education. So, guess what he's trying to achieve there? He's asking questions, shaking trees, looking for ways to improve that 0.12 effect size. He's designing systems that will raise the bar on teacher

> Complex classrooms often require complex solutions: rarely will a shortcut to growth mindset reap anything other than surface-level gains.

> Growth mindset interventions are not the only approaches to school improvement that lead to a lower-than-expected impact. Figure 6 shows some of the other influences that John Hattie has identified as having low effects on student achievement.

Influence	Effect Size	Author Commentary
Summer vacation	– 0.02	All being well, summer vacations mean adventures for children and halcyon memories for adults. Therefore, if the meta-analyses identified the effect on happiness, independence and family time rather than on student achievement then we might expect this effect to be much higher. Instead, the effect is negative (albeit a small negative) because too many teachers assume students will have forgotten so much during the long holidays that they start further back than they ought to. This is exacerbated in countries that routinely move students to a different teacher every year.
Student control over learning	0.02	When given choice, students too often choose the option they are most familiar or comfortable with. Though effects on motivation are higher (ES = 0.30), the impact on achievement is extremely low. This does *not* mean we should stop giving students control over their learning; instead, it means we should consider what we can do to influence students to choose more challenging options when given the chance. See Section 8.1 for further comments about this topic.
Teacher subject matter knowledge	0.11	This factor raises the hackles of so many in the teaching profession: how on earth can teacher subject knowledge have such a small effect on student achievement? Indeed, compare the effect size of growth mindset interventions (ES = 0.19) to subject knowledge (ES = 0.11) and, on the face of it, mindset wins hands down! Perhaps one of the explanations is that subject knowledge is only relevant in so far as it is expertly applied. In other words, subject knowledge might win a pub quiz but it won't inspire many students if it doesn't go hand-in-hand with expert pedagogy.
Teacher education	0.12	This is another one of those factors that puts the cat amongst the pigeons. How can initial teacher education have such a small effect on student achievement? (Worse still: what if the politicians find out, and think it a good idea to send in unqualified staff on minimum wages to plug the gap in teacher recruitment?) In our opinion, part of the story is that learning to teach follows a similar path to when you learn to drive: first you pass your test, then you learn how to drive. It doesn't mean we should no longer take lessons or attend graduate school; instead we should perhaps accept that the real impact comes later?
Web-based learning	0.18	Large sums of money and a significant amount of time have been invested in recent years to change teaching practices so that more use is made of web-based learning. Yet, the impact on student achievement is relatively low. Does this mean the potential impact is also low or that too many tokenistic approaches have been taken? If the only difference is that the activities are online rather than on paper (as they are in some cases) then no wonder the additional effects are low.
Reducing class size	0.21	This is the effect that John Hattie is most associated with though that is more to do with the misleading headline, 'Hattie says class size does not matter!' instead of the more accurate, 'Hattie says class size does not matter as much as expectations, behaviour, quality of instruction, response to feedback, to name but a few'. Of course, this more accurate statement doesn't make such an attention-grabbing headline so is rarely reported, but let's be clear: class size does matter. At least it does to parents and teachers, and often to students too. It's just that it doesn't affect students' achievement as much as we thought it would. It seems the quality of teaching is much, much more important. For example, which class would you want your own children to be in: a large class with the teacher who is currently the most effective, or the smallest class with the teacher who is currently the least effective in the school? Or, if you could reduce the number of students in your own classes, what would you opt for: removing six at random or choosing the two to pass on to someone else? (Hands up who has got those two picked out in their minds already.)

Source: Effect sizes taken from *250+ Influences on Student Achievement (August 2017)* available as a PDF on www.VisibleLearningPlus.com

education so that there is much more of an emphasis, and likely influence, on student learning outcomes than currently. He's not sat, as some would have him, in an ivory tower pontificating about the ills of education; he's rolling up his sleeves and doing his damnedest to improve things.

The same goes for Carol Dweck: she is not hiding away at Stanford, letting other people worry about the effects of growth mindset. She too is questioning, challenging, investigating, critiquing. She is revising her earlier work based on the challenges that have emerged. She is seeking explanations for the problems of transfer from research to practice. She continues to seek the best possible ways to implement growth mindset. So, watch this space!

2.5 • REDUCED EFFICACY 5: MINDSET AFFECTS QUALITIES OTHER THAN ACHIEVEMENT

Mindset is about how people think. It is not solely focused on improving levels of achievement. So, some of the benefits of being in a growth mindset are not going to show up in effect size scores. This doesn't make them any less valuable, of course. It simply means that there are many other benefits as well as those that can be measured. Or, as William Bruce Cameron wrote in the 1960s:

> It would be nice if all of the data which sociologists require could be enumerated because then we could run them through IBM machines and draw charts as the economists do. However, not everything that can be counted counts, and not everything that counts can be counted. (Cameron, 1963: 13)

That said, Carol Dweck and other researchers in the field have collected empirical evidence that shows people in a growth mindset are more:

- willing to take on challenges
- resilient when the going gets tough
- open to the idea that the right effort at the right time in the right direction makes a significant difference to success
- likely to attribute success and failure to a combination of factors such as talent, effort, timing, focus, perseverance and so on (rather than primarily to intelligence or lack of it)
- likely to respond to feedback constructively.

So, why *don't* these factors influence grades more? Surely a willingness to take on challenges, remain resilient when things get tough and respond constructively to feedback *will* make a significant difference to achievement? Probably, yes.

However, it will also be dependent upon the conditions being right such that the full influence can be felt. Figure 7 shows that this often isn't the case.

It is reassuring to know that Carol Dweck, John Hattie and other eminent researchers are not just presenting the data and then shrugging their shoulders; instead, they are examining the effects and asking, how can we make this better?

Being more willing to take on challenges, develop and apply resilience, and make better use of feedback are just some of the advantages of being in a growth mindset. These gains might not show up in measurable data – particularly not in the short term – but that ought not make them any less worthwhile.

Benefit of a Growth Mindset Attitude	Reasons Why the Growth Mindset Attitude Might Not Influence Achievement Scores
Willing to take on challenges	If there is insufficient challenge in the curriculum and/or pedagogy then the difference in achievement between those in a growth mindset compared to those in a fixed mindset is likely to be minimal. See Chapter 8 for further exploration of this.
Resilient when the going gets tough	Many adults are too quick to help, thus reducing the opportunity to develop, and benefit from, resilience. This is explored further in Chapter 8.
Belief that effort, strategy, perseverance and so on, will significantly improve outcomes	There may not be time to persevere long enough for gains to be measurable. Pressures from a swollen curriculum, the expected pace of lessons and commitments to other studies might cut short the opportunity to improve significantly.
Belief in the malleability of intelligence and talents	By itself, this attitude is unlikely to improve grades, and particularly not in the short to medium term. If it goes hand in hand with excellent instruction and time to invest in development then the outcomes are likely to be much greater.
Respond to feedback constructively	This is the one that is most likely to impact on grades but it assumes that feedback systems in school allow for improvements (which often they don't). See *Challenging Learning Through Feedback* (Nottingham & Nottingham, 2017) for more information.

NOW TRY THIS

1. Reviewing the five reasons we have suggested for why growth mindset is not (yet) showing a large impact on achievement, which of these do you think are most significant in your experience and why?

   - Mindset as third-hand knowledge.

   - Mindset is made to sound too easy.

   - Classrooms are complex.

   - Influences are complex.

   - Mindset isn't all about achievement anyway.

2. What other reasons would you add to this list?

3. At the end of Section 2.0, we asked you to consider whether growth mindset is still worth promoting in school despite its relatively low effect size. Would you add to or change your answer now that you've read five of the factors we think are adversely affecting mindset interventions?

4. Figure 6 shows some of the factors that John Hattie has found to have a lower-than-expected effect on student achievement. Next to each one, we have included

a commentary of possible explanations. Figure 8 shows some other factors from Hattie's database (2017) that might also be surprising. Talk with your colleagues about these factors and come up with your own commentary to explain the effects. Remember that the average effect of all 250+ factors is an effect size of 0.4 so anything less than that is below par.

▶ Figure 8: Other Influences with a Low Effect Size on Student Achievement

Influence	Effect Size	Your Commentary
Summer school	0.23	
Lack of illness	0.26	
Exercise/relaxation	0.26	
Use of calculators (maths)	0.27	
Open plan vs traditional classroom	0.01	
Non-standard dialect use	−0.29	
Student control over learning	0.02	
Ethnicity	0.12	
Humour	0.04	

2.6 • WHAT ARE THE CRITICISMS OF GROWTH MINDSET?

Indiana *pink*? Why, what a lie! It ain't no lie; I've seen it on a map and it's pink!

(authors): It would be no exaggeration to say I have written that statement from *Tom Sawyer Abroad* by Mark Twain ([1894] 1993: 270) more than 200 times in my life. Not because I wanted to but because the most common punitive response to bad behaviour when I was a teenager was to be given '50 statements' by our teachers. The more vindictive staff would even set 100 statements at a time.

Being given statements at my high school meant collecting from the school office a sheet of particularly banal sentences such as the Tom Sawyer quote above and copying them out one by one until the magic number was reached. Since I hated the place and acted up frequently, writing out statements was a weekly and sometimes daily torture.

That statement about Indiana came flooding back when I read an article in *The Spectator* magazine entitled: 'Schools are desperate to teach "growth mindset". But it's based on a lie'. The author writes: 'to claim that your performance in a cognitive task is entirely dictated by how hard you try and is nothing to do with raw candle-power flies in the face of more than 100 years of intelligence research' (Young, 2017).

However, in her book *Mindset*, Carol Dweck does not say that performance is 'entirely dictated' by how hard a person tries. Instead, she says that effort is *one* of the key ingredients to success. She also says strategy, resilience, support and desire are just as important as effort.

There are many criticisms of growth mindset. Although most are based on false premises, it is still worth sharing them here so that you are better able to respond to them if you encounter them at a later date.

The article mentioned above is one example of the growth mindset 'critiques' online. I say 'critiques' in quotes because the vast majority are based on over-simplifications of Carol Dweck's research and theories, which make it easier to discredit. The same is happening with the work of John Hattie, Dylan Wiliam and Guy Claxton, as mentioned at the beginning of this chapter.

So, rather than use this book to get you all revved up to try mindset strategies (we hope), only for you to find criticisms of mindset online, we thought it best to prepare you with some considered responses. As the saying goes, forewarned is forearmed.

Later in the book, we explore the more important or nuanced ideas but for now, we think this brief summary should help deal with the more common misrepresentations of fixed and growth mindsets.

2.6.1 • Common Critique One

As stated above, one of the most common critiques we encounter is the false assumption that Carol Dweck attributes someone's success entirely to their effort and ignores a person's innate ability.

Reality: Carol Dweck does *not* say that performance is 'entirely dictated' by how hard a person tries. Instead, she says that effort is one of the key ingredients to success. She also says strategy, resilience, support and desire are just as important as effort.

> A lot of parents or teachers say praise the effort, not the outcome. I say [that's] wrong: Praise the effort that led to the outcome or learning progress; tie the praise to it. It's not just effort, but strategy . . . so support the student in finding another strategy. Effective teachers who actually have classrooms full of children with a growth mindset are always supporting children's learning strategies and showing how strategies created that success.
>
> Students need to know that if they're stuck, they don't need just effort. You don't want them redoubling their efforts with the same ineffective strategies. You want them to know when to ask for help and when to use resources that are available. (Dweck, 2016)

2.6.2 • Common Critique Two

Growth mindset ignores the role of genetics and their influence on performance.

Reality: Carol Dweck does not ignore genetics! In fact, in almost every presentation we have heard from Carol Dweck, she has stated: 'Genetics are the starting point'. In other words, Usain Bolt smashed the 100-metre world record in 2008 because of his stunning genetics *and* his absolute dedication, training and desire to be the best (amongst other things).

> Yes, people come with different genes, and yes, genes can certainly influence our behaviour and development. But if we care about how people lead their lives – whether they lead constructive lives, how effectively they can cope when it matters, whether they can attain their goals, how they treat others – genes don't give us the answers. If we care about whether people can sustain successful relationships, succeed in school, and hold meaningful jobs, then environment matters greatly.

These depend on things we are taught. It may be that genes make it easier for some to learn adaptive skills, but under the right circumstances virtually everyone can. (Dweck, 2000: 15)

2.6.3 • Common Critique Three

Growth mindset is over-simplified nonsense; students are not going to succeed merely because they are shown pictures of brains exercising and neurons connecting together.

Reality: It is not the growth mindset research that is over-simplified; it is the reporting and implementation of it that is too often over-simplified (see Sections 2.1–2.5).

Students are not going to succeed merely because they are shown pictures of brains exercising and neurons connecting together. We often lament the fact that teachers are putting up a picture or a chart in their classrooms and expecting changes to occur. To have an impact, growth mindset practices have to infuse the classroom culture. Teachers have to embody them and not just spout about them.

Some of the other over-simplifications include:

- 'diagnosing' students with a fixed mindset and labelling them as such
- making students responsible for their mindset
- not understanding that classroom and school triggers are critically important
- focusing only on effort, which is just one of the routes to learning
- praising ineffective (or non-existent) effort.

There is also the significant issue of the high-stakes testing culture that exists in many schools. This is likely to undo any positive effect that might come from short-term or surface-level mindset interventions.

2.6.4 • Common Critique Four

Too many claims are made about the ability of growth mindset to nullify the limiting effects poverty and social injustice have on student achievement.

Reality: Over-enthusiastic advocates do indeed over-claim but Dweck herself does not. In a recent big study of 168,000 students in Chile where mindsets were examined in relation to socio-economic variables, Dweck and her colleagues discussed how these factors might affect each other:

To be clear, we are not suggesting that structural factors, like income inequality or disparities in school quality, are less important than psychological factors. Nor are we saying that teaching students a growth mindset is a substitute for systemic efforts to alleviate poverty and economic inequality. Such claims would stand at odds with decades of research and our own data. Rather, we are suggesting that structural inequalities can give rise to psychological inequalities and that those psychological inequalities can reinforce the impact of structural inequalities on achievement and future opportunity. (Claro, Paunesku & Dweck, 2016: 8667)

Importantly, the title of that paper was 'Growth mindset *tempers* the effects of poverty on academic achievement'. It does not say, 'Growth mindset cures/eradicates/ignores the

Although it is true to say that mindset messages are often over-simplified, the research underpinning these messages is not. So, critiques would be more correctly aimed at the application of mindset rather than at the theory itself.

There are indeed many over-claims about mindset. These can always be checked by referring to Dweck's own words and the research she has been involved with.

effects of poverty'. Advocates might be a little less careful but a quick reference back to Dweck's own work will show that she is very precise with her language (as you would expect from a Professor of Psychology who has all her work peer-reviewed before publication).

2.6.5 • Common Critique Five

Growth mindset is just another new 'stay-positive-at-all-costs' movement where the message is to always say yes, be happy, smile, celebrate mistakes, praise everyone. This makes people prone to over-confidence and unrealistic expectations.

Reality: Mindset is the term given to the observed phenomenon that people have subconscious (implicit) beliefs about intelligence. Some people think intelligence is an inherited, fixed quality whereas others think it is more malleable and developed. This belief exists anyway, whether or not they have read Carol Dweck's work. It is true that when in a growth mindset, a person is more likely to respond to challenge, feedback and mistakes in a more positive fashion than if they were in a fixed mindset but it does not mean they are impossibly happy, smiley people! It means they are more interested in learning opportunities than they would be if they were in a fixed mindset.

As for over-confidence, it would appear that being in a growth mindset might make you less prone to over-confidence, as this abstract from a paper by Ehrilnger, Mitchum and Dweck (2015) shows:

> Study 1 demonstrated that participants with an entity (fixed) theory of intelligence showed significantly more overconfidence than those with more incremental (malleable) theories. In Study 2, participants who were taught an entity theory of intelligence allocated less attention to difficult problems than those taught an incremental theory. Participants in this entity condition also displayed more overconfidence than those in the incremental condition, and this difference in overconfidence was mediated by the observed bias in attention to difficult problems. (Ehrilnger et al., 2015: 94)

2.6.6 • Common Critique Six

Educators are far too quick to speak with certainty about research that is not yet widely accepted. For example, educators will explain growth mindset in terms of neuroscience, even though those involved directly in neuro-research are themselves cautious in making claims about brain development and brain plasticity.

Though it is likely that educators have indeed over-claimed the certainty and efficacy of many aspects of research (and not just in terms of neuroscience or mindset), it is also true to say that talking about brain development with students *can* have a positive effect on their mindset. Indeed, many interventions from which the impact of mindset is drawn, have involved teaching students about brain plasticity. They have explained to young people how the grey matter within our brains can shrink or thicken; that neural connections can be forged and refined or weakened and severed; and that every time an action is repeated, new 'wires' or neural pathways can be created. Though these explanations are simplistic, there is evidence that thinking our brains are *able* to change at any age is more likely to lead to growth mindset thinking than to lead to fixed mindset thinking. After all, in a growth mindset, people believe that change is likely, whereas in a fixed mindset, people believe abilities and intelligence are far more static.

> In the growth mind-set classes, students read and discussed an article entitled 'You Can Grow Your Brain.' They were taught that the brain is like a muscle that gets stronger with use and that learning prompts neurons in the brain to grow new

connections. From such instruction, many students began to see themselves as agents of their own brain development . . . Other researchers have replicated our results. Psychologists Catherine Good, now at Baruch College, Joshua Aronson of New York University and Michael Inzlicht, now at the University of Toronto, reported in 2003 that a growth mind-set workshop raised the math and English achievement test scores of seventh graders. In a 2002 study Aronson, Good (then a graduate student at the University of Texas at Austin) and their colleagues found that college students began to enjoy their schoolwork more, value it more highly and get better grades as a result of training that fostered a growth mind-set. (Dweck, 2015b)

Why should [memory] retain so much better the events of yesterday than those of last year and, best of all, those of an hour ago? Why should repeating an experience strengthen our recollection of it? Why should drugs, fevers, asphyxia, and excitement resuscitate things long since forgotten? . . . Such peculiarities seem quite fantastic. . . .

Evidently, then, **the faculty does not exist absolutely, but works under conditions; and the quest of the conditions becomes the . . . most interesting task**.

James, 1890

WHEN DOES MINDSET WORK BEST?

In the previous chapter, we shared the evidence that growth mindset interventions are not working as well as expected in schools. Not yet, anyway. We also gave suggestions as to why this might be.

This chapter shows that the effects are in fact highly nuanced and make much more of a difference in some circumstances than in others. Indeed, the meta-analysis by Burnette et al. (2013) that we described in Chapter 2, can be summarised as follows:

> Implicit theories are indeed consequential for self-regulatory processes and goal achievement. However, these consequential relations are nuanced. We sought to clarify when (e.g., when facing ego threats) and how (e.g., monitoring processes) implicit theories are consequential for goal achievement. Findings suggest . . . that the literature would be better served by asking **when** and how implicit theories are consequential . . . rather than asking **if** incremental theories are generally beneficial. (Burnette et al., 2013: 680)

> Although it is clear that mindset does make a difference, the question remains 'when' does it make the *most* difference?

3.0 • GOALS, STRATEGIES AND EXPECTATIONS

On page 670 of their report, Burnette et al. (2013) shared their SOMA (Setting, Operating, Monitoring, Achievement) model showing the relationship between incremental beliefs (growth mindset) and goal achievement. Some of their findings are shown in Figure 5 of this book, which to recap shows:

- The effect of 'learning goals' on goal achievement is 0.32, which compares favourably with the effect of 'performance goals' of *minus* 0.02. The difference between these two effect sizes is 0.34.

(Note: Learning goals are often described as 'mastery-orientation'; they focus on learning and improvement, whereas performance goals or 'performance-orientation' focus on demonstrating competence relative to others, generally in an attempt to look clever or to avoid looking stupid.)

- The effect of 'mastery strategies' on goal achievement is 0.31, which compares favourably with the effect of 'helpless strategies' of *minus* 0.24. The difference between these two effect sizes is 0.55.

(Note: Mastery strategies are used by a person who responds to challenges by remaining task-focused and aiming for mastery in spite of difficulties and setbacks, whereas helpless strategies are used by a person who responds to challenges by giving up and withdrawing, acting as if the situation were out of their control.)

- The effect of 'expectations' on goal achievement is 0.41, which unsurprisingly compares favourably with the effect of 'negative emotions' of *minus* 0.32. The difference between these two effect sizes is 0.73.

(Note: Expectations refer to a person thinking, 'I believe in my ability to reach my goal', whereas 'negative emotions' are connected with the belief that 'I feel hopeless or anxious when evaluating my goal progress so far'.)

What their SOMA model shows, which Figure 6 does not, is that a person holding an incremental theory is much more likely to set learning goals for themselves, employ mastery strategies and have positive expectations of success.

As Burnette et al. hypothesise:

> Implicit theories will predict goal setting processes, with entity theorists especially likely to set performance goals oriented toward proving their ability and incremental theorists especially likely to set learning goals oriented toward developing mastery. After all, one of the most immediate consequences of believing that ability is fixed (entity beliefs) is that people will try to demonstrate that they possess the ability in question, and one of the most immediate consequences of believing that ability can be developed (incremental beliefs) is that learning has value. (2013: 659)

3.1 • MINDSET WORKS BEST WHEN GOALS ARE LEARNING-ORIENTATED

Performance goals focus on success relative to others. Learning goals focus on personal progress.

Here is the bad news: there is a *negative* correlation between incremental theories and performance goals. That is to say that if you are in a growth mindset, and you perceive the task in front of you is a 'performance-related goal' (e.g. let's see who is the best), then the benefit derived from being in a growth mindset is reduced.

Furthermore, when beating their peers on performance tasks motivates a person with an entity theory, then the negative effects of being in a fixed mindset are reduced. Thus, a person with a fixed mindset in these circumstances is likely to apply himself or herself just as much, maybe even more, than the person in a growth mindset who suspects there are no learning opportunities within the task.

Pause for a moment to consider how many tasks in school are performance-related, either by design or by ethos! Small wonder, then, that being in a growth mindset is less effective in real-world classrooms than we thought it would be.

Of course, if you can set learning-related tasks for all of your students *and* you can get them all into a growth mindset then the effects should be significant. We realise that those are two very big *ifs* but then that is what this book aims to help you with, particularly Chapters 5, 6 and 7.

3.2 • MINDSET WORKS BEST WHEN THERE IS CHALLENGE

As we mentioned in Section 3.0, mastery strategies are used by a person who responds to challenges by remaining task-focused, whereas helpless strategies are used by a person who responds to difficulties by giving up and withdrawing.

Therefore, if there is no challenge then there is no need for a growth mindset; you will simply 'get the job done' and move on. It is only when confronted with difficulties that anxieties and fears, or grit and determination, rear their heads; that is when your mindset makes a difference.

If you are in a fixed mindset then it is likely that you will focus on ways to avoid losing face. Classic strategies include making excuses, predicting failure, claiming nonchalance and so on. On the other hand, if you are in a growth mindset then you are more likely to have a go, seek feedback, try again and persevere. This is when mastery strategies are crucial.

Little challenge means little effect of mindset; high challenge is when mindset matters most. Chapter 8 explores this topic in much more depth.

3.3 • MINDSET WORKS BEST WHEN THERE IS A CHICKEN AND AN EGG!

When expectations of success are high then we are more likely to engage with a task; even more likely if it is a learning task rather than a performance-related one. This, in turn, leads to a greater chance of success.

Similarly, the more success we have previously encountered within the same or a similar context, the more likely we are to think we will be successful next time too. Of course, mindset makes a difference as Burnette et al.'s meta-analysis showed but so too does prior success.

So, there we have it: a chicken or egg situation! We are more likely to succeed if we have high expectations and we are more likely to have high expectations if we have succeeded previously. So now for the clichéd question: which comes first?

As a teacher, a leader, a parent, or indeed anyone responsible for the well-being and success of others, it is up to us to raise the bar of expectation by showing those we care for how much further they can go than they thought possible. Achieve this and we will set them on an upwards spiral. With more successful experiences under their belt, they are more likely to raise their expectations next time. With higher expectations, they are more likely to succeed. And so it goes on.

Of course, very sadly the opposite is true for so many students: negative experiences lead to low expectations, which in turn lead to lower levels of success and so on. No wonder there are so many disaffected teenagers in our schools if they have endured years upon years of a negative spiral.

> A growth mindset is more likely to exist when a person has experienced success beforehand. Success leads to a growth mindset and a growth mindset leads to success.

The good news (for those of us investing our time and energy in growth mindset strategies) is that teaching our protégés the theory of mindset can be one way to start off the upwards spiral. By showing them that talents and intelligence are malleable, they will be more likely to suppose that changing their efforts, strategy and perseverance will reap rewards.

This topic is explored in more depth in Chapter 10.

3.4 • MINDSET FOR LIFELONG LEARNING

> A growth mindset is more important when goals are less grade-orientated and more focused on engaging in the fullness of life.

This book has been very research-heavy so far. Our focus, as with all the books in the Challenging Learning series, is to bridge the divide between research and practice. So, we'd like to round this chapter off with some practical suggestions.

To begin with, we'd like to share an email from one of our colleagues. After we had completed draft one of this book, we sent the manuscript to our team to ask for their feedback. The following is part of the response from our organisation's financial controller, Beccy Morley, shared with permission:

> Reading as a parent, I actually found the beginning bit really interesting regarding misinterpretation of theory and I think parents could do with being armed with more of this stuff because teachers do sometimes cite such things and there's a tendency to believe them as the professionals (my son told me a couple of weeks ago that they'd done a diagnostic at school and he was a kinaesthetic learner! Before working here I wouldn't have been equipped to have a discussion about that, but I was, so we did, and it wasn't quite as bad as he made it sound! In fact, he was just trying to use it as an excuse!).
>
> I know that this is a book mainly for teachers, so I get that the positive benefits of growth mindset are phrased in terms of achievement. However, I think its relevance is far wider, in terms of wellbeing and developing well-rounded people able to enjoy life. Like most parents, I worry about the world the kids are going to grow up into; tech means the world is shrinking so they'll be competing for jobs with people worldwide, far more jobs will be automated, and the 'edge' is going to come from being more creative and more human – being able to combine disciplines, take risks in the interest of innovation and 'have a go'. To me, growth mindset seems to foster these things.
>
> And really, if I'm honest, I worry more about their wellbeing than their future careers and, again, growth mindset would seem to feed wellbeing by making sure they don't shut down opportunities and have as wide a range of experiences as possible.
>
> I think I've said to you before that I had the 'gifted and talented' label all through school. I don't think it made me less resilient in the subjects that I was good at, because when I struggled I had the rock-solid conviction that I'd get it in the end, but I closed off whole areas to myself that I considered weren't 'my subjects'. I'm thinking of music and sport in particular, which could arguably have given me great pleasure across the years and improved my physical health and wellbeing. It's probably only in the last five years that I've actually started doing more exercise, which I would have previously said I couldn't join in with because 'I wasn't sporty'.

Having started to do more I've realised that a lot of the Lycra-clad, sporty people are actually no more able than I am, they're just more confident of the 'subject' and happy to give it a go (not that it matters if I'm able, as long as I'm enjoying it/ feeling some benefit). I wonder what pleasure I've missed out on across the years from not playing team games, what health benefits I've missed, which more varied social connections I might have made?

The same goes for people who 'aren't numbers people' like me, whose lives are going to be 'less-well' if they end up in debt because they've avoided doing the maths, etc. I'm only highlighting this because in my mind, I guess, achievement (as in grades) is still intrinsically linked to work (i.e. what job you get) whereas really achievement should be about wellbeing, i.e. wanting students to achieve well across a range of subjects to give them the best chance of enjoying an adulthood in which they shut down as few opportunities as possible and have a wide range of experiences that feed their wellbeing (and simultaneously give them a competitive edge in the workplace).

We couldn't have put it better ourselves, Beccy. Thank you.

3.5 • MINDSET WITHOUT SHAME

If you have identified that you are sometimes, or maybe even often, in a fixed mindset then feel no shame! As we hope we've been able to show you so far, we are all a mix. And yet, there are so many people who give the impression that being in a fixed mindset is a sign of weakness or even shame. Certainly, there are students in schools teaching growth mindset who feel that mindset is yet another factor being used to explain their shortcomings (see Chapter 10 for more details).

Teachers are particularly prone to worrying what their colleagues will think if they admit to being in a fixed mindset. After all, they reason, how can a teacher in a fixed mindset show students how to get into a growth mindset?

In the early days of running workshops on mindset, we would ask everyone to think of a time they were in a fixed mindset. Almost everybody would pick an occasion involving something low down their priority list: a potential hobby they had never attempted; or something manifestly true that they've learned to shrug off (e.g. being tone deaf or hopelessly inept at building flat-packed furniture); or 'owning' a criticism that is humorously but frequently levelled at them (e.g. 'I have to make everything perfect' or 'I am a terrible prevaricator'). Interestingly, when we asked them to think of fixed mindset attitudes they had witnessed in *other* people, then all of a sudden the examples would become far more consequential: 'Management have a very fixed mindset towards performance reviews' or 'The cynics in the staff room always assume change isn't possible with *these* kids!'

> Mindset is more influential when a person recognises they are prone to both fixed and growth mindset thinking.

These are some of the reasons why we now ask delegates to think about self-efficacy first before then thinking about fixed and growth mindset examples. We have done the same thing with the 'Now Try This' suggestions at the end of Section 1.5.

Another approach to take is to name your 'Fixed Mindset Persona' (FMP), own it, talk about it and then look for ways to change it. Indeed, this was one of our favourite suggestions that came from Carol Dweck during our most recent tour with her in August 2017. The process is as follows.

3.5.1 • Recognise When You Are in a Fixed Mindset

The following behaviours are classic examples of when you might be in a fixed mindset:

- You tell yourself, 'I can't do that' or 'I've never been good at that so why would I expect success now?'
- You look for ways to get out of trying anything you are unsure of or you hide your attempts from other people.
- You feel embarrassed, self-conscious or nervous about how people might assess your talents (or lack of them).
- You make excuses beforehand so that the reasons for failure can be recalled and relied upon if indeed you do fail.
- You claim not to care whether you succeed or fail and/or you diminish the value of success.
- You encourage other people to have a go before you in the hope that they will prove how difficult it is to succeed.
- You think to yourself, 'I've managed to get this far in life without success in this thing so why worry? Life will go on as before!'

3.5.2 • Name that Fixed Mindset

When you recognise you are getting into a fixed mindset, imagine it is your alter-ego surfacing. Think of it as your FMP. Give it a name; one that means something to you. For example:

- The name of an adult from your past who exhibited a particularly strong fixed mindset towards you. Common examples include a parent, teacher, uncle or aunt, or a coach who criticised you and made you feel incompetent.
- The name (or nickname) of an ex-boss or colleague who exhibited a particularly strong fixed mindset (such as seeking praise rather than feedback; or sticking to systems that plainly didn't work because 'that's how we do it around here', rather than looking for ways to improve them).
- A fictional character from your childhood literature (e.g. Eeyore, Charlie Brown, The Grinch, Wilbur from *Charlotte's Web*) who is the eternal pessimist, routinely accepting the inevitably disappointing outcomes.
- A character in TV, film or media you know well (e.g. Homer Simpson, Statler & Waldorf from *The Muppets*, Sadness from *Inside Out*, Javert from *Les Misèrables*, Michael Scott/David Brent in *The Office*) who believes the world is unfair but that there is nothing they can do about it; is a grouch; critical of everything; or has the belief that no one is ever good enough.
- Someone in your life currently who fits the bill but who won't ever find out you use their name to evoke ideas of fixed mindset thinking!

Remember to choose a name you would associate with fixed mindset thinking rather than just someone you don't like! Some of the most negative characters in fiction might actually have been in a growth mindset. For example, Cruella de Ville or Lady Macbeth believed they could influence the people and the circumstances around them for their own material gain. As such, they probably were not in a fixed mindset.

Photograph by andrewbillingtonphotography.com

3.5.3 • Talk About Your FMP and Talk to It

Having named your FMP, talk about it and talk to it. For example, talk about what causes it to surface and what you can do about it when it does. Welcome it, hear it out, thank it for causing you to think more, and then invite it to join you on your growth mindset quest! Take it on your journey as you try a new challenge, persist with something particularly difficult and so on.

> This is not meant to sound like some new-age psychobabble. Instead, it is intended to be a bit of fun and to reduce the demonising effect that has emerged since the idea of 'fixed mindset' came to popular attention. Obviously, we would all much rather be in a growth mindset but it is not that simple. There are many reasons why we might be in a fixed mindset. So, when it does happen then normalise it rather than demonise it. Play with it and look for ways to change it. First of all though, recognise it when it comes knocking.

3.5.4 • Recognise Your FMP Triggers

When your FMP comes knocking then pause for a moment to recognise the triggers that provoked it. Some examples might include:

> **Losing control**: Feeling that you are losing control of a situation. In teaching, this might occur when students are behaving badly; having too many assignments to grade; worrying about the lack of time to cover all the topics before your students take their exams, and so on.

When someone identifies their own fixed mindset behaviour and triggers, they are more able to turn these to their advantage.

Assumptions: Assuming that you can't change things or assuming the worst intentions will come from others. For example, assuming that you are incapable of exerting any influence over outcomes; thinking that other people believe you are scared, unwilling or pessimistic; or in the case of teaching, assuming the visitor to your classroom is looking to criticise you rather than learn with you.

Imposter syndrome: Believing that everyone thinks you are a phoney or that if you succeed then it was by fluke rather than by ability or effort. Perfectionists are particularly prone to this. The good news though is that only highly capable people ever feel the imposter syndrome!

Rare criticism: If you are used to a lot of praise then you might find the rare occurrence of criticism harder to take than most. This could trigger your FMP to rear its head and begin whispering in your ear, 'Told you so! You're not that good after all, are you?'

If you are in teaching then you are unlikely to receive a lot of public praise – the media, after all, like to blame us every time young people put a step wrong. However, it is also true that the majority in our profession regard themselves to be better teachers than the majority of other teachers. Work that one out if you can! So, it may well happen quite often that a teacher expecting to receive glowing praise following a lesson observation is confronted with less fulsome comments than they were expecting. This, in turn, could very easily trigger their own FMP.

Over-simplification: Expecting that if you do a, b and c that it will lead to x, y and z, then being surprised, annoyed and disappointed when it doesn't. Classic examples in teaching include, 'I told them how to do this so I don't understand why they can't do it' and 'I talk about growth mindset all the time so I can't see why they would have such a negative attitude'. Incidentally, the FMP that emerges from this is quite likely to be connected to 'those kids can't'.

3.5.5 • Reduce the Impact of Your FMP

Each time your FMP surfaces, talk about it, talk to it and then reduce its impact. For example, if it has been triggered by a loss of control then look for small steps to regain control; or if the trigger has been a negative assumption then what evidence can you find to the contrary?

Here are some questions to help you think through next steps:

1. What part of your FMP do you have most influence over?

2. How could you adapt the part you have most control over so that it is more growth mindset focused?

3. When will you know you have made enough progress that your FMP is less dominant?

It will never be the case that the FMP will go away completely – not if you're taking on challenges. It is instead a lifelong journey that you will be taking with it.

Also, the FMP was born for a good reason: to help you do the 'right thing' and win approval as a child; for being good, smart, sporty and so on. It's just that the 'play it safe and win approval' stance is ultimately limiting.

NOW TRY THIS

1. FMP for Your Students

   Introduce the idea of Fixed Mindset Personas to your students. Talk about the reasoning behind the approach and the benefits of naming and talking to their persona. Your students could also create images of their FMP and make a display about them. Even better, they could also create Growth Mindset Personas too; name them, illustrate them and then create an equal and opposite display next to the FMP display.

2. Fixed Mindset Characters in Fiction (Fix-ional Characters?)

   Another possibility is to identify Fixed Mindset Characters (FMC) in film, television and literature. You could of course do this with your colleagues and/or your students.

   Interestingly, when we asked our own colleagues for exactly that when writing this book, some of the examples they came back with didn't fit our own definitions of fixed mindset! Then there are characters who might be in a fixed mindset at the beginning and a growth mindset at the end of the story. So, perhaps it is not as easy as it first seems.

   In our mind, an FMC is not the same as the villain or negative character. For example, The Joker, as played by Heath Ledger in *The Dark Knight*, would be one that, although deeply troubled, has the sense that he is master of his own destiny, with enough potency to change the world as he goes. To us, that is very much a growth mindset, albeit one that is used for devilish intent.

   The examples we gave in Section 3.5 (point 2) are the closest we can get to an agreement on Fixed Mindset Characters. Here are some others that we weren't so sure about (and not just because we don't know who some of them are!):

   > Bellwether from *Zootopia*
   >
   > Buzz Lightyear from *Toy Story*
   >
   > Carl from *Up*
   >
   > Chief Tui and Maui from *Moana*
   >
   > Edmund in *The Lion, the Witch and the Wardrobe*
   >
   > Elsa from *Frozen*
   >
   > Karen from *Will and Grace*
   >
   > Peter Pan
   >
   > Scarlett O'Hara in *Gone With The Wind*
   >
   > Vernon Dursley in *Harry Potter*

   We also found it interesting to note that most of the examples we could agree on – as well as those in the list above that we have our doubts about – are male characters. Everyone we asked struggled to think of many female Fixed Mindset Characters. We could think of lots of growth mindset ones but very few fixed mindset examples.

   So, perhaps that is another thing you could challenge your students or colleagues to come up with too: bonus points for female FMC examples!

HOW DOES MINDSET INTERACT WITH EDUCATION?

One of the most damaging aspects of the 'gift' mentality is that it makes us think we can know in advance who has the gift. This, I believe, is what makes us try to identify groups who have it and groups who don't – as in, boys have it and girls don't, or those who show early promise have it and others don't.

Dweck, 2012a: 7

MINDSET IN EDUCATION

As we have shown in the first three chapters, people already hold an implicit belief about intelligence. Some of us tend to be in a fixed mindset, some of us in a growth mindset and almost all of us experience both mindsets in our lives. This chapter explores the interaction between mindset and education, and addresses the following:

1. The effect that terms such as 'bright', 'gifted' and 'less able' have on mindset and expectations.

2. The assumptions that are made about why some students attain higher grades than others.

3. How mindset affects the conclusions we draw about the origins of talent, and how our beliefs about the origins of talent affect our mindset.

4. How common descriptions of schools and students are used as excuses when in a fixed mindset and as challenges to overcome when in a growth mindset.

4.0 • INTRODUCING ALISHA AND ZACK

Allow us to introduce two fictitious characters central to this story: Alisha and Zack. Their story will lead us to consider some more general thoughts about where talent comes from, which in turn will lead to a consideration of where mindset comes from.

Although Alisha and Zack have been in the same class all the way through school, it is fair to say they've been at opposite ends of the achievement scale. Alisha has aced every test she has ever taken in school. Zack has not; in fact, he has barely scraped a pass in any subject at school, particularly those relying heavily on literacy.

If we were to ask you to characterise the differences between two children such as Alisha and Zack who are at opposite ends of the grading scale then what would you say? Would you be tempted to think of Alisha as a bright child, a high achiever, perhaps even gifted and talented? Whereas, might you think of Zack as a low achiever, less able or someone who is just 'not the academic type'?

If we pushed you further and asked you to *explain* the differences between these two, then what might you say? How many people might say it's just that some children are more academically minded than others? They believe that some were put on this earth to be intellectual, and others have strengths that lie elsewhere. Some are lucky, have a natural predisposition and are wired the right way; others are not.

Indeed, what are some of the euphemisms you might expect to hear used as short hand for such contrasting competencies? Figure 10 shows some of the terms we have heard used by staff in schools.

▶ Figure 10: Terms Often Used to Describe Students

Students with high grades	Students with low grades
Bright	Slow
Brilliant	Struggler
High achiever	Low achiever
Gifted and talented	Special educational needs
Academic	Non-academic
Top group	Bottom group
More able	Less able

These are only some of the variants and you may have heard others. Furthermore, we have purposefully steered clear of the more offensive terms that might be used in playgrounds but you could perhaps think of these too.

So, what do these references reveal in terms of beliefs about talents and abilities? How many of them imply that some people 'have' these things (for example, intelligence, talents, academic minds) and others simply do 'not have' them? How many suggest that some people are capable and others are not? In other words, which of them are more likely to come from, as well as lead towards, a fixed mindset?

Then consider what effect all this will have on Alisha and Zack. Presumably, Alisha will be thought of as the one who 'has' the talent, capability, possibility. Zack, on the other hand, is more likely to be thought of as the one who does 'not have' those things.

If this were the case then what would you predict for the ways in which people might respond to Alisha and Zack? How likely is it that people will place high expectations on Alisha and low expectations on Zack? How many times will people enjoy celebrating and drawing attention to Alisha's continuing successes? As for Zack, how many people would be tempted to explain that his talents 'lie elsewhere'? Place a bet on which of these two children would be most likely to win prizes at school and be elected as school captain and you'll soon realise there are very short odds on Alisha winning!

So, what does this all mean in terms of mindset? Unsurprisingly, the more these situations exist in your school, team, organisation or family, the more likely a fixed mindset will be influencing interactions and decision-making.

NOW TRY THIS

Figure 10 shows some of the terms often used to describe students at the top and bottom of the competence scale. Here are some activities based on these terms:

1. Discuss the terms with your colleagues. Identify which terms you are comfortable using and which ones you'd rather avoid. Think of reasons why.

2. Listen out for these terms in your staff room. Which ones are used? How do people respond when they hear these terms?

3. Are there any terms you use (or could use) that would imply more malleability of intelligence and talents? For example, 'more focused/less focused' or 'determined/indifferent'.[1]

4. If you were to go to night class to learn a language you'd never used before, you would expect to start in the 'beginner' group. As you make progress, you would then look to move into the 'intermediate' group and ultimately into the 'advanced' group. These terms seem to be less value-laden than those shown in Figure 10. Discuss with your colleagues some of the possible explanations for this.

4.1 • ALISHA AND ZACK'S BACKGROUNDS

Thus far, we have only told you that Alisha gets good grades at school and Zack doesn't. So, let us give you some more information about these two. Figure 11 shows a brief comparison of some aspects of their home life and background.

▶ Figure 11: **Circumstantial Differences Between Alisha and Zack**

Alisha	Zack
Alisha's parents have high aspirations for her educationally.	Zack's parents are not too concerned about grades because there is lots of work locally.
Her mother is professor of language and her father runs the family business.	His parents work on the assembly line in the local factory.
As a family, they play lots of word games together and Alisha receives high praise if she does well.	As a family, they watch a lot of television.
Alisha is very competitive and always wants to beat her siblings at everything.	Zack doesn't care if he wins or loses.
Before she started school, Alisha was able to independently read books by Roald Dahl.	Before starting school, Zack learned a few letters and could recognise his own name.
Alisha is an articulate, confident child who enjoys interacting with adults.	Zack doesn't say very much and is particularly shy around adults.

1. Although we are asking you to think about how 'fixed' terms such as 'bright' or 'gifted' might be changed to more 'malleable' qualities such as 'focused', 'determined' or advanced, we are suggesting this is a starting point rather than a solution in itself. What is needed is not only a change in language but also consideration of the circumstances in which those terms would be used.

Given the differences in their backgrounds, how much more likely is it that Alisha will succeed at school than Zack?

The differences shown in Figure 11 are unlikely to change your opinion that Alisha is more accomplished with language than Zack. Rather, it is likely to confirm the conclusion and add some explanation to it.

However, for many people it might also confirm some of their prejudices: that Alisha is clever because she comes from an 'academic family' whereas there is little wonder Zack doesn't do well; you only have to look at where he comes from to know that he is never going to be the brightest student. We do not agree with these sentiments but we state them because, sadly, they are so very common. Worse still, 'explanations' such as these are sometimes just the tip of the iceberg. The really ugly prejudices that link race, gender, poverty, sexuality, disability, social class, cultural heritage, beauty, family traits and so on, with expectations for talents and intelligence, can be even more pervasive and pernicious.

The differences in Alisha and Zack's backgrounds go some way to showing how complex the story of talent is.

However, the opposite might be true also: that the information in Figure 11 helps to explain why Alisha has made more progress with language so far than Zack has. The emerging story might help persuade people that intelligence and abilities are not fixed; instead they are developed and nurtured over time. If that is the case then Alisha's potential has been nurtured a lot more by her circumstance than Zack's has so far.

This sort of conclusion is more in keeping with a growth mindset. Indeed, it is more likely to *lead to* a growth mindset and *come from* a growth mindset.

NOW TRY THIS

Figure 11 identifies some differences in the early experiences of our two fictitious characters, Alisha and Zack.

1. What are some of the other classic reasons for differences between students resembling Alisha and Zack in your school?

2. With your colleagues, sort through all the reasons shown in Figure 11 as well as any other possibilities you've added. Rank them according to significance, or group them according to things that can be changed and things that can't.

3. Discuss what, if anything, you and your colleagues think you can do to not let these inequalities determine the educational chances of Alisha and Zack.

4.2 • ALISHA AND ZACK START SCHOOL

When Alisha and Zack started school, they were placed in the same class. The teachers knew that Alisha was the oldest in the class and Zack the youngest but, otherwise, they knew very little about them.

That said, Alisha and Zack's teachers will also have ascertained the children's gender and race, and might have made judgements about social class and appearance. In some countries, Alisha and Zack's teachers will be given information about the children's socio-economic status and cultural heritage; if either of them has a disability then depending on the type and whether or not it has been identified yet, the teachers might

be given information about that too. In a few cases, patterns relating to family 'traits' might also have been volunteered by long-serving members of staff who taught Alisha or Zack's parents or even grandparents.

We would hope that none of these factors would unduly influence expectations but they do in some schools. Just think about the terms you have heard used to describe students and schools, and think about the negative inferences these might lead to. Figure 12 shows some of the examples we (the authors of this book) have heard when working with schools, preschools and colleges around the world.

▶ Figure 12: **Descriptions Used by Some School Staff**

I work in . . .	This student . . .
A socially deprived school (and you know what goes with that).	Comes from a tough neighbourhood (so I'm more of a social worker than a teacher).
A failing school (so I do what I can but I'm swimming against the tide).	Has a long line of unemployment in the family (so aspirations are very low).
A high-performing school (which means we've got the pressures of pushy parents to deal with).	Is from a single-parent family (so, the parent has no time to help).
A white, working-class school (and as the media tells us, that category has the lowest aspirations and most offensive attitudes).	Has behavioural problems (so any failings are purely down to bad attitudes).
A very traditional school (so we're not allowed to try anything new or innovative).	Has a lot of issues (so there's only so much we can do to help).
A school with a very weak principal (so I've got my hands tied in terms of what I can do around here).	Has failed at other schools (so it'll be a major surprise if they succeed here).

The phrases and corresponding implications shown in parentheses in Figure 12 give examples of the sorts of bias that exist in some schools. This means Alisha and Zack are not entering a neutral environment; they are entering a very subjective one. For example, the type of school they joined, and the 'types' of students who normally attend that school, will influence perceptions towards our two central characters. If, for example, behavioural problems are a rarity in the school but one of our students has ADHD then they will encounter a differing degree of bias than if they attend a school for which behavioural problems are perceived to be more common.

How does this affect mindset, and how will mindset affect the responses to these situations? The examples given in Figure 12 are often given as reasons for why change is less likely than in other contexts – for example, 'there is only so much we can do with students from socially deprived backgrounds' or 'we are not allowed to be creative because of the pushy parents we have to deal with'.

If you are in a fixed mindset then you are likely to view the examples given, and others like them, as excuses for having limited influence on outcomes, whereas if you are in a growth mindset then you are more likely to view them as challenges to overcome.

The descriptions shown here are all too common and give a sense of the fixed mindset thinking that exists in some schools.

4.3 • ALISHA AND ZACK MEET THEIR TEACHERS

Now let's introduce two of the staff at the school Alisha and Zack attend: Mr Adams and Miss Zane.

Mr Adams is an experienced teacher with a passion for language. He has studied with the Royal Shakespeare Company and is a published author of crime novels.

Miss Zane is one of the teaching assistants in the school. She generally works with the children who are falling behind in their studies and does everything she can to boost their self-esteem.

Figure 13 is *not* intended to reflect the reality in every school nor even perhaps in every country. That said, it *is* common in many contexts. Plus, it is likely to play a significant role in influencing mindset, as will be explored later.

▶ Figure 13: **Ways in Which Alisha and Zack Are Taught**

Alisha	Zack
Alisha is referred to by many staff in the school as 'gifted and talented'.	Zack is referred to by many staff in the school as 'below average'.
For literacy, Alisha is taught primarily by Mr Adams.	For literacy, Zack has many of his lessons with Miss Zane.
Alisha is grouped together with children who also enjoy and excel at language.	Zack is grouped together with children who also struggle with reading and writing.
Alisha's group ask thought-provoking and imaginative questions, and talk excitedly about the books they are reading currently.	Many of the children in Zack's group are reluctant readers and see reading as a chore rather than a pleasure.
Mr Adams has very high expectations for Alisha's group. He doesn't use extrinsic motivators because Alisha's group are already highly motivated to achieve.	Miss Zane has high expectations for Zack's group but she is in a minority amongst the staff. She uses rewards and other extrinsic motivators to keep the kids on track.
Alisha has opted to join an extension class with Mr Adams because she enjoys drama and literacy so much.	Zack doesn't think the extension class would be relevant for him even though Miss Zane has tried to persuade him otherwise.

If even half of the actions shown in Figure 13 reflect the reality for students such as Alisha and Zack in your school then what is the likely outcome? Is the gap between their varying degrees of competence likely to narrow or extend? Will this level the playing field or exacerbate it even more?

What effect will it have on mindset? Will the widening gap confirm the belief that Alisha is clever and Zack is not, or will it show just how many more opportunities Alisha has to grow her talents? As with all the sections in this chapter, the answer will depend very much on the mindset of the person being asked: those in a fixed mindset will point to Alisha's motivation, excitement for language and high performance as further proof that some kids are academically minded and others are not; whereas those in a growth mindset will argue that the enhanced opportunities to grow her talents explain why Alisha is out-performing Zack at the moment.

Students like Zack who have not yet made much progress are often given fewer opportunities in school than students like Alisha. This influences mindset and expectations.

A teacher in a fixed mindset would explain success in terms of a student's 'natural ability', whereas a teacher in a growth mindset would draw attention to a student's prior learning.

NOW TRY THIS

To help you and your colleagues think through some of the detail of Figure 13, we recommend that you use an opinion line such as the one shown in Figure 14.

▶ Figure 14: Opinion Line to Consider Varying Degrees of Agreement and Disagreement

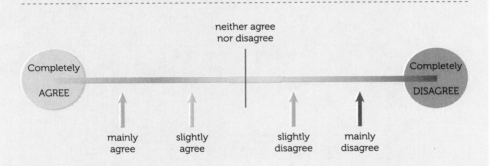

Ideally, you would create a physical representation of the diagram shown and ask your colleagues to stand at the appropriate place along the line to indicate their level of agreement or disagreement with the statements we have designed (shown below). The 'line' could be created simply enough by placing a card with the words 'completely agree' at the far left-hand side of the room, a 'completely disagree' card at the far right-hand side of the room, and then cards with the other descriptors shown in Figure 14 at intervals between the two extremes.

Once you have created the line, introduce the activity to your colleagues. Say that you will give them a statement connected to Alisha and Zack, then ask them to stand at the appropriate place along the line to represent their views.

For example, one of your colleagues might completely disagree with the first statement that, 'It is OK to call Alisha a "gifted and talented" student', and so would stand at the right-hand end of the opinion line; whereas, another colleague might slightly disagree so would stand just to the right of the middle; whereas another might agree in the most

An opinion line is a useful convention for stimulating dialogue around important concepts such as mindset. More examples can be found in *Challenging Learning Through Dialogue* by Nottingham, Nottingham and Renton (2017).

(Continued)

(Continued)

part with the statement and so would stand where the 'mainly agree' point is along your opinion line. Once people have taken their positions, you should then ask them to give reasons for their stance, to listen to counter-arguments from others, and to move along the line if they are persuaded to revise their opinion by someone's thoughts.

Here are some statements to get you started. Notice that they are designed to provoke differences of opinion so that you can get into some exploratory dialogue with your colleagues. Do not give out all the statements at once! Instead, begin with the one you think will prompt most thought, explore that properly with your colleagues and then move on to another one if time permits. There is no need to use all the statements.

1. It is OK to call Alisha a 'gifted and talented' student.

2. It is OK to refer to Zack as 'less able'.

3. It is right that Alisha should be taught by Mr Adams, an experienced teacher with a passion for language.

4. It is right that Zack is grouped together with children who also struggle with reading and writing.

5. Rewards and extrinsic motivators are an important way to keep some kids on track.

6. Extra effort should be made to encourage students from Zack's group to join Mr Adam's extension class, even if this means affirmative action/positive discrimination.

Further guidance on using opinion lines to engage people in exploratory talk can be found in Section 7.2 of *Challenging Learning Through Dialogue* by Nottingham et al. (2017).

4.4 • ALISHA AND ZACK DISCOVER THEIR TALENTS

Learning styles is an over-used and sometimes misleading idea.

(Authors): I noticed a young man at the back of a maths class recently who was flailing his arms around frenetically. All the other students were managing to ignore him, focusing instead on their own work or on trying to listen to what the teacher was saying. This went on for much of the lesson. Afterwards I asked the teacher whether this was normal, to which she replied, matter-of-factly: 'Damian is a kinaesthetic learner – he learns better when he moves'.

What a load of rubbish! The boy doesn't have a medical condition that means he *has* to move: he's simply been told he's a kinaesthetic learner, and gone along with it because it sounds fun. His teacher had asked her students to complete a learning styles questionnaire and then concluded that some were visual learners, others were auditory and the rest were kinaesthetic. She'd gone on to declare that visual learners had to see something written down to learn well; auditory learners had to hear something; and the kinaesthetic lot – well, they had to bop and groove to learn!

More recently, I attended a conference at which three schools were presenting ideas about how to engage students more effectively. Each and every one of them declared that they encouraged their students to 'work in their preferred learning style'. As you can

imagine, I was quietly retching at the back. Preferred learning style indeed! *If* there were such a thing as a preferred learning style (and that's a big if) then why on earth would we encourage our students to work in their *preferred* learning style? Why not do it in anything *except* their preferred learning style? After all, shouldn't we be looking to help our students step outside their comfort zones? Shouldn't we be encouraging them to try new things, approach things from different angles? In other words, shouldn't we be helping them to *improve* rather than simply *prove* what they're good at?

Of course, there are exceptions. A student whose confidence, mental well-being and ability to engage with the curriculum is so compromised by specific needs that they need a sympathetic, supportive and safe way back to engagement with learning, is very likely to benefit from activities tailor-made to their 'preferred learning style'. Otherwise, the evidence just does not support the general theory.

> There is no adequate evidence base to justify incorporating learning-styles assessments into general educational practice. Thus, limited education resources would better be devoted to adopting other educational practices that have a strong evidence base, of which there are an increasing number. (Pashler, McDaniel, Rohrer & Bjork, 2008: 105)

> It comes as no surprise that, within John Hattie's recent monumental survey of 150 factors that affect students' learning, matching teaching to the learning styles of students was found to have an insignificant effect, little above zero. (Coffield, 2013: 2)

> It could be that the whole idea of learning-styles research is misguided because its basic assumption – that the purpose of instructional design is to make learning easy – may just be incorrect. (Coffield, Moseley, Hall & Ecclestone, 2004)

So, what of Alisha and Zack: what stories are they telling themselves about their talents? It seems likely that Alisha might be thinking of herself as a clever, literate, confident and articulate person. Conversely, she might also be an anxious, perfectionist child, riddled by fixed mindset fears!

Zack, on the other hand, will probably be telling himself he can't do it; that he's not very literate, or clever, or articulate. This doesn't necessarily mean he will be in a fixed mindset – he could be even more determined to improve because of the gap he knows he needs to bridge. But he almost certainly will be thinking he's not very good with language, certainly in comparison with Alisha. His teachers have confirmed this by grouping him together with other students who also struggle with literacy. He then did badly in his national tests. The final nail in the coffin was when he started secondary school and was put in the bottom set for literacy. Proof, if ever proof were needed, that he's not very literate.

A common response to this state of affairs is to look for areas in which Zack could excel *instead*. Zack might tell himself that although he's no good with words, he is great at other things (for example, sport, computer games or music). Adults in his life might also encourage this thinking by saying, 'I know reading isn't your thing but you're great at . . . (for example, art, maths or seeing things from another perspective)'.

Though this might seem to be a reassuring thing to say, the inadvertent message is: 'I don't expect you will ever be good at English (but don't worry, you have other talents) . . . so therefore, you may as well stop trying in English and just put your efforts elsewhere'.

Howard Gardner explored this theme at a conference we (the authors) were also speaking at in 2009 in Kuala Lumpur. He began his keynote speech by saying he wished teachers had never come across his theory of multiple intelligences because so many of them

> Using multiple intelligence to label students as 'visual learners', 'kinaesthetic learners' and so on, is a fixed mindset notion.

> Reassuring students that they 'can't be good at everything' inadvertently lowers expectations of success in tasks they find problematic.

Multiple intelligence is a useful idea *if* it is used to remind people how multi-faceted learning is, but it becomes a fixed mindset idea if it is used to label students.

were 'obsessed with categorising kids'. An interesting opening line for a speech attended by more than a thousand teachers!

What Gardner meant by this arresting opener is that too many of us in education are grouping or responding to students according to which of the multiple intelligences they excel at. So, for example, some of us might single out some students as being mathematically or logically minded, whereas we suppose that others are more artistically or musically minded. Not that this might be a bad thing in itself but when we then ask the 'mathematically minded' to do something creative or the 'artistically minded' to do something logical, then we may already have inadvertently lowered expectations of success. This very notion was wonderfully articulated by our colleague Beccy, in Section 3.4.

Gardner's theory of multiple intelligences proposes that instead of one general form of intelligence, typically measured by IQ tests, there could be as many as eight intelligences (or nine if you include the existential/spiritual intelligence he has recently been considering):

- spatial (ability to visualise)
- linguistic (language skills)
- logical-mathematical (abstract/logical thought)
- bodily-kinaesthetic (dexterity)
- interpersonal (understanding others)
- intrapersonal (self-awareness)
- musical (sensitivity to pitch, rhythm, timbre)
- naturalistic (sensitivity to nature).

Though responses to Gardner's ideas have been mixed, *multiple intelligence* continues to be used (and misused) in schools around the world. Not that adults outside of schools are immune to this sort of thing. For example, how many times have you heard phrases such as those shown in Figure 15?

These phrases also indicate fixed mindset thinking.

(Authors): I visited a classroom in which 8- to 9-year-olds were engaged in their maths lesson. Each group was doing something slightly different: one group had earphones in and were listening to music whilst working through their maths puzzles; one group was acting out the equations as if it were charades; another group was counting with leaves

▶ Figure 15: **Common Phrases and What They Might Imply**

Phrase Used	Implication
She takes after you.	She hasn't developed the talent herself – it is an inherited trait that 'runs in the family'.
Don't worry about that: you've got other talents.	We don't expect you to excel at this.
Don't ask me, I was never any good at English either.	The lack of proficiency runs in the family and is therefore to be expected.
We can't all be academic.	You're not academic.
We need doers as well as thinkers.	You're not a thinker but perhaps you could be good with your hands.
It takes all sorts/kinds.	We should accept our lot.

and twigs and berries. I asked the teacher what was going on; she said that the group with earphones was made up of the 'musical kids'; those acting out their maths were the 'body smart kids'; and those counting with flora and fauna were the 'naturists' (I think she meant, 'naturalists'!).

Can you imagine if students were grouped according to their horoscope: strict guidelines for the Capricorns, no rules for the Sagittarians, and plenty of quiet activities for the shy Pisceans? Imagine what parents would say; imagine the furore that would erupt in the local media! Yet, grouping students according to their strengths within the *multiple intelligence* collection is apparently a good idea in the eyes of many. Give me strength!

We are not saying that *multiple intelligence* is a bad idea. What we are saying is that using *multiple intelligence* to identify a person's strengths *is* problematic. Though it might be wise for job seekers to play to their strengths, is it really a good idea for a child to concentrate solely on their strengths and to hide their weaknesses? What if their weaknesses are something as important as numeracy, literacy or emotional intelligence? Should we give them the idea that they can mask these deficiencies by emphasising their other talents? Or should we help them to believe that they can make progress in all areas of the curriculum if they put their mind to it? After all, at a job interview, you might need to *prove* what you are capable of but education ought to be mostly about *improving*.

> All humans, short of being afflicted with certain types of organic damage, are born with an astounding capacity to learn, both in the amount that can be learned in one domain and in the variety and range of what can be learned. Children, unless stifled in some way, are usually virtuosos as learners. (Pashler et al., 2008: 117)

Back to Alisha and Zack. Tempting though it might be to divert Zack's attention away from his weaknesses by focusing on his strengths, this might lead to unfortunate consequences. It could be that Zack starts thinking he is never going to be successful with language and so, to protect himself, he begins to build some of the following defences:

- **Excuses**: 'I can't help it; I don't have the brain for languages'.
- **Nonchalance**: 'I don't care; I can do other things'.
- **Defeatism**: 'What is the point? I'm never going to be good at it anyway'.
- **Blame**: 'It's the teachers' fault. They don't explain things properly'.
- **Nature**: 'My parents didn't do well at school either'.
- **Diversion**: 'Look what I can do instead'.
- **Outrage**: 'It's not fair; why do they put so much emphasis on language?'
- **Resentment**: 'How come other people are better than me?'
- **Escape route**: 'Who needs to be able to read and write anyway; computers can do it for you'.

It's not all good news for Alisha either. She might be lured into a false sense of security or, ironically, she might begin looking for easier options in learning so that she can steer clear of the possibility of losing her status as a clever kid. Indeed, some of these reactions are quite common from a child who is often told they are the best or the brightest:

- **Ego**: 'People think I am clever so I need to keep proving that I am'.
- **Fear**: 'I had better not make mistakes or else people will stop thinking I am clever'.

An over-emphasis on learning styles can lead to the idea that most people only have one way of learning successfully. This, in turn, runs the risk of missing out on other learning opportunities.

When there is too much focus on identifying people's strengths rather than on growing their talents, many students will respond with defence mechanisms such as those shown here.

- **Imposter syndrome**: 'What if people think I am a fraud?'

- **Identity**: 'If I stop being the clever girl, then who will I be?'

- **Pretence**: 'If I don't know something then I should pretend I do because clever people are supposed to be knowledgeable'.

- **Guarded**: 'I can't reveal ignorance or ask questions publicly because I'm supposed to know the answer already'.

- **Approval**: 'I want people to keep telling me how clever I am'.

- **Prodigy**: 'Being clever makes my whole family proud of me'.

- **Responsibility**: 'I will let my family down if I don't get the best scores'.

- **Shame**: 'I feel ashamed if I get something wrong or make a mistake'.

All of the examples above are more likely to *come from* a person in a fixed mindset. They are also more likely to *lead to* someone getting into a fixed mindset. That is one of the reasons we have shared them: to emphasise how much of a two-way relationship mindset and actions are. Or, as we mentioned in Section 3.3, how much of a chicken and egg situation it is.

Another reason we have shared the examples above is to show how common it is for people at either end of the success continuum to be in a fixed mindset. It is certainly not the case that those at the top of the performance tree must be in a growth mindset and those at the bottom in a fixed mindset. As we've mentioned throughout the book, we are all much more likely to experience both mindsets at different times of our lives. The challenge is what we can do about it. Coincidentally, that just so happens to be what the rest of this book addresses!

NOW TRY THIS

Figure 15 shows some of the phrases used to explain talents or lack of them. The unfortunate side-effect is that they imply a fixed notion of intelligence and talents.

1. Have a conversation with your nearest and dearest (or failing that, your colleagues!) about these phrases. Which ones have you used before? What did you mean by them? Were they accurate?

2. Are there any other phrases you've used – or heard being used – that would give similar messages?

3. Would it be better to say nothing at all or are there alternative ways to reassure someone without giving fixed mindset messages?

The chapter finished with bullet point lists of things people might say to themselves when they sense there is a threat to their ego.

1. Identify which of these examples in the bullet point lists you are most prone to using. Explain to someone else why you think that is.

2. Are there any examples in either list that you think are less negative than others? Which ones and why?

WHAT IS YOUR CURRENT REALITY?

Do not ask what teachers do.

Instead, ask students what their teachers value.

DO YOU HAVE A GROWTH MINDSET CULTURE?

Perhaps the three most important questions to ask ourselves in professional development are:

1. What are we trying to achieve?
2. How much progress have we made so far?
3. What should we do next?

Coincidentally, these are the same three questions at the heart of great feedback as well as great learning. So, they should be well-rehearsed inside schools.

5.0 • WHAT ARE WE AIMING TO ACHIEVE?

To help you answer all three questions shown above in terms of growth mindset development, we have created the set of descriptions shown in Figure 16.

The descriptions in the main column (second column in from the left) should help you to answer the first question shown above: What are we trying to achieve?

Then to answer the second question above (How much progress have we made so far?), we invite you to place a mark in one of the four columns in the 'current reality' section. For example, for the first descriptor ('There is an atmosphere of exuberant discovery'), if you think the opposite is true, that the atmosphere is 'listless and mundane', then place a mark in the 'opposite is true' column. If, however, there are some signs of exuberant

The descriptions in Figure 16 give an idea of what would be happening in a school with a growth mindset culture. You can use the table to identify how much progress you have made so far towards each of the descriptors.

discovery, then place a mark in the 'some signs' column; whereas if the atmosphere is mostly exuberant discovery then place a mark in the 'mostly true' column; or if, as one would hope, the atmosphere is always one of exuberant discovery then place your mark in the 'always true' category. Further guidance to this process is given in Section 5.1.

You could place your mark individually, based on your own assessment; or you could work with your colleagues, your students or invite an impartial observer to make notes for you. Ideas about who to ask to complete this snapshot of your current reality is given in Section 5.2.

Once you have placed a mark in one of the four current reality columns for each of the 34 descriptors, the next thing to do would be to think about the third question shown above: What should we do next? More guidance for this is given in Section 5.3.

▶ Figure 16: **Descriptions of a Growth Mindset Culture**

Aspect of Culture	Evidence of a Growth Mindset Culture (Figures in brackets show the section of this book that offers advice about how to make this aspect of culture a reality.)	Current Reality			
		Opposite is true	Some signs	Mostly true	Always true
First impressions	1. There is an atmosphere of exuberant discovery. (1.3)				
	2. Everyone is engaged in intellectual risk taking, persevering and supporting each other towards collective improvement. (3.0)				
	Notes				
Abilities					
Your beliefs	3. You believe that abilities are grown and developed, and that *all* your students can make excellent progress. (6.0)				
Students' beliefs	4. Students believe that school is about learning rather than about deciding who is best and who is not. (Chapter 3)				
Student awareness	5. Students understand there are many reasons for varying ability levels and can identify some of the different influences. (Chapter 4)				

Aspect of Culture	Evidence of a Growth Mindset Culture	Current Reality			
		Opposite is true	*Some signs*	*Mostly true*	*Always true*
Organisation	6. Your systems and structures are designed around the growing of talents rather than the classifying and labelling of talents. (6.3)				
	Notes				
Mastery					
Trial and error	7. Students understand the value of trial, error and practice and the ways in which these lead to mastery. (10.1)				
Progress	8. Systems are in place to look for, draw attention to and celebrate progress. (6.2)				
Mistakes	9. Students treat mistakes as part of the learning process and examine them thoughtfully. (10.0)				
Resilience	10. Students are resilient in their learning. They do not give up easily nor do they show signs of 'learned helplessness'. (9.1)				
	Notes				
Challenge					
Learning zone	11. Students' behaviour shows that they are willing to get out of their comfort zone and into their Zone of Proximal Development. (8.2)				
Struggling students	12. Students are given deliberate opportunities to make mistakes, solve problems and struggle during lessons. (10.0)				
Positive attitudes	13. Students talk positively about the challenges they are undertaking and the progress they are making as a result. (8.2)				

(Continued)

(Continued)

Aspect of Culture	Evidence of a Growth Mindset Culture	Current Reality			
		Opposite is true	*Some signs*	*Mostly true*	*Always true*
Student choice	14. When given a choice, students will pick the options they think will stretch them most. (8.1)				
	Notes				
Flopped Learning (see Chapter 10)					
Failure mindset	15. Students believe that making mistakes, then examining and correcting them, leads to deeper learning. (10.1)				
Parents' attitudes	16. Parents believe failure can be positive because it can stimulate deeper learning. (10.3)				
Strategies for learning	17. Students understand that effort is not enough; that they *also* need to select and apply the appropriate strategy for learning. (10.4)				
Pedagogy	18. Flopped previews are used to engage students before new topics begin. (10.5)				
	Notes				
Feedback					
Using feedback	19. Students have a positive disposition towards feedback and use it effectively to deepen their learning. (10.2)				
Quality feedback	20. Feedback is high quality and is timed effectively to help students make more progress in their learning. (10.2)				
Informing pedagogy	21. You use assessment formatively to inform how, what and who to teach next. (10.2)				

Aspect of Culture	Evidence of a Growth Mindset Culture	Current Reality			
		Opposite is true	*Some signs*	*Mostly true*	*Always true*
Groupings	22. You divide your students according to on-going, formative assessment (rather than in static ability groups). (6.0)				
	Notes				
Metacognition					
Applying mindset	23. Students can identify an example of when being in a growth mindset helped them with their learning. (1.1)				
Self-awareness	24. Students recognise when they are in a fixed mindset and can think of ways to move more towards growth mindset thinking. (1.1)				
Learning to learn	25. Students talk positively about learning *how* to learn and can identify instances when learning strategies have helped them to master something. (7.1)				
Effects of language	26. You have identified the language for growth mindset you wish to teach and can explain and justify the anticipated effects. (7.1)				
	Notes				
Self-efficacy					
Influencing outcomes	27. Your students believe that they can significantly influence outcomes. (9.3)				
Self-regulation	28. Students display a high degree of self-regulation and an awareness of how their thinking affects their efficacy. (9.3)				

(Continued)

Aspect of Culture	Evidence of a Growth Mindset Culture	Current Reality			
		Opposite is true	*Some signs*	*Mostly true*	*Always true*
The power of yet	29. The power of 'yet' is alive and well, with all students knowing they can make improvements with the right attitude and strategy. (7.0)				
Examples	30. Attention is drawn to examples of efficacious behaviour by students and role models in society. (9.3)				
	Notes				
Adults					
Role model	31. You model growth mindset attitudes and strategies in all interactions with students, their parents and your colleagues. (10.7)				
School-wide	32. The language and principles of growth mindset are shared with all adults working within your organisation. (10.7)				
Professional dialogue	33. Growth mindset is the foundation for all professional dialogue about teaching, learning and leadership. (Chapter 10)				
Parents	34. Students' parents understand the principles and language of growth mindset and how this can affect their child's development. (10.3)				
	Notes				

5.1 • HOW MUCH PROGRESS HAVE WE MADE SO FAR?

In the introduction to this chapter, we recommended that growth and development should be guided by three questions. To answer the second of these, we recommend that you select the right-hand column in Figure 16 that best fits the current context. To explain the options, they are:

Opposite is true: Select this one if your current reality is in opposition to the target situation. For example, description 2 states: 'Everyone is engaged in intellectual risk taking, persevering and supporting each other towards collective improvement'. If, however, the reality is that everyone is playing it safe, taking no risks, giving up easily and trying to belittle the efforts of others, then ticking the 'opposite' box would be the appropriate thing to do.

Some signs: Select this one if your current reality shows some signs of the target situation. For example, the target situation might be seen in a few of the classrooms but not many, or with a few of the students but not yet most of them. For example, description 9 states: 'Students treat mistakes as part of the learning process and examine them thoughtfully'. If this is the case for some of the students but it is by no means the norm then ticking the 'some signs' box would be most appropriate.

Mostly true: Select this one if your current reality shows that, despite some signs to the contrary, it is generally the case across the school. For example, description 15 states: 'Students have a positive disposition towards feedback and use it effectively to deepen their learning'. If this is the case for most of the students but not all then you should tick the 'mostly true' box.

Always true: Select this one if your current reality matches the description shown in all aspects of school life.

To determine how much progress you have made towards creating a growth mindset culture, we recommend you use this key in conjunction with the descriptors in Figure 16.

5.2 • COLLECTING YOUR EVIDENCE

When thinking about your culture for mindset, you could complete the table shown in Figure 16 based on your own professional judgement. Even better, you could *also* ask a colleague or friend to gather evidence for you by going on a learning walk and meeting a cross-section of students and colleagues. The following guidance should help whoever is collecting the evidence.

Gather evidence in the following ways:

Learning

- Observe student learning.

- Ask students about the activities they are engaged in (with particular reference to descriptors 7, 9, 10, 15 and 24 in Figure 16).

- Gauge students' levels of understanding and interest in their learning.

This is really important: ask your students anonymously about the classroom values and ethos so that they are more likely to tell the truth. Otherwise, teachers can fool themselves about their students' levels of engagement, and their students' perceptions of practices and values.

This page shows some of the many ways to collect evidence to identify how much progress you have made towards a growth mindset culture.

Ethos

- Ascertain the atmosphere in the room (with particular reference to descriptors 1 and 2 in Figure 16).

- Observe the attitudes of staff and students towards each other and towards their learning (with particular reference to descriptors 3, 11, 12, 23 and 25 in Figure 16).

- Notice what messages are portrayed by displays and general ambiance.

Organisation

- Think about the messages portrayed by the ways in which the classroom is organised.

- Find out how students are grouped (ask students for their assumptions too).

- Take photos (if permission granted).

Student voice

- Find out about students' beliefs in connection with the descriptors in Figure 16 (particularly 4, 5, 7, 9, 13, 14, 15, 19, 20, 21, 25, 30).

- Listen to a cross-section of students, not just those who love school but also those who barely tolerate it.

Staff voice

- Ask staff about their beliefs in connection with all the descriptors in Figure 16.

- Listen to a cross-section of staff, not just those who are super supportive of growth mindset thinking.

5.3 • WHAT NEXT?

> Once you have identified how much progress you have made thus far, the next step is to decide what to do next.

To help you answer the third of the guiding questions (What should we do next?), we recommend that you read the rest of the book! To help you know which parts specifically to read, we have included section references next to each of the descriptions shown in Figure 16.

Before you start reading these, please allow us to remind you that if you work in a school then you set the culture. Politicians, parents and school leaders have some influence but it is *you* who sets the tone for *your* students.

If you are sceptical about this then cast your mind back to your own high school days. As a teenager, you moved from class to class to class, encountering different teachers for different subjects. We bet you knew exactly which teachers had high expectations for you and which ones didn't even know your name; which ones had a good sense of humour and which ones you suspected had not laughed since childhood. It is the same today: our students know which is which.

Now let us ask you this: did you change your behaviour and expectations depending on who was teaching you at the time? Did your peers also adapt? How often was it that the same class of students was well-mannered and attentive with some teachers, then distracted and disruptive with others? The kids were the same but the teacher had changed and so the culture also changed.

Many parents know this only too well too. How many parents have seen their own children blossom with a new teacher? Or sadly, go the other way and suddenly go off school and develop an intense dislike for the experience? That is how influential school staff are: they can make or break the experience for their students.

That said, there is a significant difference between what we might be concerned about and what we can actually influence. For example, you might be concerned about the home life of one of your students but have very little influence over it. But you *are* able to influence the school life of that same student. The same can be said of nature and nurture: you might be interested in the nature of your students but it is the nurture that you can significantly affect.

We make this rather obvious statement not to be patronising but to reiterate the point: you set the culture of your classroom; you decide how to nurture and how not to. Your leaders set the culture of the school; parents of the home; administrators of the district. But *you* are the one who affects the nurture in your classroom.

This contrasts with phrases such as, 'What can I do? Parents have much more influence than I do!' or 'What if I get students into a growth mindset this year but then they go to another teacher or another school next year and it is all undone?' Of course, these can be very real concerns but if they become an excuse for inaction or for a lack of will to try then that becomes part of the problem too.

At this stage, it would be worth looking back at Chapter 4 to see which of the influences on Alisha and Zack you would be able to respond to if they were students in your class. For example, Figure 10 shows some of the terms often used to describe students, such as bright, gifted, low achiever, non-academic and so on. It is your choice whether or not to use those terms. Similarly, Figure 13 identifies some of the all-too-common responses to students. These include grouping by ability rather than the more learning-led grouping that comes from on-going formative assessments; setting high expectations for Alisha but not for Zack; and referring to Alisha as 'gifted and talented' but to Zack as 'less able'. Again, it is within your sphere of influence to choose whether or not to use these terms. So, we repeat, *you set the culture*.

Although some people will say there is not much an individual can do to change a culture, we would argue otherwise.

If you are a member of staff in a school, then you are very influential. You set the culture in your classroom.

Your students know which members of staff love questions and which don't; who listens and who doesn't; who believes in them and who doesn't. They then adjust their behaviour and expectations accordingly. If that doesn't make you influential then we're not sure what does.

HOW CAN YOU BUILD A GROWTH MINDSET?

Another misunderstanding [of growth mindset] . . . is the oversimplification of growth mindset into just [being about] effort. Teachers were just praising effort that was not effective, saying 'Wow, you tried really hard!' But students know that if they didn't make progress and you're praising them, it's a consolation prize. They also know you think they can't do any better. So this kind of growth-mindset idea was misappropriated to try to make kids feel good when they were not achieving.

Dweck, 2016

PRIVILEGE PROGRESS

In Section 3.1, we showed that mindset works best when goals are learning-orientated. To make this a reality, a great starting point is to promote the possibility of progress. Show your students, your colleagues, your children that improvement is possible; probable, even, with the right strategy, effort and determination.

Before we show you some ways to achieve this, we think it is a good idea to go back to the origins of intelligence testing to shed some light on why so many schools might have more of a performance-focus than a learning-focus currently.

> Any organisation wishing to develop growth mindset should look for ways to value and draw attention to progress.

6.0 • THE ORIGINS OF INTELLIGENCE TESTING

A French psychologist, Alfred Binet (1857–1911) invented the first practical IQ test with his student, Théodore Simon, in 1904. By creating the Binet-Simon test, they were able to meet the French Ministry of Education's desire to identify those students most in need of alternative education. Though this might seem unremarkable at first glance, bear in mind the prevailing wisdom at the time was to place 'slow' children into an asylum, rather than to adjust pedagogy to the needs of the child. So, Binet's work was pretty radical for its time.

As an aside, you might be interested in the types of tasks devised for the 6- to 14-year-olds who took the test. Some of the simplest tasks assessed whether or not a child could follow a beam of light or talk back to the examiner. More challenging tasks included asking children to repeat back seven random digits and to find three rhymes for particular French words. There were, however, some 'interesting' elements in which the children were asked what was wrong with the following statements:

> The original IQ test, created by Alfred Binet, was intended to support the development and adjustment of pedagogy. It was never about labelling people.

1. An unfortunate bicycle rider smashed his head and died instantly; he was taken to the hospital and it is feared he may not recover.

2. A railroad accident took place yesterday. It was not a serious one; only 48 people died.

3. Yesterday the body of an unfortunate young woman, cut into eight pieces, was found on the fortifications. It is believed she killed herself. (Binet & Simon, 1905: 252)

These rather macabre statements aside, one of the most interesting aspects of Binet's work was the caveats he gave for his test, and for testing more generally. These can be summed up as follows.

6.0.1 • Caveats About Testing

Binet noted that objective tests can be an alternative to the subjective assessments so often made by teachers, parents, principals and physicians. He noted that 'teachers in standard schools might denigrate troublesome students' competence to have them removed from the classroom; conversely, teachers in special schools might exaggerate their students' achievements to boost their own success as instructors. Parents might overstate the accomplishments of their children to avoid the embarrassment of special school placements or understate them if they wished to escape responsibility for the child' (Siegler, 1992: 182).

However, Binet also noted that even objective tests are at the mercy of the subjectivity of those administering the test. For example, he observed that 'while one principal claimed he didn't have a single abnormal child in his school, the principal of another school nearby counted 50 of them in his' (Binet & Simon, 1905: 280).

One thing Binet made clear is that tests should not be done in isolation and then over-relied upon for months, even years to come. Instead, if testing is to be used then it should be used frequently, partly because all tests are fallible but mainly because intellectual development progresses at variable rates. So, a child scoring poorly in one test might, only a few months later, score very highly in another. This unpredictability would, in part, be explained by the different rates of maturation and educational experiences in between times (Binet & Simon, 1905).

6.0.2 • Caveats About Intelligence

Binet also emphasised the remarkable diversity of intelligence and the subsequent need to study it using qualitative, rather than solely quantitative, measures. Ironic then that Binet's name is so strongly associated with IQ scores, which reduce intelligence to a single number. Maybe Alanis Morissette could have used Binet as an example in her song, Ironic, rather than singing about things that really weren't ironic!

Back to Binet though. Not only the grandfather of IQ testing but also perhaps the grandfather of growth mindsets, Binet also stressed that intellectual development progressed at variable rates and could be influenced by the environment. He asserted that intelligence was not based solely on genetics, was malleable rather than fixed, and could only be compared between individuals if they had comparable circumstances. As he wrote in 1905:

A few modern philosophers seem to lend their moral support to these deplorable verdicts when they assert that an individual's intelligence is a fixed quantity which cannot be increased. We must protest and react against this brutal pessimism . . . With practice, training, and above all method, we manage to increase our attention, our memory, our judgement, and literally to become more intelligent than we were before. (Binet & Simon, 1905: 301)

So far, so good. Until, that is, 1908, just four years after the Binet-Simon test was created.

6.0.3 • From French into English

A change in direction for IQ testing began with the translation of Binet's work from French into English. This was led by H. H. Goddard, a champion of the eugenics movement that aimed to improve the genetic composition of the human race through a process of selective breeding. Goddard promoted the test for reasons antithetical to Binet's thinking. He stated that IQ testing could be used as a measure of 'genetically determined' intelligence; that it tested a construct of 'general intelligence' and that it could be used to separate 'superior' people from the 'inferior'. Specifically, he found utility in mental testing as a way to support his belief in the 'superiority of the white race' (Siegler, 1992: 179–190).

Goddard's interpretation of Binet's work was met with approval. In the late 19th and early 20th centuries, the idea that society ought to be built upon people's relative merits rather than on inherited position was gaining traction, immortalised in the phrase, 'the American dream'. However, the people in positions of power did not want to let their privilege disappear without a fight. So, to them, the idea that an IQ test could be used to determine the 'superior' from the 'inferior' was an attractive one. After all, they wanted to ensure that only the 'right' people could live the American dream.

Lewis Terman, a professor of psychology at Stanford University, took on the mantle by standardising the Binet-Simon test with a sample of 2,300 children in the United States. When he and his colleagues at Stanford published the new Stanford-Binet test, they stated that:

> High-grade or borderline deficiency . . . is very, very common amongst Spanish-Indian and Mexican families of the Southwest and also among negroes. Their dullness seems to be racial, or at least inherent in the family stocks from which they come . . . Children of this group should be segregated into separate classes . . . They cannot master abstractions but they can often be made into efficient workers . . . from a eugenic point of view they constitute a grave problem because of their unusually prolific breeding. (Terman, 1916: 91–2)

The new Stanford-Binet scale was no longer used solely for advocating education for all children, as was Binet's objective. A new objective of intelligence testing was illustrated in the Stanford-Binet manual, with testing ultimately resulting in 'curtailing the reproduction of feeble-mindedness and in the elimination of an enormous amount of crime, pauperism, and industrial inefficiency' (Terman, 1916: 84).

6.0.4 • Mindset and Intelligence Testing

There were, of course, many other protagonists in the development of IQ testing and the wider debate about the nature of intelligence. These include Francis Galton, Francoys Gagné, Cyril Burt, Jean-Jacques Rousseau, Reuven Feuerstein and, of course, Carol Dweck. However, we have chosen to focus on Terman and Binet in this chapter; partly because of the particularly significant roles they have played in influencing current attitudes about intelligence, and partly because their attitudes paint a clear picture of fixed and growth mindsets.

Terman's goal was to classify people on a scale, so that they could be assigned a suitable job or, in the case of children, be put on an appropriate job-track. He believed IQ is inherited, stable and generalisable. He also believed that IQ is the strongest predictor of a person's ultimate success in life. As such, it is clear that Terman had an entity theory of intelligence.

Binet's goal was to identify children who were in need of additional support. He believed that IQ is significantly influenced by the environment and builds at variable rates

> However, when Binet's test was translated into English, there was also a significant shift in value-base, from growth to fixed mindset thinking.

according to experience and maturity. He rejected the idea of a general form of intelligence, stating instead that intelligence is remarkably diverse, in terms of origin, function and applicability. As such, it is clear that Binet held an incremental theory of intelligence.

Bear in mind that these examples should be treated with care. We do not share them to imply that people in a fixed mindset are unethical (for that is how Terman is frequently judged today). Nor do we wish to suggest that people such as Binet, who very obviously held a growth mindset, are holier than thou. Instead, we recommend making the comparison between fixed and growth mindsets without thinking *how* these two men, particularly Terman, *applied* their beliefs. Look again at the summaries given above. Then consider how beliefs such as these manifest themselves today.

NOW TRY THIS

Section 6.0 has shared some of the varying beliefs upon which intelligence testing has developed. Lewis Terman's work is linked to testing that has a performance-focus; Binet's work is linked much more closely with testing that has a learning-focus.

It would be a good idea at this point to consider the following questions in conversation with your colleagues:

1. What do your students think tests are for?
2. In what ways are beliefs about testing different today than when you were a child (if at all)?
3. What are the main performance-focused activities that take place in your school (or organisation) currently?
4. What are the main learning-focused activities that take place in your school (or organisation) currently?

6.1 • ADMINISTERING TESTS THE GROWTH MINDSET WAY

As the IQ story shows, tests are neither good nor bad; it is how they are used that will determine whether they support fixed or growth mindset values.

At the beginning of this chapter, we said that we would look at the origins of intelligence testing to shed some light on why so many schools might have more of a performance-focus than a learning-focus currently. We finished that section by asking you to consider how your school (or company) is set up. Now let's look at a way to use testing in a growth mindset way.

Consider the example tests for 11-year-olds shown in Figures 17 and 18.

If an 11-year-old were to score full marks on either test, would you praise them for it?

Did you hesitate in answering the question about whether to praise the student because you suspected it was a trick question? If you did then you were right to do so because it *was* a trick question!

Although it might seem the normal, and indeed right, thing to do to praise a student for getting full marks on a test, consider the implications if that test was well within their comfort zone. What if they didn't have to think very much about it or needed no effort to get everything right? What would telling them, 'well done' do for their beliefs about success? To many students it would imply that what matters most is getting everything right. Which again, on the face of it, seems reasonable enough but what if that comes at the expense of learning? In other words, what if they learned nothing but still got everything right? In those circumstances, it would mean performance is being valued more than learning.

► **Figure 17: Example Knowledge Test**

The Water Cycle
Explain the following items:

1. River

2. Reservoir

3. Evaporation

4. Condensation

5. Precipitation

6. Transpiration

7. Infiltration

8. Percolation

9. Surface-flow

10. Through-flow

How would you respond to a student who aced a test such as this one? Would you congratulate them for getting 100%?

► **Figure 18: Example Spelling Test**

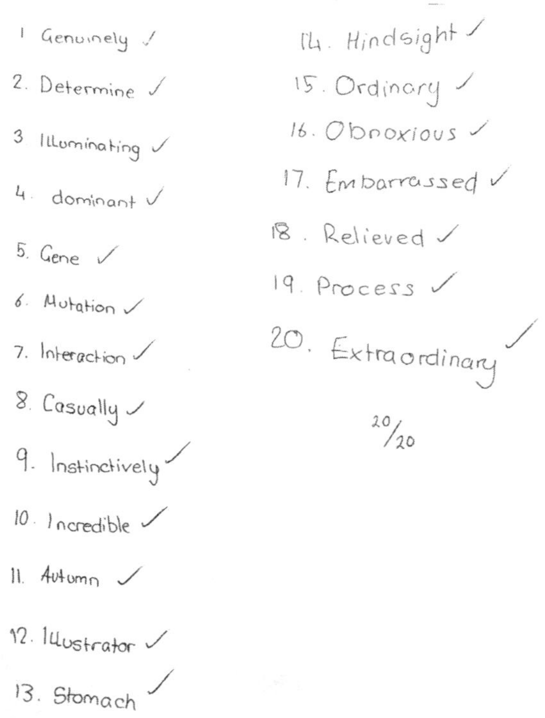

How about this test? Would you praise a student for spelling all the words correctly?

1. Genuinely ✓
2. Determine ✓
3. Illuminating ✓
4. dominant ✓
5. Gene ✓
6. Mutation ✓
7. Interaction ✓
8. Casually ✓
9. Instinctively ✓
10. Incredible ✓
11. Autumn ✓
12. Illustrator ✓
13. Stomach ✓

14. Hindsight ✓
15. Ordinary ✓
16. Obnoxious ✓
17. Embarrassed ✓
18. Relieved ✓
19. Process ✓
20. Extraordinary ✓

20/20

Of course, many of us in teaching would say that we would never give a test to child if we thought it was too easy for them. Certainly, that is our aim anyway. But is that the reality? Flick through some students' books and see how many of them have got full marks on every test they have taken. Are you sure that they have had to work hard and learn lots for every test or might it be that sometimes, or even often for some students, they have found things particularly straightforward and easy?

So, here is the alternative: get rid of tests!

Then . . . introduce twice as many tests.

By that we mean, do not give a test in isolation. Instead, give a pre-test first *then* the 'real' test some time later. In between times, your students know what they need to focus on and what they already have 'in the bag'. It also allows you to find out how competent your students are on the planned-for test before they actually take it, such that you can give them more challenge if they already know most or all of the answers. This, in turn, means you can increase your students' opportunity to make progress, thereby shifting the emphasis from a performance-focus to a learning-focus.

So, the answer to, 'Should we praise a student for getting everything correct?' becomes: 'It depends!' If there has been a learning-focus and your student has made progress, then yes! If not, then it might be better to encourage them to look for a more 'interesting' challenge (see Chapter 8 for more details).

This approach isn't fool-proof but its intentions are much more orientated towards growth mindset than the common approach of single tests. Of course, some of your more 'tactical' students might aim to get a purposefully low score on the pre-test so that you don't give them any additional challenge but you can call them on this and say, 'well, if you want easy stuff, I can get you easy stuff. I'll ask the lower grades what they are studying then you can have all that baby stuff if you like!' In our experience, students will be quick to say no to that 'offer'!

To give you the best chance of success, we recommend the following steps:

1. Give your students the test or activity you have planned for them ahead of time. Call this the pre-test (or 'practice', 'preview' or 'survey' if you don't like the idea of too many tests).

2. After they have completed the pre-test, show them the right answers (or the right way to perform the skill) and ask them to score their own performance. This gives them their pre-test score.

3. If some students score very highly on the pre-test then give them additional challenges so that they have the opportunity to make progress. If some score very lowly then reassure them that they now have lots of opportunity to make progress before the actual test. Incidentally, we are assuming that you have not chosen a test that is so complex that they won't be able to make any gains at all!

4. Now give your students time to study and practise. Depending on the type of test, this might be a few days to fit in some self-study or time within school.

5. Finally, give them the actual test. Calculate the progress they have made from start to end and draw attention to that score.

Figures 19 and 20 show examples of this in practice. Figure 19 shows the pre-test and post-test from a 13-year-old pupil at Dulwich Prep school in London, UK. Figure 20 shows the progress of Juliet, a 9-year-old student at Brudenell Primary School in Leeds, UK. Juliet is originally from Italy and has only recently moved to England.

► Figure 19: Pre-Test and Post-Test Example from a
13-Year-Old Student

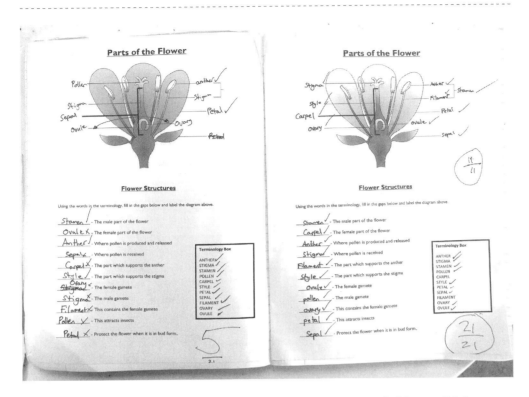

► Figure 20: Progress Made in Spelling by a 9-Year-Old
Student

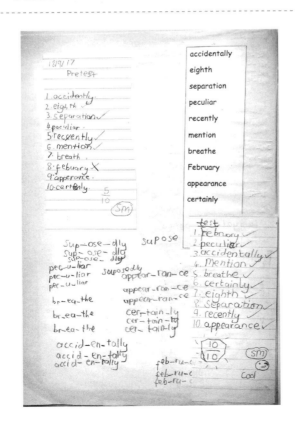

6.2 • DRAW ATTENTION TO PROGRESS

Drawing attention to progress doesn't need to involve tests. It could also look at progress in art, in sport, in student attitudes and so on. The examples over the next few pages show this in practice in schools we are working with on long-term projects.

It is important to note that growth mindset approaches to learning do *not* equate with giving more tests for the sake of it. Instead, they equate with focusing on the progress made *between* tests. So, it is not the number of tests given that is important, but rather the purpose of when and why those tests are given.

In the minds of many, tests have a bad reputation. Tests can increase anxiety, be used inappropriately to shame those with low scores, and can detract from valuable curriculum time – that is, if the tests are used, implicitly or explicitly, to demonstrate competence *relative to others*.

However, if tests are used to identify what to teach next or what to concentrate on before next time, then the emphasis changes to demonstrating competence *relative to prior achievement*. This changes the focus from performance-orientation to learning-orientation, which, as we showed in Section 3.0, can change the possibilities of success from an effect size of minus 0.02 to plus 0.32.

Sometimes it also helps to disassociate the term 'test' in this context from the ones that generally heap pressure on young people. National or state exams, for example, that typically are used to measure the achievement of students – and very often to rank schools and teachers – give testing a bad name. They are the epitome of high-stakes, performance-orientation. As such, they are rarely a welcome activity.

The testing we mean here, though, is the type you have control over. We mean the tests that you select, maybe even create, to use as part of curriculum instruction. With these tests, we are saying you should speak of them as starting points for improvement rather than as end-point checks. Use them 'formatively' rather than 'summatively' (see Nottingham & Nottingham, 2017, for further explanation).

Imagine you were going to take skiing lessons or learn how to play a musical instrument. Presumably, your instructor would begin by saying, 'Show me what you can do then we'll go from there'.

► **Figure 21: Progress Made in Art by Aaron, Aged 12**

▶ Figure 22: Progress Made in Art by Fateha, Aged 12

That is exactly the sort of impression we advise giving your students when they take your teacher-made tests: let's find out what you know or can do already so that a) I know what to teach you next, and b) we can work out how much progress you are making.

Not that tests are the only way to show progress of course; far from it. There are many opportunities to draw attention to the progress your students are making.

Figures 21 and 22 show the progress two students at Åsgård school in Norway are making in art. In each case, the image on the left is their first attempt and the image on the right, their improved version after feedback from their teacher and their peers.

We love that this school in Norway celebrates their students' progress in art by displaying their students' first attempt next to their improved versions. Compare that with the sorts of displays typically shown on school walls, an example of which is shown in Figure 23.

Figure 23: Display Sharing Students' Completed Art

► Figure 24: Display Sharing Students' Progress in Art

The display in Figure 23 is very well presented, colourful and attractive. However, it only shares students' finished pieces of artwork. So, in a sense, it draws attention only to the achievement of their 9- and 10-year-olds rather than to their progress. How much better would it be if they put the children's earlier sketches next to their completed artwork as the Norwegian school has done? That way, the display would still be showcasing the artwork of the children *and* it would also be celebrating the progress they had made to create such beautiful pieces of art. Figure 24 shows an example of this. The display might not be as aesthetically pleasing as the one shown in Figure 23 but it emphasises that Dulwich Prep, the school in which the photo was taken, values learning as much as it does achievement.

The same school uses this approach with their youngest students. Figures 25 and 26 show the progress in understanding of one of their 4-year-olds. All the images in the photographs were drawn by Sam. The notes next to the images were written by his teacher and were based on what Sam told her he knew about science. Figure 25 shows what he thought science was at the beginning of the school year. Figure 26 shows how much more he understands about science, having explored the topics of magnets, slime and floating with the rest of his class.

You can read more about this and see other examples from Dulwich Prep at: http://mailchi.mp/843d48799609/teaching-and-learning-newsletter.

Sticking with the early childhood theme, the examples shown in Figures 27 and 28 come from a pre-school in Copenhagen. This is one of the ways Bente Bahrt, a teacher at Dronninggårdskolen in Rudersdal, encourages children to develop their dexterity. In other activities, Bente encourages the children to be creative to express themselves in different ways, but in this activity, the focus is on staying within the lines when colouring in. Figure 27 shows a reference sheet identifying what progress looks like with colouring in. Figure 28 shows one of the girls identifying how much progress she thinks she has made so far. Incidentally, 'Trinmål for at farve' means 'Targets for colouring'.

► Figure 25: What 4-Year-Old Sam Understands About
           Science at the Beginning of His School Life

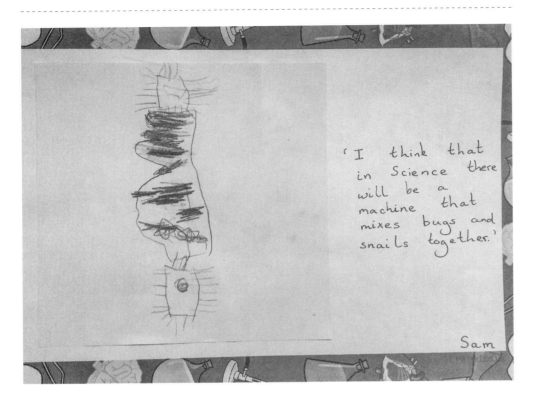

► Figure 26: What Sam Understands About Science After
           Studying the Subject for a Few Weeks

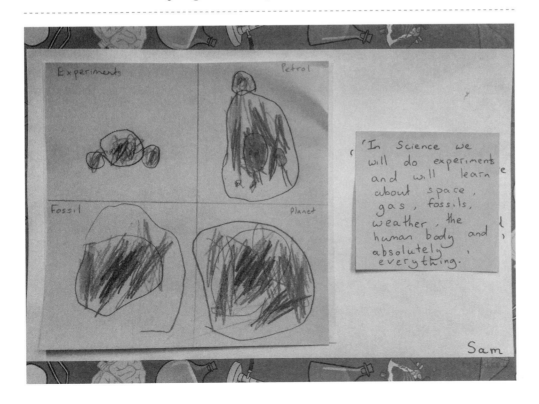

► Figure 28: A Child Identifying Her Progress So Far

6. Privilege Progress

The examples we have given so far show progress across the space of a few days. It would also be a good idea to draw attention to progress made over a few months or even over a full school year. Figure 29 shows the progress Jessica, a pupil at Brudenell Primary School in Leeds, UK, is making with her language skills. Jessica wrote the first piece at the end of her first full year at school, aged 5. She wrote the second piece ten months later. Her teachers purposefully gave her the same image to build a story from so that they could look at the progress Jessica was making.

▶ Figure 29: Progress Made in 10 Months by Jessica, Aged 5/6

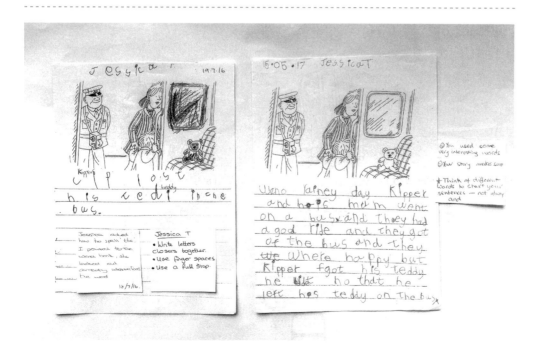

(Authors): Figures 30 and 31 show some of the progress made by my eldest daughter, Ava. In Figure 30, Ava was asked to identify some of the uses for taxes. In Figure 31, she was considering what influences a person's sense of identity. As a parent, it is nice to see the move from a practical concept (what taxes are used for) to a more abstract concept (influences on identity). It is also pleasing to see that her handwriting and spelling have also improved from example one to example two. Talking with Ava about these differences led to a nice discussion about learning, citizenship and identity.

▶ **Figure 30: Concept Map by Ava, Aged 10**

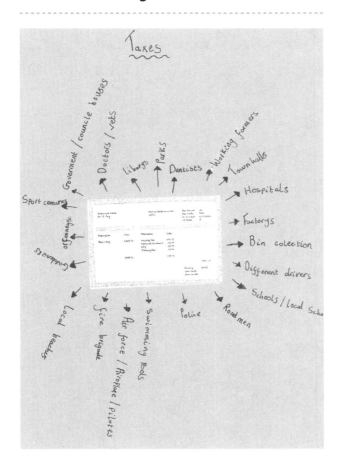

▶ **Figure 31: Concept Map by Ava, Aged 11**

NOW TRY THIS

Here are some other ideas for collecting and sharing evidence of progress with your students.

1. Engage 'mark-up' when your students create digital documents so that they – and you – can easily see the amendments they have made, and therefore the progress they are making.

2. Use collaborative documents such as Google Docs so that you can give feedback in the moment rather than waiting until your students have finished their assignments. This shifts the emphasis more onto improvements and progress rather than only on the finished product. This is explored more in Section 6.4.

3. Every month, return to something that your students have created previously. Then invite them to use their newly improved skills and understanding to edit their original creations to make them even better than they were before. Examples include essays, paintings, models, scientific write-ups and so on. This should show them how much progress they have made in the intervening period.

4. Invite your students to browse through their books to see what progress they think they have made. You could get them to identify their favourite examples.

5. Record your students performing a skill in sport, drama, group work and so on. Share the recordings with them and ask them to identify what they would like to improve next. Record their subsequent attempts and highlight the improvements.

6. Similarly, record some of the activities students are engaged in. Look for signs of increasing confidence, curiosity, reasoning, interpersonal skills and so on.

7. During PE lessons, record your students' performances over a few months – for example, how fast they can run 100 metres, how far they can jump, how accurately they can throw a ball and so on. This will allow you to focus on the progress they are making as well as their performances in competitions.

8. Create thinking journals in which your students record their reflections following different learning activities. They can add further ideas over time or extend their original ideas that they recorded earlier in their journal. These journals will show your students, their parents and you how their ideas are gaining in complexity over time.

9. Host 'learning conferences' in which students show their parents the progress they have been making recently. This gives your students the opportunity to show examples of what they have been learning and improving. If used in conjunction with some of the other ideas here then each student should have ample examples to showcase.

6.3 • PROGRESS–ACHIEVEMENT QUADRANTS

One way to think about progress is to draw a quadrant diagram as shown in the examples in Figure 32. The x-axis represents progress. The y-axis represents achievement.

The x-axis represents how much progress your students are making. This should provoke a lot of debate with your colleagues about how much progress you would expect of your students. For now, we will use the 'hinge point' that John Hattie recommends of 0.4 effect size. This is the average amount of progress students make in one year, according to Hattie's analysis of more than 1,400 meta-analyses, involving 80,000 studies in education (Hattie, 2017). Of course, you might want to select your own 'hinge point' or find an alternative to effect size measurements, but we will come back to that later.

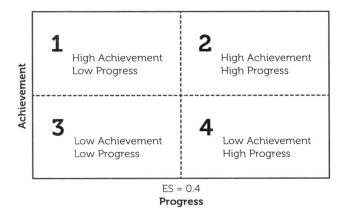

ES = 0.4
Progress

A progress–achievement quadrant can be used to promote dialogue about student learning.

The y-axis represents the achievement of your students. You will notice that we have not added a scale to the example shown in Figure 33 because it will be dependent upon context. For example, the scale might be representative of test scores, or a performance grade in music or dance, or a sporting achievement such as the distance they have been able to swim in a given time. The dotted line that intersects this achievement axis shows the level above which achievement is deemed to be good (above the pass rate) and below which achievement is identified as low (below the pass rate).

(Authors): Recently, I was an official timer for a swimming gala. The qualification times for the swimmers varied according to age: 14-year-olds needed to swim 100 metres in under 1 minute 15 seconds; whereas 9-year-olds were expected to swim 50 metres in under 1 minute 5 seconds in order to qualify for the second round. So, in this case, the scale along the vertical axis could be distance swum in 60 seconds. A quadrant for 14-year-olds would place the dotted line at 80 metres, whereas a quadrant for 9-year-olds would place the dotted line at 46 metres.

These two diagrams show differing achievement scales on the y-axis. The left-hand diagram has a scale of zero to four (commonly used for 7-year-old students in England), whereas the right-hand diagram has a scale of two to six (commonly used for 11-year-old students in England).

A more familiar scale to most teachers would be the levels or grades expected of their students. For example, in England, it is expected that 7-year-olds will achieve a Level 2 in reading, writing and maths; whereas 11-year-olds are expected to achieve a Level 4 in each of the subjects. So, if we were to draw a quadrant for that context then the achievement scale would be curriculum levels. A quadrant for 7-year-olds would place the dotted line at Level 2, above which achievement would be thought of as good, and below which achievement would be thought of as low. A quadrant for 11-year-olds would draw the dotted line at Level 4. Figure 33 shows these examples in practice.

The four quadrants in Figures 32 and 33 represent the following:

The four quadrants shown in Figures 32 and 33 can be described as shown here.

1. The top left-hand quadrant is where students with high achievement levels and low progress would be placed. Classic reasons for a student being placed there would include thinking of themselves as clever, highly skilled or a top-grade student who does not need to try. They are resting on their laurels and/or not being challenged enough.

2. The top right-hand quadrant is the best place for students to be. This is where both their achievement and progress scores are high. It is often the highly motivated, hard-working students who would make it into this quadrant. It doesn't necessarily

mean they are in a growth mindset but, nonetheless, the outcomes (accordingly to the evidence collected) are good.

3. The bottom left-hand quadrant is the worst place for students to be. This is where both their achievement and progress scores are low. Classic reasons for students being in this quadrant are if they have had a bad start to education, and/ or they are suffering from low expectations (from themselves, their families or their teachers).

4. The bottom right-hand quadrant is where students have low achievement but high progress. Typical reasons for being in this quadrant are when students have had a slow start but are now gaining momentum. Perhaps there were low expectations or ineffectual support mechanisms before but now things have improved enough for students to begin catching up.

> People with an achievement-focus worry if their students are not in quadrants 1 or 2. People with a learning-focus worry if their students are not in quadrants 2 or 4.

▶ **Figure 33: Example Quadrants Showing Different Achievement Scales According to Age of Students**

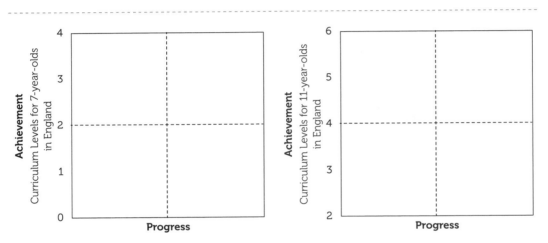

When people have a performance-focus, they aim for their students to get into quadrant *1 or 2*. When people have a learning-focus, they aim for their students to get into quadrant *2 or 4*.

What is the focus in your school? What is the focus in society? How many times have you heard the phrase, 'It's the grades that count!'? Or how many schools – and school systems – spend huge amounts of time and resources on measuring achievement but not on ascertaining progress? When this happens, it suggests that there is more of an achievement-focus than a learning-focus.

Similarly, how many schools send report cards home, identifying the grades students have achieved? Meanwhile, how few schools send report cards home, identifying the amount of progress each student has made? Of course, most schools send grades together with *comments* about progress but then which do parents trust more: grades or comments? Rightly or wrongly, grades appear to be more objective and are therefore generally relied upon more than the seemingly subjective comments are.

So, what can we do to shift the emphasis towards a learning-focus and therefore a growth mindset? In Section 6.4, we will look at some of the solutions that schools we know have tried. Sorry to say, we will also examine the problems with each approach too! For now, we invite you to use the following 'Now Try This' suggestions with your colleagues to help you reflect on the use of the quadrants shown in Figures 32 and 33.

NOW TRY THIS

1. Even if you are unable to collect data relating to progress and achievement for now, it shouldn't stop you using the quadrants. Select a relevant domain (for example, reading, verbal language skills, understanding of numbers, athletic ability or something else that is important) then use everything you know about your students – how well they are doing, how well they apply themselves, how much progress they are making compared with each other and with previous cohorts, and so on. Basically, use your professional judgement to place your students into the diagram shown in Figure 32.

2. Having done that, share your thinking with a colleague. It would be particularly useful if you explained the following:

   - Why have you placed your students where you have?

   - What made you place particular students in quadrant 2 as opposed to quadrant 1? (and vice versa)

   - Similarly, what made you place particular students in quadrant 4 as opposed to quadrant 3? (and vice versa)

   - Most importantly, what does this all mean in terms of how you might respond to different students going forward? For example, more challenge for some; a radical rethink for others; and encouragement for some to keep going exactly as they are because they're making really good progress!

3. A useful exercise is for two of you to think about the same group of students. Firstly, place the students into your own copy of Figure 32, then compare your thinking with each other. What are the significant differences? Do you each see different things in certain students? Is it possible to come to an agreement about which quadrant each student is in?

This commentary accompanying Figure 34 shows how effective an achievement–progress quadrant can be for stimulating dialogue and adjusting pedagogy.

Figure 34 shows an example of what the quadrants might look like when student data is added in. This particular example comes from our colleague, Marianne Skogvoll. She used to be the deputy principal at Åsgård school in Ås, Norway, before she joined the Challenging Learning team. Marianne leads a lot of the long-term development work we do with schools, pre-schools and colleges across Scandinavia. To give our partner schools an idea of how effect sizes can be used to make decisions about leadership and learning, Marianne used a standardised reading test with 5th grade students (10- and 11-year-olds) at the beginning of a reading project in January and then at the end of the project in April. She then used the effect size calculation as recommended by John Hattie to identify the locations for each of the points shown in Figure 34. If you would like to use the same method, then go to www.visiblelearningplus.com/resources and download the 'Visible Learning Effect Size Add-in'.

It is not the numbers that are most important though; it is the story behind them and what you might do next that makes this approach part of a learning-focus. The following commentary that Marianne sent along with her calculations shows this very well:

1. In regard to the students in the **top left-hand quadrant**:

   Before I did the calculations, we had just had student/parent conferences. To this group of students, I would say things such as: 'You are doing very well' or 'Keep up the good work'. But now, when I look at their progress scores, it suggests they

were *not* doing 'good work'; instead, they were probably taking it too easy and relying on prior knowledge to get good grades rather than learning new things and making even more progress.

2. In regard to the students in the **top right-hand quadrant**:

   What made this group of students do so well? We don't know. In fact, we had no tradition for investigating the reasons why some students make excellent progress; instead, we were just happy that they did! This meant we lost valuable information, both to us, to them and to their peers.

3. In regard to the students in the **bottom left-hand quadrant**:

   We normally think we are pretty good at spotting kids who are in quadrant 3 but there were some surprises in there for us as well. In fact, for kids who are so far behind, we often focus mainly on the progress that they are making rather than the grades they are not getting. Strange how we thought this would help kids in quadrant 3 but not in all the other quadrants!

4. In regard to the students in the **bottom right-hand quadrant**:

   By focusing on the grades they are not getting (yet) rather than the excellent progress they are making, we do a disservice to those in quadrant 4. The students, their parents – and yes, their teachers – in general compare to the top achievers rather than compare to where they were before. OK, so they haven't got the good grades yet but they are heading in the right direction (which is more than can be said for those in quadrant 1 who are taking it too easy).

► **Figure 34: Progress Made in Reading by 5th Grade Students from Ås, Norway**

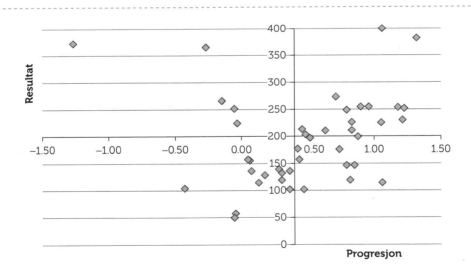

Notice how the above commentary reflects a move from a performance-orientation towards a learning-orientation. Great stuff! Keep doing this and it would be reasonable to assume that a growth mindset will become ever more evident amongst the staff and students of Åsgård school. Is it the same in your school? If not then what can you do about it?

Another of our colleagues, George Telford, used to be principal of Yinnar School in Victoria, Australia. He would do a very similar thing to Marianne, but his data used to come from the differences between two sets of national test scores. In Australia, students in Years 3, 5, 7 and 9 take the 'National Assessment Program – Literacy And Numeracy'

This gives another example of how useful achievement–progress quadrants can be.

(NAPLAN) tests. So, George would use the scores his students got in Year 3 and Year 5 (for example), work out the improvements and then calculate an effect size. This meant he could do a similar analysis to the one shown above from Marianne. In addition, he would also look for 'where' as well as 'when' this growth happened, as he explains here:

We were generally very pleased with the growth that our students were making but for me, the equally important point was 'where' was the growth? I wanted to identify whether, for example, the students at the beginning of Year 3 were making really good progress in numeracy but not in literacy, or perhaps the other way around later in Year 4. If so, then I wanted to know so that we could do something about it. Although taking national tests every two years might seem too frequent in the eyes of many, it also seems a long period of time to be carrying on in our own merry little way if it turns out latterly that there was a better way of doing things, if only we'd known earlier. So, for me, the NAPLAN data was never about patting ourselves on the back; it was about seeking out the stories hidden in amongst the numbers and then adjusting our teaching and learning accordingly.

(Authors): Sticking with the Australian theme for a moment, I was recently presenting to a group of high school teachers and college lecturers in New South Wales. As I waited for the day to begin, I watched all the delegates taking a seat and noticed in particular a group who took the back row. Much the same as with the teenagers I used to teach, it was those who were least interested in the topic of the day who took up residence at the back of the room. Indeed, these teachers also kept their coats on, their hoodies up, and barely cracked a smile all day; just as the hardest-to-reach kids do. Throughout the day, this group seemed to be trying their best to let me know how uninterested they were; they didn't just disengage, they made damned sure I knew they had disengaged! God love 'em.

Then, when I started talking about the achievement–progress quadrants, one of them stood up. I thought he was about to leave but instead he interrupted the flow of the day by roaring: 'What you don't get, James, is . . .' (he was spitting his words out with venom) . . . 'you can't make a silk purse out of a pig's ear!'

'Ohhh-kay,' says I. 'What makes you say that?'

'So long as some kids have got a hole in their backside' (I'm paraphrasing here to spare your blushes), 'they will never achieve. Some kids were put on this earth to be good with their hands, not with their heads. Some are never going to win the competition'.

There followed a moment of deafening silence. I could see some of the other delegates wondering how I, a prisoner of mother England, was going to respond; his pals were puffing their chests with righteousness that at last someone had named the elephant in the room; others seemed more worried that I might think this guy represented a typical Aussie outlook!

Having heard similar sentiments back home in the UK, sometimes even worse, I wasn't as bullied by his assertion as I might have been. So, after a brief pause, I responded:

My first thought is to wonder why you choose to remain in the teaching profession? Surely, such pessimism will only make you unhappy and, worse still, discourage your students from trying anything outside their comfort zone?

There is, however, just one thing I agree with you on and that is, 'not all students can win the competition'. If it is indeed a competition – and most grading systems around the world seem to be exactly that – then there *will* only be a few winners. Not everyone can get an A grade or 4.0 GPA unless we change from the usual

norm-referencing to criterion-referencing, and I don't suppose that is going to happen soon.

However, and here is yet another excellent dimension of a learning-focus – *everyone* can make great progress irrespective of how well other people are progressing. You can make great progress without negatively affecting my chances of making great progress. With an achievement-focus, it is different: if you get one of the few A grades available then it makes it less likely that I will also get an A grade. But we can both make superb progress; that is not a competition. Progress is not about the *inter*-personal competition (competing against other people). If it is a competition at all, it is about an *intra*-personal one (competing against yourself to beat your personal best).

He snorted his reply: 'Get real. We're *not* all equal and never will be. Whilst you're getting your students to think about progress, my students are preparing for the real world. They are going to be tested. Those who get the best grades will get the best jobs; those who don't won't. So why raise their expectations. You're dealing in false hope and should be ashamed of yourself'.

I thought about my reply for a moment and then responded:

I agree that we're not all equal.

(I made a weak joke at this point about the superiority of Brits versus Australians, in an attempt to lighten the mood a bit. Thankfully it seemed to work, at least a little).

However, I think all students deserve an equal *opportunity* to make good progress. The more progress they make, the better chance they have of getting those good grades. As we've already agreed, they won't all get top grades – too much depends on where they are starting from, how much time they have before the exams, and who else is in that particular cohort competing against them that particular year. But one thing's for sure, if we write them off now as having no chance and – worse still – if they agree with that damning assessment, then of course they're not going to get those top grades.

At least, if we keep most of our attention on progress and half an eye on grades then they stand a fighting chance of doing OK rather than giving up prematurely.

As for grades being directly linked with jobs, I'm not sure that's true. There are just too many people who have done well in life despite not getting good grades. Many employers would say it is an attitude towards learning, a determination to get the job done, an openness to feedback and so on, that is valued more in the workplace than grades. Of course, good grades will help you get into university or get a job interview, so they are still important. But isn't it those 'aptitudes' such as willingness to learn, listen, focus and so on that are prized just as much, if not more so? And perhaps we develop those things more when we keep learning how to learn rather than when we look only to the exams at the end of our school days?

> In the usual, norm-referenced systems that most schools operate, not every student can get a top grade, but everyone can make excellent progress.

Afterwards, I made sure to have a coffee with him and we chatted things through. He seemed resigned to the idea that despite wishing he could have more of a learning-focus, too many things prevent him from doing so. These included the pressures of exam boards; the attitude of his line-managers who, in his opinion, cared only about grades; the clear link between career progression of teachers and student grades (meaning no one wanted to teach the 'dumber classes', as he called them, because they 'never get good grades'); and the state's willingness to publish league tables of student grades, thus emphasising again and again that 'it's the grades that count'. By the end, he was a little more optimistic and I was a little more pessimistic but we shook hands and went our

own ways. About the only thing we did agree on is that progress leads to higher grades. It is not a case that *either* students make good progress *or* they get good grades; one leads to the other.

NOW TRY THIS

Looking at Figure 35 and Marianne's accompanying commentary, talk about the following questions with your colleagues:

1. How do you identify the students in quadrant 1 in your school? What can you do to move them into quadrant 2?

2. How many of your students are in quadrant 2 just now? How did they get there? What can you do to make sure they stay there, and how can you help other students to move into that quadrant with them?

3. How do you identify which of your students are in quadrant 3? What can you do to move them into quadrant 4? (Note: Ideally, you would want to move them into quadrant 3 but, as our Australian friend pointed out, this is extremely unlikely in the immediate future. So, first things first, how do you get students from quadrant 3 into quadrant 4 – and then *eventually* from quadrant 4 into quadrant 2?)

4. How do you reassure the students (and their parents) who are in quadrant 4 that they are making good progress, even if the good grades aren't there (yet)? And what can you do to stop them from sliding back into quadrant 3 but instead push on to quadrant 2?

6.4 • DIFFERENT FORMS OF PROGRESS

> Too many people feel obliged to focus on achievement grades, particularly when information about progress is unavailable.

(Authors): I don't want my students to have an achievement-focus. I don't want my own children to either. The problem is, when our three children bring home their report cards, guess what my wife and I look at: their achievement grades! Of course, we would rather look at progress information but the report cards don't include that. There are comments such as, 'she applies herself well'; 'he is making good progress'; and 'she is a joy to teach'. All of which are pleasing but they don't tell us *how much* progress they are making. So, how do we know which quadrant they are in? Simple answer: we don't.

Of course, that might sound like a particular concern, relevant only to authors of educational books. But it's not. Although most parents wouldn't talk in terms of the four quadrants, nearly all of them want to know their child is doing well. They might not say, 'I want to be sure my child isn't left in quadrant 3' but they will mean exactly the same thing when they say, 'I don't want my child left behind'.

So, back to the report cards: do the lovely comments about attitude, trying hard, being a joy to teach and so on, tell us which quadrant our children are in? Nope. But do the grades at least reassure us that they are not being left behind? Well, yes, if the grades are good. We don't want to over-value grades but at least they are a mechanism for determining

whether or not our child is doing OK. So, we look at them, talk about them and congratulate our children for them when they do well. Talk about an achievement-orientation!

What is the alternative though? We don't want to ignore the report cards. If we do, we run the risk of giving our children the impression that grades never matter. They do matter. Just not as much (in our eyes, at least) as enjoyment, progress, desire to learn, friendships, health (physical and mental), curiosity, confidence and so on.

Here, then, are what some schools have tried, together with the associated pros and cons.

6.4.1 • Standardised Assessments of Progress

This is one of the best ways to provide a score that can be relied upon by staff, students and parents. The approaches generally use baseline assessments that measure competence and confidence in learning. Students' learning is then monitored over subsequent years and value-added progress measures calculated. By comparing achievement grades with these progress scores, you can be confident about which quadrant each student is in. This, in turn, allows you to challenge, support and target-set ever more confidently and accurately. It also means you are putting your money where your mouth is: setting a learning-focus in your school that values progress as much as achievement.

The Centre for Evaluation & Monitoring (www.cem.org/midyis) is one of the many organisations providing standardised measures of progress.

> Here are some of the many ways to draw attention to progress.

6.4.2 • Calculate Progress

You could do as our colleague, Marianne, did and calculate the amount of progress your students are making. Generally, this involves giving your students a test at the beginning and end points.[1] Marianne used the Carlsten test (www.brittmark.no/carlsten) which is common in Norway but there will be many equivalents available to you. Your local educational psychologists can probably help in selecting the right test(s).

As mentioned earlier, if you would like to use effect size to help you calculate progress then the Visible Learning Plus site gives a great guide. It even offers an add-in for spreadsheets so that the clever numbers can do the work for you. See www.visiblelearningplus.com/resources.

> Beware the common pitfalls of awarding scores for effort.

6.4.3 • Beware Effort Scores

Many schools we have come across have started giving effort scores. These are well intentioned but, sorry to say, misguided. Though they come from a good place (wanting to provide a counter-balance to achievement grades), they rarely work. Here is why:

How do you know how much effort students are putting into something? It might be relatively obvious when observing sport but what about reading, writing and maths? If a child stares out of the window, are they deep in thought (high effort) or daydreaming (low

---

1. Though we say, 'beginning and end', it would be even better to give it at the beginning and *middle* point. It is much better to leave yourself time to use the data formatively rather than to look back at it summatively. So, if, for example, you are going to measure progress in reading then do a baseline at the beginning of the year and then the next test three to four months later. With that information, you can calculate improvements, place your students into the different quadrants and then plan what to do next. With time still left in the academic year, you can decide who needs more challenge, who needs more encouragement to keep going as they are, who needs a whole new approach, and so on.

effort)? If they ask lots of questions, are they engaging in the subject matter (high effort) or just aiming to please (high effort for the wrong thing)?

Added to that is that most effort scores seem to be assigned to students based on a general impression that the teacher has about them. So, the effort has not even been observed; it's been inferred from a whole range of factors, most of which are implicit. Sounds pretty damned subjective, doesn't it?

Then there are the beliefs of students to contend with. Both of us authors have asked students in many countries what they think effort scores mean, and indeed what the best combination of academic grades and effort scores are. Do you know what most students have replied: high grade, low effort, because that means you are clever! And the worst? Low grade, high effort, because that means you really are stupid!

To some people, this shows how cynical students are, particularly the high school students. In our mind though, it's just common sense, especially if fixed mindset is in the air: why would you let your teenage peers know you are putting effort into something? Adolescence is hard enough without everyone thinking you're a teacher's pet! The best way forward is to pretend to be nonchalant, even if you are putting in lots of effort behind the scenes. That way, when you do well, you can say it's because you're naturally clever; whereas if you do badly you can fob it off as something you didn't care much about anyway.

We are, of course, *not* recommending this attitude! It is just that it exists in so many high schools anyway. Sadly, high grades with low effort seem to be revered a lot more than high grades, high effort, as if effort was the imposter's way to achieve! This will be explored in more depth in Chapter 8.

6.4.4 • Beware Attitude Grades

Similar problems occur with attitude grades. They are so subjective that they can become relatively meaningless.

(Authors): My eldest daughter used to receive attitude grades at her old school. A week or two before her academic grades were sent home, we would receive a report card identifying her attitudes towards each subject. The first time we received them, she was identified as having an excellent attitude in some subjects and good in others. We asked her what this meant: she didn't know. We asked her why she thought she had been given a 'good' rating in six of the subjects and excellent in the other five. Again, she didn't know but she wondered if it had something to do with how much she smiled in different subjects, or which ones she found more interesting and which ones less so.

So, I phoned the school to find out what they meant. I asked what a pupil needed to do to move from good to excellent, what the scale was, and whether there were indeed any criteria for each 'level'. I bet you're thinking you'd hate to have me on the parent body but please be assured, I was gentle with my probing. Honestly.

After the phone call, I was none-the-wiser than I was beforehand. So, I put the report card away in a drawer with the assessment, 'must try harder'.

You know what happened next, don't you? Ava was given 'excellent' for every subject for the rest of the year! This of course was not what I was seeking; I just wanted to know how the system works. Perhaps the hike in scores was coincidental – or because my

> Grades for attitude are also problematic.

daughter wore a permanent smile on her face in all subjects, always. But I'm guessing it was just to shut me up.

Now, though, my son is going through the same school and they have morphed the attitude ratings into effort grades. What did his first report card say? That Harry is Mr Joe Average, with a 'C' grade for effort in every single subject!

In my mind, this throws up yet another problem with attitude ratings: how expressive of their emotions are different students? I was going to use the terms 'introverted' and 'extroverted', but these terms are laden with so many critiques that I will stick with the terms 'expressive' and 'demonstrative' instead.

My son is a much more private person than either of his sisters are, and nowhere near as gregarious. Though you'll never find a more loyal or loving soul, it often takes quite a long time for new people to get to know him because he keeps things very much to himself. So, a new teacher and a new class will be met with a quietly assured but far less demonstrative child than if either of the other two Nottingham children were in the class. I don't know for sure of course, but I suspect this influences the attitude grades he receives just as much as his sister's very different personality influenced her 'good' and 'excellent' grades a few years earlier.

6.4.5 • Progress Points

The schools that have tried effort scores and then rejected them again, have started to work out a system for 'progress points'. This looks very different in art than it does in maths, but each faculty is working on creating a system for their students.

Some schools are awarding progress points throughout the year; some at particular times such as mid-term and end-term points.

Some schools have a team competition running in which all students are part of one of four 'houses', Harry Potter-style. Students then earn progress points for their team and whichever house has the hightest number of points at the end of each term are the winners. A nice aspect of this approach is that students starting further back often travel further than those who begin with high grades at the beginning of the year. So, all of a sudden, everyone wants the kids with lower grades in their team. Teachers included.

> A growth mindset culture can be supported with the use of 'progress points'; these tend to work much better than effort or attitude grades.

NOW TRY THIS

Have a discussion with your colleagues about the following questions to do with progress:

1. Which of the recommendations and cautions described in this section stand out for you most, and why?

2. Do you have data already available that you could use to calculate effect size scores? If so, then what's the plan for putting it into action?

3. If you were to create a system of progress points then how would you make it work in your school?

6.5 • YOUR STUDENTS ARE ALREADY MAKING PROGRESS

> The point is not to see *if* your students are making progress because they almost certainly will be. Instead, the key is to check that they are making really *good* progress and to adjust things if they're not.

Here is the good news: your students are already making progress. Spending time with others, observing, listening, thinking – all of these help your students to grow and learn.

Here is the bad news: your students are already making progress. We describe this as bad news only in that it means we can't pat ourselves on the back too heartily when our students know, understand and can do more at the end of the year than they could at the beginning. It would be bizarre if they couldn't.

Our aim, therefore, ought *not* to be *just* helping our students do their best; they can do that without our help. Instead, if we want a learning-focus then we should help them to love learning; to wonder more; explore more; be more than they ever expected. That is *not* the opposite of saying, 'be comfortable in your own skin'. There are many times when 'being' is enough; when relaxing is the best thing to do; when accepting is better mentally as well as physically.

A performance-focus might help with this but a learning-focus will help even more.

The examples in this chapter should help you with that pursuit. If you can *also* calculate some effect size scores then that should help to ratify progress as the main focus of education. The most important thing, though, is to build a learning culture that privileges progress and celebrates growth. For, as the motto for our company, Challenging Learning, states:

> Proving is good; improving is better.

NOTES

Recently, someone asked what keeps me up at night. It's the fear that the mindset concepts, which grew up to counter the failed self-esteem movement, will be used to perpetuate that movement. In other words, if you want to make students feel good, even if they're not learning, just praise their effort! Want to hide learning gaps from them? Just tell them, 'Everyone is smart!'

The growth mindset was intended to help close achievement gaps, not hide them. It is about telling the truth about a student's current achievement and then, together, doing something about it, helping him or her become smarter.

Dweck, 2015a

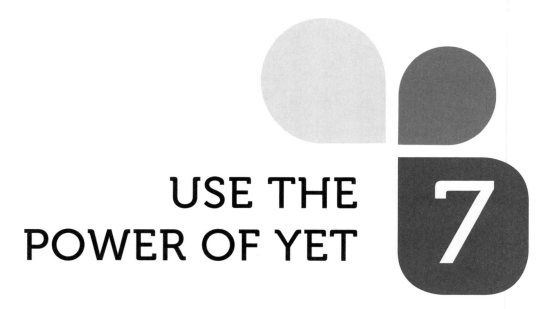

USE THE POWER OF YET 7

7.0 • THE POWER OF YET

In November 2014, Carol Dweck gave a presentation to the TEDx event in Norrköping, Sweden. Bosse was part of the organising committee and James had the privilege of introducing Carol on the night. That 10-minute presentation has now been watched almost seven million times in the three years it has been on the TED.com website. The fact that our introduction has been cut from the beginning of the video is not a source of disappointment. Honest.

The title of Dweck's presentation that night was, 'The power of yet'. It has been changed online to 'The power of believing that you can improve', which is a shame because it is nowhere near as catchy or as powerful. Nevertheless, the point of the presentation is to say that 'yet' can have a significant effect on attitude. Instead of saying, 'I can't do this', Dweck recommends that we say, 'I can't do this *yet*'.

That three-lettered word, 'yet', changes the possibilities. 'I can't play the guitar – yet' gives the impression that I could play the guitar if I put the right amount of effort, time and dedication into it; whereas saying, 'I can't play the guitar' sounds so final.

If a student says, 'I can't do it' then you could say, 'not yet'. This acknowledges their current reality and adds a sense of possibility that they *might* be able to in the future.

Compare this to the common response when a student says they can't: many of us will say, 'yes, you can'. This might seem just as good but all too often – particularly in cases of low self-esteem – students respond by thinking either a) this adult is lying to me or b) this adult doesn't understand what I'm going through. Then, some students will even try to *prove* that they can't do it!

> Saying, I can't do this 'yet' emphasises the possibility of progress.

Photographs by Göran Hedlund

> Telling your students they can't do something 'yet' acknowledges their situation but also indicates there is a way forward.

So, instead of saying 'yes, you can', in most cases it would be better to say, 'no, you can't. Not yet'. This works particularly well when used in conjunction with the learning-focus ideas recommended in the previous chapter.

So, when you get chance, take a look at the video online at TED.com. It begins with:

> I heard about a high school in Chicago where students had to pass a certain number of courses to graduate, and if they didn't pass a course, they got the grade 'Not Yet'. And I thought that was fantastic, because if you get a failing grade, you think, I'm nothing, I'm nowhere. But if you get the grade 'Not Yet' you understand that you're on a learning curve. It gives you a path into the future. (Dweck, 2014)

7.1 • THE POWER OF YETIS

> Yetis help learners identify what to do next after they've decided they can't do something yet.

With a small leap of the imagination, we have come up with yetis to use when students are 'not there yet'. This chapter explains how they can be used.

There are two sets of yetis: one for older students (see Figure 36) and one for younger students (see Figure 37). In our opinion, the older set works for teenagers, and the younger set for 5- to 12-year-olds.

The best time to use the YETI steps is when your students have made good progress towards their learning goals but have not yet finished. As such, they fit in very well with stages three to six of the Seven Steps to Feedback Success (see Section 10.2).

For students of all ages, we have found the following method works best:

1. Introduce YETI as an acronym.

Y You

E Evaluate

T Target

I Improve

Before using yetis, check that 'You' are ready to learn; 'Evaluate' how much progress you have made so far; agree a 'Target' for improvement; and then select the appropriate YETI to help you to 'Improve'.

2. Explain to your students that you will prompt them to use each YETI stage until they are used to the process. After that, you hope they will use the process as and when they think their learning could benefit from some YETI thinking.

3. Introduce each stage as follows:

YETI – You

Before selecting the best yeti for your purpose, check that *you* are:

- open to learning
- determined to improve
- willing to have a go.

(Note: You could also add 'in a growth mindset' to this list if your students are conversant with the term and know it isn't just another way to criticise them when they don't succeed.)

Y**E**TI – Evaluate

Evaluate how much progress you have made towards your learning goal. This includes thinking about the following questions:

- Which success criteria have you accomplished brilliantly, which have you yet to reach, and which ones have you not addressed yet?
- In what ways is your thinking affecting your learning? (Meta-cognition)
- Is there something you can think of that will make things much better?

YE**T**I – Target

Set targets for yourself that will help you to improve, deepen or extend your learning. For example, you could:

- Identify what you are aiming to accomplish in the time that you've got.
- Clarify what the end result of your learning will look, sound and feel like.
- If learning with others, agree together what you want your learning outcome to be.
- Then, depending on the age of your students, introduce the yetis shown in Figure 36 or 37. In both cases, the 'I' in YETI stands for:

YET**I** - Improve

Select the yeti (or strategy) that will be most effective in helping you to reach your target.

▶ Figure 36: Yetis for Older Students (approx. 12–18)

1. Accuracy Yeti

Improve the accuracy of what you are doing; check for errors; be meticulous about the details; check the reliability of the sources you have used; be precise with your language; create a version that is faithful to the original.

2. Analysing Yeti

Consider the merits of each idea or action; create criteria; judge; examine; compare and contrast; identify or estimate the effectiveness; measure; calculate.

3. Applying Yeti

Apply techniques you have used successfully in previous contexts to this new situation; apply knowledge from one curriculum area to another; use someone else's recommendation to help you enhance your learning.

4. Classifying Yeti

Sort, classify, code, rank, group, separate, grade or categorise your options, ideas, information or attempts. Use strategies such as odd one out; diamond, pyramid or linear ranking; Venn diagrams; or concept targets.

(NB. All of these strategies are covered in depth in *Challenging Learning Through Dialogue* by Nottingham, Nottingham and Renton, 2017)

5. Comparing Yeti

Compare your learning with someone else's learning; identify the differences between your results and those you were aiming for; compare your views with someone else who has opposing views; find similarities and differences.

6. Connecting Yeti

Connect your learning to other people's learning; combine two or more ideas into one; demonstrate causal links or correlations; find similarities and differences; identify general patterns.

7. Creative Yeti

Think of innovative ways to make progress; look for new solutions; design a better way forward; come up with new ideas; create a new composition or sequence; modify an input to see if the output changes, find interesting angles to think about your learning, think outside the box.

8. Describing Yeti

Describe what you are doing; give details; explain your learning to others; recount; illustrate; represent; define; outline what you are aiming for, how much progress you have made and what you intend to do next.

9. Extending Yeti

Look for ways to extend your learning; try different techniques to see if the quality of your learning improves; think of alternative ways to demonstrate your learning to others; find generalisations and exceptions.

10. Organising Yeti

Organise your learning so that it is more meaningful; rearrange the parts to add clarity to the whole; rationalise your thoughts or actions; sequence actions or ideas to improve the flow; create headings and subheadings; label; catalogue.

(Continued)

(Continued)

11. Questioning Yeti

Identify the questions you still have; predict what questions other people might ask about your learning; investigate possibilities; create an hypothesis using 'if . . . when?'; create how, what, where, when and why questions, which will enhance your learning.

12. Reasoning Yeti

Identify reasons; find cause and effect; rationalise; find convincing proof; decide why one approach is better than another; solve equations; create a rationale; form a judgement; decide on the next logical steps.

13. SPaG-Yeti

Check your Spelling, Punctuation and Grammar.

Younger Yetis

▶ **Figure 37: Yetis for Younger Students (approx. 5–12)**

YETI Learning 1	YETI Learning 2
Listen *(Hear, Receive)*	*Talk* *(Discuss, Debate, Self-talk)*
©2017 www.challenginglearning.com	©2017 www.challenginglearning.com
YETI Learning 3	YETI Learning 4
Work Together *(Collaborate, Co-operate)*	*Give Reasons* *(Explain, Justify)*
©2017 www.challenginglearning.com	©2017 www.challenginglearning.com
YETI Learning 5	YETI Learning 6
Remember *(Recall, Retell)*	*Think* *(Reflect, Consider, Contemplate)*
©2017 www.challenginglearning.com	©2017 www.challenginglearning.com

These yetis are more suited to primary school students. As with the first set of cards, you could photocopy them or download them, cut them out and then make them available as a set of cards for your students to choose from.

(Continued)

(Continued)

YETI Learning 7 *Choose* *(Decide, Conclude)*  ©2017 www.challenginglearning.com	YETI Learning 8 *Take Turns* *(Share, Include)*  ©2017 www.challenginglearning.com
YETI Learning 9 *Make Links* *(Make Connections, Associations)*  ©2017 www.challenginglearning.com	YETI Learning 10 *Ask Questions* *(Query, Inquire)*  ©2017 www.challenginglearning.com
YETI Learning 11 *Answer Questions* *(Respond, Reply)*  ©2017 www.challenginglearning.com	YETI Learning 12 *Explore* *(Research, Investigate)*  ©2017 www.challenginglearning.com

7. Use the Power of Yet

YETI Learning
13
Order
(Prioritise, Rank)

YETI Learning
14
Analyse
(Examine, Compare/Contrast)

YETI Learning
15
Concentrate
(Focus, Give Attention To)

YETI Learning
16
Classify
(Categorise, Group, Sort)

YETI Learning
17
Evaluate
(Judge, Assess)

YETI Learning
18
Predict
(Expect, Suggest, Hypothesise)

(Continued)

(Continued)

YETI Learning 19 *Create* (Invent, Imagine)	YETI Learning 20 *Define* (Identify, Describe)
 ©2017 www.challenginglearning.com	 ©2017 www.challenginglearning.com
YETI Learning 21 *Apply* (Demonstrate, Use)	YETI Learning 22 *SPaG-Yeti* (Check Spelling, Punctuation and Grammar)
 ©2017 www.challenginglearning.com	 ©2017 www.challenginglearning.com
YETI Learning 23 *Check Accuracy* (Be Precise, Find Mistakes, Check Sources)	
 ©2017 www.challenginglearning.com	

NOTES

The whole idea that students should always answer teachers' questions correctly is actually rather odd. If the students are answering every one of the teacher's questions correctly, the teacher is surely wasting the students' time. If the questions are not causing students to struggle and think, they are probably not worth asking.

Dylan Wiliam, 2014

CHOOSE CHALLENGE

8.0 • MINDSET MATTERS MOST WHEN THERE IS CHALLENGE

In Chapter 2, we discussed the meta-analysis of 85 studies connected to mindset by Burnette et al. (2013), which identified that mindset matters most when faced with challenging situations. To remind you, the difference between a person responding to challenge by remaining task-focused, compared with a person giving up too easily, is an effect size of 0.55. So, when there is lots of challenge, mindset really matters. But when challenge is low then the impact of mindset on learning outcomes is also low.

This situation might seem unworthy of repeating; after all, it seems obvious that mindset will matter most in times of challenge. However, there is another complication: when students are given control over their learning, or offered a choice of learning tasks, too many of them pick the easier option. This leads to a double-whammy: students learn less by opting to stay in their comfort zone *and* they miss out on the opportunity to experience how their mindset can make a significant difference to learning.

This chapter focuses on how to encourage your students to choose challenge and thereby experience situations in which mindset really matters.

8.1 • WHEN STUDENTS PICK THE EASIER PATH

Take a look at Figure 38, showing two paths through the woods: which of those paths would you choose? We ask you this because if you were to look on www.visiblelearning-plus.com at the list of 250+ influences on student achievement compiled by John Hattie, then you would find the typical effect of 'Student control over learning' is an effect size of 0.02 (Hattie, 2017).

Bearing in mind the typical effect of all factors influencing student achievement that Hattie has collated is an effect size of 0.4, it shows just how pitifully small 0.02 is. Indeed, you could say that giving students choice slows down their rate of learning!

▶ Figure 38: Easy Path or Challenging Path?

Let's be careful here: Hattie is *not* saying, 'don't give students control over their learning'. Instead, his analysis leads to many questions, of which one would be, 'Why would giving students choice result in decreased learning?' And perhaps more importantly, 'Is it happening in my class or school?'.

(authors): To be honest, when I first read that giving students choice reduces learning, I thought: 'What a load of rubbish! That can't be true. Students love choice. When I give my students control over their learning, they have a greater sense of ownership. They engage in things they have chosen far more willingly than when they are simply instructed to do something. So, Hattie must be wrong!' But then I got to thinking that perhaps that was a defensive position to take and, instead, I should look for reasons why students might pick the easier option and then identify what I can do about it.

NOW TRY THIS

Before we go any further, please take the opportunity to come up with your own reasons why students might pick the easier option when given the choice. Assume the research findings are correct for now, rather than react the way James did initially!

Reason 1:

Reason 2:

Reason 3:

We will now look at some of the reasons we have come up with. As you read through them, consider which mindset – fixed or growth – they would more likely link to.

(authors): Recently, I took my children on a family bike ride. My 3-year-old sat on the back of my bike and never stopped talking the whole journey! My 10-year-old jumped on her bike and away she pedalled confidently. My 7-year-old had just got a new bike for his birthday and you know how that goes: buy a frame that's a bit too big so that the bike will last longer! So, he jumps on the bike that is too big for him and away he wobbles! He keeps going but he wobbles way more than my heart would have liked.

As we were cycling, I thought to myself: which one is learning most about bike riding on this journey?

The answer of course is my son, Harry. He was out of his comfort zone and was therefore having to concentrate more than his sisters. He was learning how to handle a bigger bike; he was learning more about balancing. He was learning about using gears (this was the first bike he'd ever ridden that had more than one gear). Our girls were enjoying the ride but they were not learning anything like as much as their brother was.

A similar comparison would be to think about driving your car. When you drive from home to work every day, you can do so almost on autopilot. You don't have to think about your driving because it comes easily to you. So, when you drive on familiar roads in a familiar car then it is well within your comfort zone. Therefore, you are more likely to be 'doing' rather than 'learning'.

Compare that type of everyday driving to driving somewhere completely different, perhaps in a busy city in a foreign country where they drive on the wrong side of the road! How much more would you have to concentrate then? How much more would you be learning by being *out* of your comfort zone?

Now, let's say that you give me a lift when driving in that foreign city. What would you think of me if I said, 'shall I do it for you?' Of course, some people might readily agree but most would presumably think I was being patronising or that I had very low expectations for your success. Yet, how many times do we do such things to our students? When they are struggling with something, when they are out of their comfort zone, then how many of us might be tempted to offer our help; show them how to do it; in some cases, even do it for them for the sake of efficiency?

If we do any of that then what is the implication? Does it say that struggling is good or that struggling is to be avoided? Does it encourage students to persevere or does it suggest that whenever they get stuck, they should ask for help?

Back to the bike riding for a moment: what would you have thought of me as a father if I had said to Harry: 'Son, I think you're wobbling too much. Why don't you get off and walk? Or why don't I ask your sister to run alongside you holding the frame so that you don't wobble too much?' If I had done that then presumably you would have thought, there goes an over-protective parent. And yet, how many times do we, as teachers, do something similar by offering our help to 'wobbling' students? How often do we seat a more competent student next to a 'wobbling' one so that they can help show them the way?

- -

All of this might seem reasonable in the moment; after all, we don't want to leave our students to flounder. But what does it also imply about struggle or 'wobbling'? Does it say, 'the more you wobble, the more you learn so keep at it until you get there'? Or does it say, 'whenever you wobble, ask for help and someone will rescue you'? Presumably the latter and, in which case, no wonder so many students pick the easier option when given the choice; after all, 'wobbling' is to be avoided.

Take another example: which of the following scores would your students say they are most likely to be praised for?

6/10   10/10

Presumably, most students would say they are more likely to be praised for getting ten out of ten; if they get six out of ten then they are generally told, 'Try harder next time!' or 'Have another go'.

Which 'path' does that encourage students to take next time: the easy path or the challenging one? After all, the chances of getting ten out of ten (and being praised for it) are much higher when they take the easier option.

Finally, consider what happens when a student makes a mistake: how many of us are likely to share that mistake with others so that everyone can benefit from the learning experience? Some would perhaps, but most people we ask say they couldn't share the mistake with others in case it embarrasses the mistake-maker. In those situations, many teachers tell us they tend to help the student in question correct their mistake and then move on. No drama. No sharing with others.

What might those actions imply? Does it suggest that mistakes are learning opportunities or things to be embarrassed about? If the latter then, again, no wonder so many students pick the easier 'path' when given the choice. If mistakes are to be avoided then the sensible choice is to go for the path least likely to result in errors. The easy path it is then.

Three points of clarification before we move on to look at how to encourage students to choose the challenging path more often:

1. We are *not* suggesting that mistakes should be celebrated! We have noticed in too many classrooms the notion that 'mistakes are good' is promoted. We think that is inaccurate, or, at the very least, over-simplistic. Mistakes are *not* good in themselves. The learning opportunities that can come from mistakes are generally good but the mistakes themselves are not. Of course, we want our students to step out of their comfort zone because that is where they will learn more, and when they do, they are more likely to make mistakes. So, mistakes can be a sign that something good is happening; and if our students then examine their own and each other's mistakes then something *great* is likely to be happening. But to say, 'mistakes are good' is not something we would support, at least not without these caveats.

2. We are also *not* suggesting that mistakes are always a sign that your students are out of their comfort zone. Mistakes can also come from carelessness or lack of focus when doing something relatively straightforward. Even so, they can still be a source of learning if approached with the right attitude.

3. If you *are* able to share your students' mistakes with others, without fear of embarrassment or shame for the mistake-maker, then it is very likely that you are well on your way to creating a 'growth mindset culture'. If not, then you are not there. Yet!

8.2 • ENCOURAGING STUDENTS TO CHOOSE THE CHALLENGING PATH

James's story about his family bike ride involved just three children and, even then, only one of them was out of their comfort zone. In schools, there are way more than three children per classroom! So, how on earth do you get all your students out of their comfort zone?

That is why we began this chapter by talking about student choice. If we can persuade students that the better *choice* is the more challenging option then we won't have to do all the leading ourselves; the students will seek out the challenging opportunities for themselves. This, in turn, will make it more likely that a growth mindset will come into play.

For example, if James's eldest daughter had said, 'Can I go on the mountain bike trail, please and then see you at the other end?' or 'Can I have a go at riding your bike, Dad?' then she would have been much more likely to learn from the experience; much more likely to need to be in a growth mindset; and much more likely to reflect back on the experience with a sense of achievement as well as the sense of pleasure she had from the original bike ride.

Have you seen those time-lapse videos available online showing how many more people choose to ride the escalators rather than walk up stairs? The videographers then make the steps more appealing by transforming them into a keyboard so that people taking the stairs play a tune. As soon as the giant keyboard is in place, more and more people opt for the stairs rather than the escalators. They choose the stairs because it has become the fun option and, in so doing, they do a little bit more exercise than they would have done otherwise. A win-win for everyone.

So, how might that apply to the classroom? It wouldn't be enough to create a giant keyboard, even if we had the budget – which we probably don't.

A good starting point is to break the link between challenge and 'difficulty'. Far too many people already associate challenge with things being difficult. If, for example, we say to our students, 'I'm going to challenge you' then very many of them take that to mean, 'I'm going to make things much more difficult for you'.

So, instead, do everything in your power to persuade your students that 'easy is boring, challenge is interesting'.

Referring back to Figure 38, if you ask your students, 'Which path looks more difficult?' then they will typically pick the one on the right. If, however, you ask, 'Which one looks more *interesting*?' then although they will still pick the one on the right, many more of them will be more inclined to try it out because 'interesting' is more appealing than 'difficult'.

To reinforce this, you can say to your students when they are doing something with ease, 'Wow, you're finding this really easy, aren't you? Shall we make it more interesting?' That will imply that easy is boring, challenge is interesting. It will also make it more likely that your students will rise to the challenge if they think things will get more 'interesting' rather than more 'difficult'.

Similarly, if you see your students 'wobbling' then do not rush to their aide. Instead, encourage them to persevere. Congratulate them for not giving up. Perhaps recommend that they use one or more of the yetis in Chapter 7, but do not 'rescue' them or make things easier – unless, of course, they are failing altogether but then that is not the same as 'wobbling'.

Thinking back to the bike riding example: if James's son falls off, it would be rather perverse to congratulate him and say, 'keep going!' However, it would also be wrong to stop him trying altogether or to do it for him. Instead, we should help him up, get him to dust himself down, give advice about what to do differently to increase the likelihood of success, and then get him back on the bike straight away. As all parents know, the last thing we would want is for him to give up there and then as it will be doubly difficult in the future to get him back on the bike again.

None of this requires a significant shift in planning, curriculum or classroom organisation. Instead, it means an adjustment in what to look out for. Rather than looking for students who are struggling in order to offer our help, we could instead look to encourage those same students to keep going; and rather than looking for the students who are succeeding with ease in order to praise them for doing well, we could instead look to increase the level of challenge so as to make things more 'interesting' for them.

This will not change attitudes overnight but it will be a step in the right direction. Indeed, talking of 'steps', think about the change in behaviour of people who get one of those exercise monitors: they start looking for opportunities to take more steps. Rather than take the escalators, they take the stairs; rather than circle around and around in their car looking for a parking spot closest to the front door, they park further away and add a few more steps to their tally. Travelling from one gate to another in a large airport, they look for places to walk rather than travellators to ride.

In other words, if we change the goal then the behaviour follows suit. If our goal is to arrive at our destination as efficiently as possible then we look for the path of least resistance: whereas if our goal is to get fitter then we seek out the opportunities for exercise. And so it is with education: if our goal is to help students succeed as painlessly as possible then we look for every opportunity to guide, support and demonstrate; whereas if our goal is to help students learn as much as possible then we look for opportunities to encourage, challenge and get them 'wobbling' whenever we can.

That is not to say that success is a bad thing of course: it is generally a very good thing. Instead, what we are saying is that a focus on completing the task might lend itself to the adult doing it for the child (think how many parents do their children's homework for them just so that it's out of the way!); whereas a focus on seeking out the learning opportunities might not be as efficient in terms of completing tasks quickly but in the long term, it is a far more effective way to help students to grow and flourish. It is also much more in line with the learning-focus we wrote about in Section 3.1.

In Chapter 5, we shared descriptions of what would be happening within a growth mindset culture. The aspects shown below relate directly to this chapter. Talk with a colleague about how much progress you have made towards these goals and what you can do next to bring them alive even more.

- Students understand the value of trial, error and practice and the ways in which these lead to mastery.

- Students are given deliberate opportunities to make mistakes, solve problems and struggle during lessons.

- Students talk positively about the challenges they are undertaking and the progress they are making as a result.

- When given a choice, students will pick the options they think will stretch them most.

8.3 • MINDSET THROUGH THE LEARNING PIT

Introducing your students to the Learning Challenge can be a really useful way to make challenge more appealing. At the heart of the model is the 'learning pit'.

(authors): I created the Learning Challenge in 2003 to give my students a way to describe being out of their comfort zone without feeling bad about it. Even though I had talked a lot with them about wobbling being good because it means you're improving, and that mistakes are not something to be ashamed of because they are actually opportunities to learn, still many of my students felt bashful about admitting that they were struggling. So, I had to find a metaphor to describe this situation in such a way that there would be no feelings of guilt or failure. So, the Learning Challenge was born. I have written about it in depth in *The Learning Challenge: How to Guide Your Students Through the Learning Pit* (Nottingham, 2017).

> The Learning Challenge can help to build a growth mindset culture.

The aim of the Learning Challenge is to get participants out of their comfort zone. This is a deliberate and strategic objective. It is neither incidental nor casual. It is not something that happens parenthetically. The very purpose of the Learning Challenge is to step outside the familiar to explore ideas and experiences that are neither effortless nor soothing. And that is why the idea of a pit works so well.

Some people have suggested that a mountain might be less negative, but in our opinion that metaphor doesn't work so well. When someone is at the top of a mountain, they can see for miles around and choose their next route with ease. Whereas when you are 'wobbling' or out of your comfort zone then you have the sense of confusion you would feel when you're in a pit, not the one of clarity you would have at the top of a mountain.

When your students get into the pit, you should expect them to feel uncomfortable. We don't mean anxious. We don't mean overwrought or afraid. We mean the opposite of contented. We mean needled: spurred on to think more, try more and question more. A pit ought to be uncomfortable without being frightening. It should be provocative without

being aggressive. Students should be able to see there is the potential to climb out – even though they might not be out. Yet.

The original Learning Challenge looked like the one shown in Figure 39. There are now many wonderful illustrations of the model, some more accurate than others. Indeed, if you do a search online for the 'learning pit' these days, you are likely to find millions of hits.

▶ **Figure 39: The Learning Challenge**

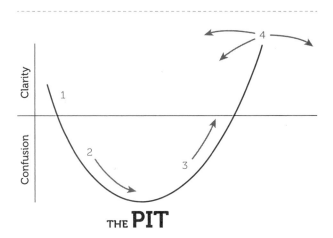

The stages of the Learning Challenge are, broadly speaking, as follows:

Stage 1   At this point, your students have surface-level knowledge of the subject matter, or they have a basic level of competence with the particular skill you are aiming to teach them.

Stage 2   Your students will go into 'the pit' when they start to question their first thoughts, find contradictions in their earlier assumptions, or begin to 'wobble' with the skill they are trying to learn.

Stage 3   After being 'in the pit' for some time (and that 'time' might be minutes, hours or sometimes even days or weeks, depending on the context), some of your students will begin to climb out of the pit. They will do this by making sense of their learning, connecting to prior knowledge, finding a way to perform the skill more adroitly, or deepening their understanding of the complexities of the concept they are examining.

Stage 4   The students who have reached stage four can then help those who are still in the pit to climb out by encouraging and guiding them. (To really build a growth mindset, you should ask the students who are being helped to challenge their helpers; remind them not to accept easy solutions. Remember: easy is boring, challenging is interesting!) After having helped others, students at stage four should also reflect on their learning journey, look for connections, and then seek out ways to transfer their new knowledge, understanding or skill to another context.

Your students' mindset will influence their response to each of these four stages. Equally, each of the stages can, over time, influence their mindset. We explored this a bit in Section 3.3, but now let's look at this relationship in more depth.

Figure 40 captures some of the thoughts that go through the minds of participants during a Learning Challenge experience. As you can see, it's not all sunshine and roses. That is not a bad thing though because the very purpose of the Learning Challenge is to take participants out of their comfort zone. So, if your students are not saying things such as, 'This is not as easy as I thought', or 'I'm confused', then perhaps your students are not even in the pit!

The thought bubbles for the character in Figure 40 show the sorts of ideas that go through someone's mind when going through a learning pit.

▶ **Figure 40: How Thinking Changes Through the Learning Challenge**

The Learning Challenge focuses on effort, having a go, taking risks, trying new strategies, seeking advice, looking for challenges, questioning yourself and others, persevering and making progress. All of these are as essential to the Learning Challenge as they are to a growth mindset. However, they are more necessary at some points of the Learning Challenge than at others. Figure 41 shows this in more detail.

The more a person goes through the learning pit, the more likely they are to get into a growth mindset.

▲ Figure 41: How Mindset Affects the Learning Challenge Journey

1 In Your Comfort Zone

The impact of mindset is less noticeable here because things are relatively straightforward. You are able to complete tasks without feeling the need to consider your strategy or to check your assumptions. You are more likely to be 'doing' or 'being' rather than questioning or checking.

2 At the Edge of Certainty

Mindset is becoming more important now. You are now right at the edge of your comfort zone. If you are in a fixed mindset, then you will be looking for ways to avoid going any further. If you are in a growth mindset, then you will be more willing to push forward and to step out of your comfort zone.

3 Going into the Pit

Mindset plays a significant role in determining your actions at this stage. If you are in a fixed mindset, then you are much more likely to take evasive action or to give up. If you are in a growth mindset, then you will enjoy the 'wobble' or at least reassure yourself that you are learning.

4 Being in the Pit

Being in the pit means you are in somewhere between your comfort zone and your panic zone. If you are in a fixed mindset, then you will think of this as your 'failure zone', and be more likely to give up, reassure yourself that you don't need to be able to do it anyway, or ask someone to rescue you. If you are in a growth mindset, then you will think of this position as your 'learning zone' and will seek out ways to overcome the obstacles or to meet the challenge head on.

5 Climbing Out of the Pit

If you are in a fixed mindset then you will probably have given up by now or sought refuge in excuses. In a growth mindset, you will continue to persevere, try out different strategies, use the most relevant 'yetis', welcome feedback and coaching, determine what is working and what is not, and apply more effort to the actions that seem most effective.

6 Enjoying Success

You are much more likely to reach this stage if you have been in a growth mindset during your learning journey. In a fixed mindset, you will probably have given up or taken a short cut to finish the task. In a growth mindset, you will have been more focused on progress and learning, and so now you will reflect on the reasons why some strategies worked for you and why some didn't, and what you can take to the next learning opportunity.

7 Reviewing and Transferring

In a fixed mindset, you will be relieved to finish. In a growth mindset, you will look for opportunities to transfer your improved knowledge, understanding and skills into other contexts; you will also be more willing to seek out, and go into, the next learning pit.

Next Pit

The Pit

NOW TRY THIS

To find out more about the Learning Challenge and how you can use it to encourage a growth mindset in your students, we recommend the following actions:

- Watch the animated video of the Learning Challenge at www.youtube.com/watch?v=3IMUAOhuO78.

- Download some of the images and resources available at www.thelearningchallenge.co.uk and share them with your students.

- Invite your students to create their own illustrations of the Learning Challenge. Make sure the exit of the pit is at a higher point than the entrance to the pit, as shown in Figures 39, 40 and 41. Otherwise, give them free reign to explore their own interpretations.

- Display the best illustrations of the pit together with the yetis shown in Chapter 7. Then encourage your students to refer to these as they engage in challenging tasks, asking them prompt questions such as, 'Which yeti could help you to climb out of the pit right now?' or 'How is your mindset influencing your decision-making?'

Praise is one of the most commonly used forms of reward. It is convenient, is nearly effortless, and makes the recipient feel good. However, praising children for being smart carries unintended consequences: It can undermine their achievement motivation in a way that praising their effort or performance does not.

Zhao, Heyman, Chen & Lee, 2017: 1

BE CAREFUL WITH PRAISE

9.0 • DIFFERENT TYPES OF PRAISE

Praise is a powerful motivator. At least that is what many people say. Yet, the research on how praise affects students' motivation and achievement is somewhat contradictory.

On the one hand, many studies have found that praise can effectively reduce behavioural problems and encourage students to learn (Harris, Wolf & Baer, 1967; Madsen, Becker & Thomas, 1968; O'Leary & O'Leary, 1977) whereas other, more recent studies have found it to be largely ineffective (Beaman & Wheldall, 2000; Brophy, 1981). Some have even found it to be dysfunctional (Barker & Graham, 1987; Birch, Marlin & Rotter, 1984; Meyer, Bachmann, Biermann, Hempelmann, Ploger & Spiller, 1979; Mueller & Dweck, 1998). Add to this the complication that it is difficult to separate out the effects of praise from other factors such as teacher attention, special privileges, student personality and so on, and the way forward is unclear.

One of the possible explanations for such contradictory findings is that the *type* of praise matters more than *if* praise has been given. The biggest difference can be noticed between praise that is directed at the person (e.g. good boy, clever girl) and praise that focuses on an aspect of a person's performance (e.g. good effort, clever idea).

Jennifer Henderlong Corpus and Mark Lepper (2007) conducted two studies to identify the motivational consequences of person versus performance praise. The first focused on differences in the way girls and boys responded to feedback. The second was with 5-year-old children in a nursery school in California. In this second study, the children were given four interesting puzzles, two of which were designed to lead to success and two to failure. The children were then asked to indicate how much they enjoyed the puzzles by pointing on a scale of five schematic faces ranging from a frowning face to a smiling face.

> Praise can be a powerful motivator, but it can also be a hindrance to learning.

> This research from Henderlong Corpus and Lepper shows how different types of praise affected children's motivation.

Next, perceived competence was measured by children's responses to the question, 'Are you good at these kinds of puzzles or not so good at these kinds of puzzles?' Finally, attributions for failure were measured by children's responses to the question, 'Did you have trouble on the second puzzles because you didn't try hard enough or because you aren't good enough at these kinds of puzzles?'

As children worked on the two success puzzles, they were praised three times – once after completing the first puzzle, once during the second puzzle, and once after completing the second puzzle. Children in the **neutral** feedback condition were given a positive sounding 'OK' at each of these points, whereas the other children were praised as follows:

Praise statements for children in the **person** condition:

    'You're really good at this!'

    'You must be good at puzzles!'

    'You are a great puzzle-solver!'

Praise statements in the **product** condition:

    'Good job on that one!'

    'You're getting a lot of pieces!'

    'You finished one again!'

Praise statements in the **process** condition:

    'You must be working hard!'

    'You're really thinking!'

    'You're finding really good ways to do this!'

This being a research study, the children were of course randomly assigned to one of the four conditions: person, product, process or neutral.

The next stage of the study involved two 'failure' puzzles that were impossible to solve successfully because the pieces had been switched. The children were given 75 seconds for the first one before being told, 'Time is up. Let's move onto the next one'. No other comments were made. Then after another 75 seconds attempting the last puzzle, the children were told, 'Time is up. You didn't finish the puzzles'. The children were then asked the same questions as before: how much did you enjoy the puzzles, and are you good at these puzzles or not? They were also asked which of these three reasons best explained why they had done badly on the last two puzzles:

    'I didn't try hard enough'

    'I'm not smart enough'

    'I ran out of time'

After this, the children were asked to sit at an activity table and to play with anything they wanted to. Figure 42 shows the proportion of children who chose to continue with the puzzles rather than choosing to play with something else. As you can see, all types of praise led to children continuing with the puzzles compared with those who received neutral feedback but the most beneficial was the product-related praise followed by the process-related praise.

The more significant results, however, were noticed days and weeks later (average time lapse of 10 days) when the children were observed engaging with the puzzles during

regular classroom activities. The amount of time varied considerably so the researchers converted it (using logistic regression) into the scale shown in Figure 43.

As you can see, the children receiving product and process praise spent much longer on the puzzles days later than those children who received person praise. That said, all types of praise resulted in children spending longer on the puzzles, compared with the children who received no praise at all. Bear in mind, though, that these experiments were with pre-school children whereas when Henderlong Corpus and Lepper ran similar experiments with upper-elementary children, they found potentially harmful effects of person praise, particularly on the motivation of girls.

As the paper summarises: 'the research suggests that praise linking children's performances to their personal traits should be used only with caution because of the vulnerability it may create when children are subsequently faced with challenging experiences' (Henderlong Corpus & Lepper, 2007: 506).

Incidentally, if you are worried about the effects of the 'failure' part of the experiment, then you will be relieved to know the children were told afterwards that no one could have solved the puzzles because the pieces had all been mixed up. The 'mistake' was later corrected and the children were given time to complete the puzzles successfully.

▶ Figure 42: **Proportion of Children Engaging with Puzzles**

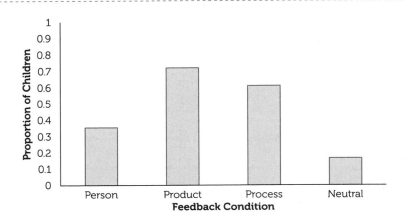

▶ Figure 43: **Amount of Time Children Spent on Puzzles**

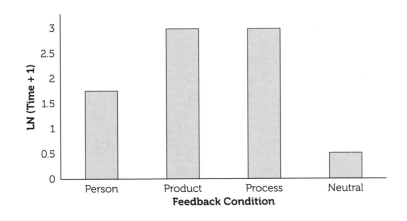

9.1 • TO PRAISE OR NOT TO PRAISE?

It is worth remembering that praise is a 'positive judgement'. Though the 'positive' part feels nice, problems may often result from the 'judgement'.

Answering the question about whether or not to praise is a fool's errand; notions of praise, when to give it, how much to give, and whom to give it to is so wrapped up in culture, historical era and personality. Yet this *is* a book about growth mindset, and mindset both influences, and is influenced by, praise, so we feel at least partly obligated to say a few words about it.

Of the many studies on praise we have read, we chose to share the Henderlong Corpus and Lepper (2007) findings for a couple of reasons. Firstly, the results are statistically significant; so that's a good start. Secondly, the recommendations are not about either do or don't; instead, they are about *type* of praise. That compares favourably with some of the more simplistic texts in the field, some of which say *never* praise while others say praise *lots*. That seems to us a false dichotomy. Students are complex creatures (staff even more so), so to say, 'this will always work' and therefore 'the opposite can never work' masks the splendid diversity of education.

(Authors): A significant proportion of the motivation for what I do today comes from being told time and again by my teachers at school, 'you'll never make anything of yourself'. Indeed, if you were to look up the lyrics to 'Hello Sir' by Robbie Williams (1997), you'd find my thoughts on this matter mirrored perfectly. If this was a bar room chat then I might even recite the words for you. For now, though, I'll simply make the point that even the worst of strategies – such as telling kids they're worthless – might actually become a positive influence for some. And thus, the most positive of strategies might not work for everyone. Not that we're advocating experimentation with negative strategies, even if it did inadvertently work for Robert Peter Williams and me.

So, let's keep praising kids. It might be the mantra of the most negative staff not to praise but it certainly is *not* what we're recommending here. One might imagine an ultra-grumpy member of staff sat in the corner of the staff room who never praises. The one who has told every enthusiastic newbie to stop trying hard; the one who retired years ago but forgot to tell anyone; the one who has taken it upon themselves to tell everyone of the futility of education. They might see it as *their* role never to praise but it is not one we recommend.

These different forms of praise have been found to influence motivation in different ways: person praise tends to be the most problematic, whereas process praise tends to be the least problematic.

Praise says, 'I have noticed you; I am encouraging you; I think you are praiseworthy'. Those are warming sentiments for (almost) everyone.

However, if you look again at Figures 42 and 43, you will see quite clearly that product and process praise are more effective at engaging children than person praise is. So, if you really want to use praise to motivate your students to engage more and try longer then product and process praise are the way to go. Figure 44 gives some examples of all three categories.

On the face of it, all of these types of praise seem positive and, in the moment, they typically do feel good. However, as Kamins and Dweck (1999) and Kempner, McDonald and Pomerantz (2003) have shown, using person praise may lead to children assuming they are worthy creatures only when they have succeeded, and therefore not so worthy when they have failed.

For example, some adults might tell a child they are clever, brilliant, bright or talented when things go well. Which feels nice. However, when things go badly and there's no praise then does that mean the opposite is true? Is the child now stupid, thick or incapable? Of course not, but then how many children might *infer* that?

Person praise	Product praise	Process praise
Praises the person	Praises the end result	Praises the actions
Nouns such as artist, linguist, mathematican, player	Nouns such as result, answer, model, outcome	Verbs such as thinking, trying, working, developing
Examples		
You're a brilliant swimmer	Brilliant result! Well done	That's brilliant swimming
You are a fantastic mathematician	Fantastic: your answers are all correct	Fantastic: you've answered them all correctly
Wow, you are so clever!	That's a very clever answer	That was a really clever way to solve the problem
What a brilliant artist you are	What a brilliant piece of artwork you've created	What a brilliant way to add perspective to your art
You are the best player on the team	You were the best player in that match	You played brilliantly in that match

Failure rarely feels good; but *if* a child is likely to think the opposite when things go wrong then maybe *all* types of praise are risky? Well, yes and no; some risks seem to be greater than others. For example, if a child is going to think the opposite – hopefully they won't but if they did – then would you rather use praise that risks them going from a clever person when successful to a stupid person when they fail, or from having *done* a clever thing when successful to having *done* a stupid thing when they fail? Or from being a nice person when things are jolly to a nasty person when things are not, or from doing a nice thing when things are good to doing a nasty thing when things are bad?

To many people, this might seem to be an overly sensitive exaggeration of the possible downsides of person praise. Think about it for a moment though: how many people do you know who succeeded many times early in their lives who have since found set-backs extraordinarily difficult to deal with? How many teenagers in high schools who have previously been told they are clever or bright have hit a crisis of confidence when things go wrong for them?

Think about Alisha and Zack, the two fictional characters we introduced in Chapter 4. Alisha has been told many times over how brilliant she is. She has been praised for being a brilliant linguist, for being a clever child; she has even been labelled as a 'gifted and talented' student. Imagine if she ever hits significant problems that she can't see a resolution to. What is she likely to say to herself if she is asked to read texts that she just can't understand? Worse still: imagine if she moves on to college or university and finds she is no longer the brightest student in the class. How is she likely to react if she discovers that many of the students in her class *are* able to deeply understand the literature but she is *not*? What then? It seems to us it would be quite likely that Alisha would start to question her intelligence, begin to wonder whether she's been living a lie all these years and fear that she is now in danger of being 'found out'.

Kamins and Dweck (1999) used a series of role-play scenarios to illustrate this point. They asked students to imagine receiving person, product or process praise after completing a task successfully. They then asked the children to act out their subsequent responses to failure. Children who had been given person praise acted out greater signs of helplessness than those who were given process praise, with those receiving product praise falling somewhere in the middle.

NOW TRY THIS

1. Say, Avoid, Cringe

Ask your students or colleagues, or both, to group the following phrases according to the category of praise (person, product or process) they best fit into.

▶ Figure 45: Say, Avoid, Cringe

1. A+ work
2. Amazing artist
3. Amazing result
4. Brilliant effort
5. Brilliant listener
6. Brilliant listening
7. Clever boy
8. Clever strategy
9. Extraordinary talent
10. Fabulous piece of work
11. Good girl
12. Great strategy to use
13. How good is that!
14. I love what you're doing
15. I love your determination
16. Inspired idea
17. Lovely thing to say
18. Making great progress
19. Outstanding performance
20. Perfect answer
21. Spectacular work
22. Talented musician
23. Ten out of ten
24. That's your best answer yet
25. Top of the class
26. Unbelievable work
27. Well worked through
28. What a scientist you are
29. Wonderful painting
30. You are a genius
31. You are doing really well
32. You are getting better
33. You are the best
34. You've got it

2. Role-Play

As we noted, Melissa Kamins and Carol Dweck (1999) used a series of role-play scenarios to invite children to act out how they might respond to failure after receiving different types of praise for doing well. If your students are mature enough then you could also try this with them.

Before the lesson, photocopy the cards shown in Figures 46, 47 and 48. Cut out each statement and place them into an envelope. Make sure you place all the cards from Figure 46 into one envelope; all those from Figure 47 into a different envelope, and all those from Figure 48 into a third envelope.

At the start of the lesson, ask your students to pretend being successful at something of their choosing. Tell them it would be best if they moved away from reality and instead picked something they have never tried but would love to be brilliant at. Examples might come from sport, music, acting, computer games, science and so on. Give them time to act out these successful situations for a few minutes amongst their friends.

Now divide your students into three groups and give each group one of the three envelopes. Ask each group to divide the cards amongst themselves, making sure that half the group get a card and the other half do not. Then invite those without cards to act out their successful situation again. Whilst they do that, the students with cards should use the statement on their card to praise the people in their group. Make sure they are effusive with their praise but that they only use the phrase that is printed on the card they have.

What you should see now is three groups of students in three different parts of the room. Each group will have half the students acting out scenes of success whilst the other half are moving within their own group, praising all the actors for their success.

After a few minutes, ask the students to swap roles so that the actors take the cards and those with the cards now become the actors. Make sure that your students don't swap groups! They should only swap roles within their own group.

Once they have all had a turn at acting and praising, ask your students to put the cards back in the envelopes. Then ask them to imagine failing at the thing they have just pretended to be brilliantly successful at. Really lay it on thick when introducing this part. Say something along the lines of, 'Now imagine you are completely and utterly failing at the thing you were succeeding at before. Imagine that everything that could go wrong is going wrong. Of all the failures in the world, your failure is amongst the worst!' Once in that mindset, ask your students to give each other negative feedback. Tell them they should give the very opposite messages to the ones they have just been saying when praising each other. They shouldn't be aggressive or rude but they should criticise in an equal and opposite way to how they were praising each other previously. Once they've had a bit of fun with that (and it should be light-hearted and fun), give each group a large sheet of flipchart paper and ask them to record the phrases they used when criticising each other.

Finally, ask each group to show the other groups their flipchart paper so that everyone can see the phrases used. Ask appropriate facilitative questions such as:

- What are some of the differences in the ways each group criticised each other?
- If you were to pick five phrases that you would hate to hear, what would they be?
- Which phrase is the worst one?
- How many phrases can you spot that you think are OK to use?
- Which one is the gentlest?
- Is it ever OK to criticise?
- Is it always good to praise?
- If you are prepared to give and receive praise, then should you also be prepared to give and receive criticism?
- Should the age of a person be considered when thinking about when and how to praise or criticise them?
- What links can you spot between the words of criticism you came up with and the words of praise you found in the envelopes?
- Did the type of praise affect the type of criticism you gave?
- If you were to group the types of criticism, what categories would you choose and why?
- What would your advice be to people when thinking about praise and criticism?
- How different would school be if there was no praise or criticism?
- Do praise and criticism have to be spoken?
- Would anyone be willing to demonstrate how you could give praise or criticism without speaking?
- What questions do you still have?

3. Grouping

You could use this activity as an alternative to activity 2 or as a follow-up to it. Divide your students into groups of three or four. Give each group *all* the cards shown in Figures 46,

These cards can be used to stimulate dialogue and reflection amongst your students and/or your colleagues.

(Continued)

47 and 48 in one envelope. Ask them to group them and then to give each category a description. Do not give any more instructions than that so that they have to think about the connections and possibilities themselves. If any of your students do ask, 'What categories do you want us to use?' then simply say, 'It's up to you to decide'.

As your students are sorting through the cards, circulate around the groups asking questions that will deepen their thinking or cause them to consider alternatives. For example, ask them why they have put some phrases together but separate from other ones. When they explain their thinking, try to find a problem with their proposal. Not that you are trying to correct them; instead, you are encouraging them to think about alternatives and implications.

When the groups seem to be making good progress with sorting the cards, ask them to pause for a moment. Then get volunteers to explain to everyone else in the room what their group is doing and why they have chosen that particular method. This should give other groups additional ideas to add to or alter what they have chosen to do.

After you have given more time to finish, ask all the groups to report back to each other. Ask facilitative questions such as:

- How have you grouped the cards?
- What terms did you use to describe each category?
- What similarities and differences are there between what your group has done compared to other groups?
- Which was the most difficult category to name and why?
- Were there some phrases that could have gone into more than one category? How did you decide which one to place them in?
- Which is the best category?
- What do you think 'best' means?
- What other criteria could be used to decide what 'best' means? (Your students might come up with ideas such as: nicest, easiest to remember, most encouraging, most likely to make people feel proud.)

Now ask your students to write the equal and opposite words of criticism onto each card. For example, they might write 'terrible performance' on the 'brilliant performance' card, and 'you're the worst' on the card that says, 'you're the best'. Once they have done that, ask them questions such as:

- Which phrases were the easiest to come up with?
- Which phrases were the most uncomfortable to come up with and why?
- Which of the categories had the most phrases that were uncomfortable to come up with? Why do you think that might be?
- Looking at the cards with their equal and opposite phrases written next to them, which are the top five cards to use? And bottom five?
- If you were to receive words of praise and criticism from only one category, which would you choose and why?
- Which would be the worst category to receive words of praise and criticism from?
- What are your thoughts about praise now?
- What questions do you still have?

A-1

You're amazing

©2017 www.challenginglearning.com

A-2

You're gifted

©2017 www.challenginglearning.com

A-3

You're the best

©2017 www.challenginglearning.com

A-4

I wish I was as brilliant as you are

©2017 www.challenginglearning.com

A-5

You must be the world's number 1

©2017 www.challenginglearning.com

A-6

You're a natural

©2017 www.challenginglearning.com

(Continued)

▶ Figure 47: Cards to Give to Group B

B-1

That's the best I've ever seen

©2017 www.challenginglearning.com

B-2

Brilliant performance

©2017 www.challenginglearning.com

B-3

That's stunning

©2017 www.challenginglearning.com

B-4

What a result!

©2017 www.challenginglearning.com

B-5

That must be the best performance ever

©2017 www.challenginglearning.com

B-6

I wish I could do that

©2017 www.challenginglearning.com

C-1

Look at you go!

©2017 www.challenginglearning.com

C-2

That is brilliant

©2017 www.challenginglearning.com

C-3

I love how you're doing that

©2017 www.challenginglearning.com

C-4

Amazing effort

©2017 www.challenginglearning.com

C-5

Fabulous technique

©2017 www.challenginglearning.com

C-6

What you're doing is superb

©2017 www.challenginglearning.com

9.2 • PRAISE AND CHEATING

Praising someone's ability (e.g. you are smart) can lead to people worrying that if they fail, it means they are stupid. This, in turn, makes it more likely they will use cheating as an option to avoid failure.

We introduced this chapter with a quote from a research paper by Li Zhao, Gail D. Heyman, Lulu Chen and Kang Lee (2017). They ran a trial with 300 children in China, aged 3 to 5 years old. They were asked to guess whether the number on a hidden card would be more than, or less than, six.

After their first guess, all the children were told they were correct (even when they weren't) and then given one of three randomly assigned types of praise, similar to the other experiments mentioned in this chapter:

1. Ability praise: 'You are so smart'.
2. Performance praise: 'You did very well this time'.
3. Baseline group: No praise was given.

After that, the children each took five goes at guessing. The game was rigged so that every child got the same success rate: two wrong and three correct. The children were told whether or not they had been successful but were not given any more praise.

Before their sixth guess, the researcher asked each child to promise not to peek at the card then left the room for 1 minute. A hidden camera recorded the children's actions whilst waiting for the researcher to return.

Figure 49 shows the percentage of children who cheated, either by getting out of their chair to look or leaning over the barrier to view the card.

▶ Figure 49: **Percentage of Children Who Cheated Following Different Forms of Praise**

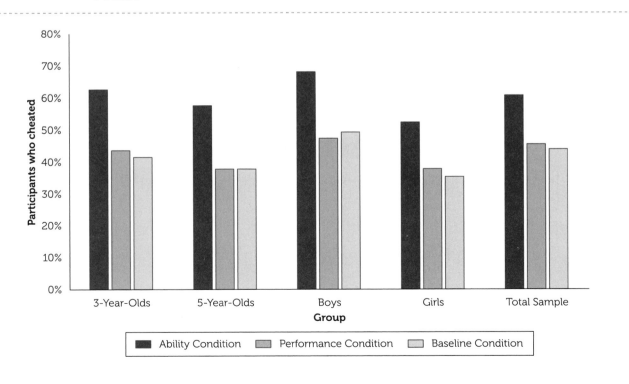

As Figure 49 shows, there was more cheating in the 'ability condition' (those children who, after the first trial, had received praise relating to ability) than there was amongst the children in the other two groups. The researchers calculated this to be a statistically significant difference. The other significant effect they found was how many more boys cheated across all three conditions than girls. There was also a minor difference in cheating amongst the children who received performance praise ('You did very well this time') compared with those children in the baseline, but the effect size was insignificant.

As Zhao et al. state:

> It is likely that ability praise promotes cheating because, unlike performance praise, it is a generic form of language that implies the presence of a stable ability (e.g., smartness) that underlies performance. In our study, ability praise may have motivated children to cheat in order to uphold the positive trait assessment or the reputation of being smart. (2017: 1868)

Again, the advice is: if we are going to praise our children or our students then we should focus on their actions rather than on them as people. So, instead of saying such things as, 'clever girl' or 'good boy', we would say, 'clever idea' or 'good strategy'.

It is even more powerful when we are praising actions that people quite clearly have influence over, as the next section about self-efficacy shows.

> Self-efficacy is a measure of how much influence someone believes they have.

9.3 • PRAISE AND SELF-EFFICACY

As we described briefly in Section 1.5, self-efficacy is the belief a person has in their ability to 'effect' or bring about a new outcome. Stanford psychologist Albert Bandura (1977) proposed the term as an alternative to the more widely used term of 'self-esteem'. Whereas the latter relates to how a person 'esteems' or likes their 'self', the idea of self-efficacy relates more to a person's potency and influence.

In her meta-analysis on teacher efficacy, Rachel Eells summarises the various works of Albert Bandura (1977–2000) stating, 'Efficacy involves more than positive thinking or optimism. It is tied to the construct of agency (the ability to make things happen) and to action' (Eells, 2011: 5).

Students who rate themselves very highly and yet are defeatist when faced with challenges could be said to have high self-esteem but low self-efficacy. Indeed, it is these students who tend to be quickest to shrug their shoulders and say something along the lines of, 'I don't care that I can't do it; I'm happy as I am'. In some circumstances, that might sound reasonable but what happens when it is actually coming from a fear of failure rather than a genuine disinterest? What if the shoulder shrug is a defence mechanism rather than a show of contentment? This is where self-efficacy comes in. If we help our students to develop their self-efficacy then they will be more likely to make decisions from a position of aptitude rather than aversion. Knowing they are in a position to 'effect' or create a new outcome *if they wish to* is preferable to avoiding new experiences because of a sense of foreboding or fear.

Figure 50 summarises the differences between low self-efficacy and high self-efficacy. As you read through it, make a note of the similarity between fixed mindset and growth mindset.

► Figure 50: Comparison of Low and High Self-Efficacy

People with **low self-efficacy** tend to be:	People with **high self-efficacy** tend to be:
1. Rigid in their thinking	1. Flexible in their thinking
2. Fearful of new and unfamiliar situations	2. Keen to experience new situations
3. Wary of change	3. Open to change
5. Cautious of other people	4. Cooperative with others
6. Keen to prove themselves	5. Keen to express themselves
7. Reassured by the familiar	6. Excited by challenge
8. Evasive in what they say	7. Honest in what they say
9. More likely to give up	8. More persistent
10. Easily frustrated	9. Tolerant
11. Less equipped to cope	10. Quicker to recover

As Figure 50 shows, there are many parallels between fixed mindset thinking and low self-efficacy; and between growth mindset thinking and high self-efficacy.

As you will have noticed, the similarities in the traits of low self-efficacy and fixed mindset include: both are wary of change; both prefer to *prove* rather than *improve* themselves; and both are more likely to be frustrated by challenges.

Conversely, the similarities in behaviour between those with high self-efficacy and those in a growth mindset include: having better coping strategies; being open to new situations as well as to change; and choosing growth and expression over playing it safe or showing off to others.

So, what of praise and its effect on efficacy? As we showed earlier in the chapter, person praise may lead to students assuming they are worthy creatures when they have succeeded, and therefore not so worthy when they have failed. This negative implication of person praise can, over time, lead to traits 2, 5, 6, 8, 9 and 10 in the left-hand side of Figure 50; whereas process praise can lead particularly to traits 2, 6, 8 and 10 in the right-hand side of Figure 50.

Keep this link in mind when thinking about praise: will it help your students to build their sense of self-efficacy? If so, then it is probably worth using. If not, then can it be adapted so it *is* more linked with dimensions that are under their control?

In summary, the key to beneficial praise is:

- If you praise your students for something they have control over (effort, focus, determination and so on) then you are more likely to empower them to learn and grow.

- Whereas if you praise your students for something they assume they have been 'given' (such as cleverness, a 'natural' talent, a gift and so on) then you might inadvertently cause them to believe they have no influence over their successes and failures.

Interestingly, it appears that boys often have a greater sense of self-efficacy than girls. This is not always the case of course, and might not be particularly prevalent in some countries but take a look at this quote from Carol Dweck:

> Confusion is a common occurrence in maths and science, where, unlike most verbal areas, new material often involves completely new skills, concepts, or conceptual systems. So we created a new task for students to learn, and for half of the students we placed some confusing material near the beginning.
>
> What we found was that bright girls didn't cope at all well with this confusion. In fact, the higher the girl's IQ, the worse she did. Many high IQ girls were unable to learn the material after experiencing confusion. This didn't happen to boys. For them, the higher their IQ, the better they learned. The confusion only energized them.
>
> Because our high IQ girls had done wonderfully well when they didn't bump up against difficulty, what we're looking at here isn't a difference in ability, but a difference in how students cope with experiences that may call their ability into question – whether they feel challenged by them or demoralized by them. (Dweck, 2006a: 47–48)

Part of the difference might come from the amount of criticism that boys receive compared to girls. Not that criticism is in itself beneficial for self-efficacy, but consider the implications of the following examples:

> 'John – if only you could sit still for a minute and listen then you'd do much better'.

> 'Paul – if you put as much effort into your work as you do into messing about then you could really achieve'.

> 'Ringo – as for you, young man, you need to focus more! I'm fed up of repeating myself for your sake'.

All of the messages are stating that by concentrating more, trying harder, listening better and so on, the outcomes will improve. Those are strong self-efficacy messages. It is a pity they come in the form of criticism but, nonetheless, they are influence-driven messages. They are also much more powerful than the person-focused messages that girls so often receive: 'good girl', 'clever girl' and so on.

Not that it is 'always boys, this' or 'always girls, that' – and indeed some countries such as Sweden are working hard to reduce gender imbalances – but *if* boys are receiving more of the type of criticism shown and girls are receiving more of the type of praise shown, *then* it might go some way to explaining the situation Dweck and her colleagues found, as shown in the quote from 2006 above.

9.4 • PRAISE, REWARDS AND MINDSET

In Section 8.1, we asked you to think about the two paths shown in Figure 38. The left-hand path was the easy one and the right-hand path the more challenging of the two. We then explained how too many students pick easy options when given a choice because they expect to be rewarded for getting things right and for not making mistakes.

> Praise can influence self-efficacy for better or for worse, depending on the type used. Person praise (e.g. you are a clever child) is likely to decrease self-efficacy; whereas process praise (e.g. that was a clever thing to do) is likely to increase self-efficacy because it focuses on actions, which are more adjustable than personality.

> Although criticism is generally thought of as a bad thing, if it focuses on actions (e.g. that was a silly thing to do) then it could have a positive effect on self-efficacy.

However, imagine if the students we asked you to think about were not yet of school age. Imagine if they were 2-, 3- and 4-year-olds: now which path would they choose? Anyone who has ever worked with, or brought up, young children will know that it is nigh on impossible to stop them taking the more challenging paths! Not because those paths look more challenging but because they look far more interesting. Why go for the boring route when there are adventures to be had on the other side?

In other words, the youngest children need no carrots dangled or promises of rewards at the end to persuade them to take the challenging route; the sheer pleasure of the adventure is enough. So why then do older students seemingly need the carrot (or the stick) to get them to engage in learning?

> No one asks how to motivate a baby. A baby naturally explores everything it can get at, unless restraining forces have already been at work. And this tendency doesn't die out, it's wiped out. (Skinner, 1948: 114)

Interestingly, in their meta-analysis of the effects of feedback on motivation, Edward Deci, Richard Koestner and Richard Ryan (1999) found a *negative* correlation between extrinsic rewards and learning (–0.34). They also found that rewards undermined intrinsic motivation, particularly for interesting tasks (–0.68), although they did find a small positive when the students were engaged in uninteresting tasks (0.18). So, it seems that extrinsic rewards such as merits, stars on a behaviour chart or the promise of grade credits only really work when tasks are uninspiring. If we are over-using extrinsic rewards – or maybe even if we are needing to use them at all – then perhaps we should first question the quality and meaningfulness of the tasks we are setting?

Indeed, as Ann Boggiano and her colleagues discovered:

> Children who adopted an extrinsic rather than an intrinsic orientation toward schoolwork were more likely to do poorly on overall achievement, as indexed by national test scores, even when controlling for achievement scores from the previous year. (Boggiano, Main, Flink, Barrett, Silvern & Katz, 1989: 24)

So, the best rewards in schools should be the joy of learning; the intrinsic pleasure derived from discovering and developing; and the satisfaction of making progress. This is easy to say, of course, and much more difficult to achieve, particularly with those students who are hooked on extrinsic motivators. However, the more we maintain a focus on learning for the pleasure of learning, the closer we will get to reigniting the intrinsic motivation almost all students had when they were pre-schoolers.

> Although some forms of praise are better than others, it is also true that all types of praise risk decreasing intrinsic motivation.

9.5 • WHEN TO PRAISE

In Section 8.1, we invited you to imagine you were driving a route you know very well; perhaps your journey from home to work. You see the two authors of this book walking along the street so offer us a lift to escape the rain, for which we thank you!

What would you think if we then praised your driving skills, saying: 'Wow, you're doing really well. We are very impressed with your driving ability'. After reading the previous section, you might be tempted to analyse the type of praise we're giving you. There is an even greater chance, though, that you would also wonder why we are patronising you. Why would anyone praise you for doing something that you can do so easily?

Yet, how often do people do that to students: praise them for doing something they can do with ease? When students complete a puzzle or an errand, how often do adults

say, 'brilliant, well done you' even though the task was straightforward for them? When students sit up straight, win a game, use a piece of technology, ride a bike, how many adults praise them for doing it even though it required very little effort? If it is patronising to praise adults for doing something they can do with ease then presumably it is also patronising to praise students when they do something with ease?

Back to your driving for a moment. Again, as we did in Section 8.1, let us ask you to imagine driving somewhere completely different, perhaps in a foreign country with very different driving laws. Driving in these conditions will take you out of your comfort zone but imagine you persevere anyway and make a good go of it. What if you were to give us authors a lift on that occasion too? How much more welcome would our praise be now? Presumably, it would no longer feel patronising; instead, it will feel deserved and encouraging.

It is the same for students: praising them when they are attempting something out of their comfort zone is supportive, encouraging and not in the least bit patronising. Praise them when they do something with ease though and it can be diverting and condescending.

So, the time to praise is when your students are out of their comfort zone, not when they are in it, as this will make it more credible and meaningful. Doing it this way will also support the learning-focus that is likely to put your students in a growth mindset.

In all cases, praise should be specific and genuine. And it should not be over-used. Praise is rather like currency: the more of it that exists, the less valuable it becomes.

> Praise can seem patronising if offered to someone completing a task with ease, whereas it is much more welcome (and effective) when used at a time when the person is out of their comfort zone.

9.6 • PRAISE IN PRACTICE

(Authors): Please don't respond the way I first responded when reading about mindset: I stopped praising my students for fear of getting it wrong! I thought to myself that seeing as I had made the mistake of calling every student clever, talented or smart, I should give up the day job and go back to working on a pig farm. Obviously, that is not what Carol Dweck suggests. Instead, her research recommends that we redirect our praise towards students' actions. It's as simple as that. It's also as *frustratingly simple* as that.

It just sounds so easy to stop saying 'good girl' and 'clever boy', but it really isn't; particularly after years and years of using person-focused praise. So, the next time you say, 'good girl' or 'clever boy', follow it up with some process praise: 'good girl' will then become, 'good girl . . . for sticking with it until you mastered it', or 'clever boy' will become, 'clever boy . . . for working out what went wrong and correcting your mistake'. It's not ideal but it's probably a lot better than stopping praising altogether.

As for other forms of praise, we shared examples in Figure 45 of phrases often used to praise students. These ranged from 'amazing artist', 'brilliant listener' and 'extraordinary talent' to 'making great progress', 'that's your best answer yet' and 'you are the best'. In this last section of Chapter 9, we will share our thoughts on which ones to say and which ones not to.

> It would almost certainly be a mistake to stop using praise altogether. Instead, if the right type of praise is used in the right way at the right time, it can sit comfortably within a growth mindset culture.

9.6.1 • Person-focused Praise

Phrases that are person-focused and should therefore be avoided, include:

- Amazing artist
- Brilliant listener

- Clever boy
- Good girl
- Talented musician
- You are a genius
- Top of the class.

9.6.2 • Product-related Praise

Phrases that are product-related and could therefore be used, in the right circumstances,[1] include:

- A+ work
- Amazing result
- Fabulous piece of work
- Outstanding performance
- Perfect answer
- Spectacular work
- Ten out of ten
- Wonderful painting
- You've got it.

Product and process praise can be nicely used together. This is particularly true if you praise the outcome (assuming it is praiseworthy) and then link it to the process that was used to create the successful outcome.

9.6.3 • Process-related Praise

Phrases that are process-related and could therefore be used, in the right circumstances,[2] include:

- Brilliant effort
- Brilliant listening
- Clever strategy
- Great strategy to use

---

1. So long as the caveats mentioned in this book are observed then these product-related phrases could be used in a learning-focused classroom. The caveats include ensuring: that the product has come as a result of learning rather than simply doing (see Section 3.1); that students have stepped out of their comfort zone to create the product (see Section 8.3); and that a sense of progress is apparent, whether measured or observed (see Section 6.3).

2. Process-related phrases are perhaps the most risk-free of the types of praise covered here. However, the same caveats as shown for the product-related phrases would apply here too. It is also extremely important to use them genuinely; for example, if you were to say, 'brilliant effort' to a student who had performed very well but hadn't actually needed to put much effort in to do so, then the credibility of your message is likely to suffer. Added to that is tone of voice, relationship between you and your student, purpose of the praise and so on – but of course that is the same for *all* the types of praise mentioned across the whole chapter.

- Inspired idea
- Lovely thing to say
- Making great progress
- That's your best answer yet
- Well worked through
- You are doing really well
- You are getting better.

Process praise can, in the right circumstances, support a growth mindset culture. It can also be used in conjunction with product praise.

9.6.4 • Context-related Praise

The following phrases are less clear and would need additional caveats, some of which are shown below this list:

- Extraordinary talent
- How good is that!
- I love what you're doing
- I love your determination
- Top of the class
- Unbelievable work
- What a scientist you are
- You are the best.

Notes to Accompany Context-related Praise

- Extraordinary talent

Many people make the mistake of thinking that it is a fixed mindset action to praise, or even comment upon, talent. This is simply not true; Carol Dweck's work does not deny talent. Instead, we should recognise that talent but only in the context of it having been grown. So, for example, you could say, 'you have developed an extraordinary talent for . . . ' or 'they must have put in years and years of deliberate practice to build that amazing talent'.

- How good is that!

The only reason we have put this one in the 'depends on the context' category is that it is not clear what 'that' is! If 'that' refers to a brilliant outcome then it would go into the product-related category and be subject to the same caveats as all the other examples in that group. If, however, 'that' related to an action then it would fit more comfortably into the process-related category; and so on.

- I love what you're doing

At first glance, this might seem to fit directly into the process-related category because it is focused on a student's actions. However, we have put it into the 'further consideration' section because of the 'please me' tone. Instead of saying, 'I love what you're doing', it would have been better to say, 'what you're doing is great'. This would have made it less about pleasing the teacher and more about the process of learning; or, in other words, more intrinsically motivated than extrinsically motivated.

- I love your determination

Some of the types of praise shown in Figure 45 can't easily be placed into person, product or process praise, and therefore need more explanation, as shown here.

It would be better to say, 'Your determination is fabulous' rather than 'I love your determination', for the same reasons as the previous example.

- Unbelievable work

This begs the question: what is meant by 'unbelievable'? If it is used to imply a lack of authenticity then that is something very different from being used to suggest it has gone above and beyond all reasonable expectations. Furthermore, what does 'work' refer to? Is it focused on the action of *working*, or on the outcome of the work; in other words, the product? Then there is the tone of voice, presence or absence of sarcasm, irony and so on. As such, we'll leave this phrase in the 'to be decided' category!

- What a scientist you are

At first glance, this would sit most appropriately in the person-focused category. However, it depends on circumstance. In some classrooms, 'being a scientist' is shorthand for asking questions, challenging assumptions, creating hypotheses, exploring cause and effect, triangulating evidence, and so on. If your students share this meaning then calling them a scientist would definitely go into the process-related category. Similarly, if it is used as shorthand for the outcome of precise research then it could go into the product-related category.

- You are the best

This can mean so many things that it could go into any one of the three categories mentioned. Are they the 'best' for going out of their way to help? If so, then it belongs in the process-related category. Does it mean they have achieved the best results in a specific instance when compared to a particular group? If so, then it belongs in the product-related category. And if it means they are the best generally compared to others then it belongs in the person-focused category.

9.6.5 • Recommendations for Praise

Who would have thought praise was so complex? In summary though, here are some guidelines to help you through the maze.

1. Praise the process, not the person

In many cases, using a verb rather than a noun is more productive; for example, 'great reading' rather than 'great reader', or 'brilliant thinking' rather than 'brilliant thinker'.

2. Praise things that can be readily influenced

Focus on factors that your students are more obviously in control of; for example, praise ideas, actions, use of language, determination and so on. Avoid praising personal attributes that are less easily manipulated; for example, great personality, or references to looks, athletic build, coming from a good family, and so on.

3. Be specific

Praise that is too general can result in inadvertent consequences. For example, 'Well done, that's great!' seems to be a good thing to say but if your students don't know what the 'what' was that was great, then it might be misinterpreted. Was it the attention they were giving the task, in which case it would be process praise; the fact that they were getting it right, in which case it would be product praise; or the belief that they are the best at it, in which case it would be person praise? Each of these will lead to quite different conclusions about what they think is important.

Following the recommendations shown on this page should help you to keep praise consistent with a growth mindset culture.

4. Be genuine

Ensure that praise is given when it is deserved and when it is genuine. For example, don't praise effort if your students haven't needed to put effort in to finish the task; and don't say an outcome is excellent unless it quite clearly is. If your students feel patronised or undeserving of praise then they are likely to question your motives or to think you have lower expectations for them than they hoped you would.

5. Don't over-praise

It is nigh-on impossible to say exactly *how much* praise to give because it will depend so much on the people involved, their relationship, the situation and the purpose for the praise, and so on. However, it is worth bearing in mind that praise might be like currency: the more of it that exists, the less valuable it becomes. Let's not be so difficult to impress that we never give praise; but similarly, let's not be so easily impressed that we give the impression that anything goes.

6. Ask questions

Very often, students just want you to appreciate what they are doing; they do not need praise so much as attention. A powerful way to do this is to ask questions such as, 'What strategy have you used?'; 'What are the main learning points for you so far?'; 'How does this compare to what you were doing last time?'. These, and others like them, reduce the feelings of judgement and increase the sense of engagement.

It may not be sufficient to teach parents a growth mindset and expect that they will naturally transmit it to their children. Instead, an intervention targeting parents' failure mind-sets could teach parents how failure can be beneficial, and how to react to their children's setbacks so as to maintain their children's motivation and learning.

Haimovitz & Dweck, 2016: 867

FLOPPED LEARNING

10

'Flopped learning' is our way of referring to learning from mistakes (or flops). We created it as a play on words from the better-known instructional strategy of 'flipped learning'.

'Flipped learning' reverses the traditional approach of 'in-class instruction followed by out-of-class practice' to 'out-of-class instruction (normally delivered online) followed by in-class practice'. 'Flopped learning' involves a similar reversal, from the traditional 'instruction to *avoid* making mistakes' to 'instruction from *examining* mistakes'. We also use it to refer to a broader idea that 'flops' (including mistakes, errors and failure) *enhance* learning rather than undermine learning.

This chapter identifies some of the ways in which 'flopped learning' can help your students to get into a growth mindset. It examines the impact of attitudes towards failure; the fact that mistakes can lead to enhanced learning; how feedback, effort and grit can enhance – and be enhanced by – flopped learning; and why parents' views of failure influence their child's mindset more than their own mindset does.

> Flopped learning is a play on words from the better-known 'flipped learning'. We are using the term to emphasise the learning opportunities that can come from making flops (mistakes).

10.0 • FLOPS LEAD TO ENHANCED LEARNING

We are using the term 'flops' in this chapter to capture many of the terms that are, at times, used interchangeably and, at other times, contrastingly. Terms such as 'mistakes', 'failure', 'errors' and 'faults' are sometimes used to identify *any* inaccuracy, whereas, at other times, used to distinguish, for example, between minor 'mistakes' and longer-lasting 'failure'.

When using 'flops' as a general term, it might then seem strange to begin this section with the heading, 'Flops Lead to Enhanced Learning'. After all, *accuracy* is privileged in schools, not *inaccuracy*. Praise and rewards are more generally handed out to students who get everything right, not to those who make lots of flops.

However, if you were to consider learning to walk, learning to read, learning to socialise, learning to 'be' and so on, then it seems clear that learning rarely happens without flops. Indeed, some of the most significant learning experiences in our lives don't just *include* flops but actually *come from* flops. So, why don't we encourage flops more in schools, maybe even create activities in which flops are part of the plan?

Most teachers, of course, already respond positively to flops when they crop up but we are recommending more than that; we are suggesting that you design lessons for your students such that flops are inevitable. Though that might seem perverse, we are not alone in proposing this. For example, Barbie J. Huelser and Janet Metcalfe (2012) ran a series of tests that found participants learnt more from errors followed by corrective feedback than they did from just studying:

> Producing an error, so long as it is followed by corrective feedback, has been shown to result in better retention of the correct answers than does simply studying the correct answers from the outset. (Huelser & Metcalfe, 2012: 514)

Huelser and Metcalfe also found that students made more use of metacognitive monitoring strategies after they had made errors. Bearing in mind other researchers have found that metacognitive thinking, such as reflecting on the why, when and how of a particular strategy, is closely linked with improved learning outcomes, then errors that lead to increased metacognition ought to be viewed as particularly beneficial.

A good starting point for flopped learning is to say to your students that you do not want them to ask for help in the early stages of a lesson. Instead, they should have a go without your help. Meanwhile, you will circulate around the room looking for the best 'flops' to share with the whole class. So, even if they are not quite sure what to do, they should take their first attempts anyway.

As you circulate around the room, if you find that no one is 'flopping' then it might be that you need to increase the level of challenge (see Chapter 8). If your students are flopping though, you should make a note of the ones that could lead to learning for other students. Then, at an appropriate point in the lesson and with the appropriate students (maybe a small group or perhaps the whole class), you can share the best flops and tease out the points of clarification, correction or implication that could lead to enhanced learning for everyone.

This approach should go hand in hand with an emphasis on 'flops' being at the heart of great learning. Tell your students that you have purposefully designed learning activities that will take them out of their comfort zone and cause them to flop. Every time they flop, they should see this as a way to enhance their learning, not as a way to limit it. Indeed, if they are not flopping very much then the chances are, the tasks are too easy.

When your students do flop, they could use an adapted version of the popular, 'Three Before Me' convention. Typically, 'three before me' means students should use the following three steps before asking their teacher for advice:

1. Brain – think about it yourself.

2. Browse – in a book or online.

3. Buddy – ask a friend for help.

This can be altered to create 'Following a Fabulous Flop', as shown in Figure 51.

FOLLOWING A FABULOUS FLOP

FIGURE OUT

figure out what caused the flop

FRIEND

share your flop with a friend so you can learn together

FOCUS

focus on your next steps (maybe use a Yeti to help)

10.1 • FLOPPED PRODUCTS

The idea of a Minimum Viable Product (MVP) is an interesting concept. It is a prototype that is released early, with the expectation of provoking feedback from early adopters. By its very nature, the product is far from being the finished article; it is instead enough of a hypothesis-in-action to stimulate invaluable feedback. Many will be flops of course and yet, as such, will be just as valuable to the design process as many, more successful models.

The purposes of MVPs vary from industry to industry but here are some of the features common to most:

- They permit the testing of a prototype at very low cost.
- They accelerate, and sometimes deepen, the rate of learning because of the diversity and volume of feedback sources.
- They limit the amount of wasted design hours, creating something that might have no market value.
- They build a sense of engagement with early adopters.
- Early adopters willingly offer feedback because of the pride they feel in influencing outcomes.
- They often reveal aspects of the design that might otherwise have been missed or spotted too late.
- The feedback received can be used in earlier stages of development.

Think about the potential of this within flopped learning: you could get your students to create their own MVP that is then shared with their peers. The MVP wouldn't need to be a product, as such. It could be a draft assignment, an early rehearsal, a first plan for a piece of work, the rough sketch for some artwork, and so on. By calling it an MVP, it will remove the thought that only corrected, thought-through or perfected work should be shared with an audience.

This idea of 'prototype – feedback – improvements' also fits in very well with our notions of 'flopped feedback'.

> Many successful people – Einstein, Thomas Edison – have said they've learned more from their failures than often from their successes. So many huge break-throughs came after a number of huge failures that provided learning experiences. So you're not going to reward someone just because they failed, obviously not. But what did the journey teach them that will help them and others in the company become successful the next time?
>
> So as people are engaging in a process, in a project, they're monitoring what worked and what didn't with an eye toward the future. And the more they can feed that back into the company to make it more a communal learning experience, the more that is reward worthy. (Dweck, 2012b)

10.2 • FLOPPED FEEDBACK

Releasing a Minimum Viable Product or beta-version is an increasingly popular way for companies to gather invaluable feedback from their markets. A similar attitude can be taken within a flopped learning culture by inviting students to examine early drafts and to give each other feedback about how best to improve.

'Flopped feedback' is our design for feedback that is learning-orientated rather than performance-orientated. It builds on 'The Seven Steps to Feedback Success' that James wrote about in his book, *Challenging Learning Through Feedback* (Nottingham & Nottingham, 2017).

If you look back at Section 10.0, you will notice that Huelser and Metcalfe demonstrated that errors led to enhanced learning *only if* they were followed by corrective feedback; without that feedback, errors stayed as errors. Sounds simple enough. Unfortunately, though, feedback is anything but straightforward, as James and Jill Nottingham showed in their recent book about feedback. Here are some of the warnings they wrote about:

1. Feedback *can* be one of the most powerful influences on learning but rarely is.

2. Hattie's analysis of thousands of studies suggests average percentiles on learning outcomes of between 50% and 83% improvement.

3. Students typically receive lots of feedback but it rarely leads to the impact cited by Hattie because of a lack of quality or application or both.

4. According to Graeme Nuthall (2007), 80% of the verbal feedback students receive on a day-to-day basis comes from their peers and most of it is incorrect.

5. Far too many teachers wait until students have completed their tasks before giving formal feedback; this significantly reduces the likelihood that students will use the advice meaningfully.

6. Too many students have yet to be taught how to give and receive feedback; this is despite studies showing that when students learn how to offer and respond to feedback, the effect can be even more powerful than feedback from teachers.

7. Feedback is too often mixed with praise or criticism, and is viewed with suspicion by students who think of it as too subjective.

So, that is some of what is going wrong with feedback in many schools. Here, then, are ways to increase the likelihood that feedback will be much more powerful – and will fit in with the idea of flopped learning.

10.2.1 • Three questions to drive feedback forward

At the heart of feedback should be an emphasis on answering these three questions:

1. What am I aiming to achieve?
2. How much progress have I made so far?
3. What should I do next to improve?

Some people talk about 'feedforward' and 'feedback'; and some even of 'feed-up' and 'feed-down'. We do not recommend this practice. Using these terms leads many people to think that 'feed-back' only involves looking back; whereas feedback has to answer all three questions mentioned above for it to have a chance of significantly improving learning outcomes. This includes the 'looking forward' question, 'What should I do next to improve?'.

10.2.2 • Feedback is not criticism

Feedback should be viewed as information to help answer the three questions mentioned above; that's it. It's not praise, it's not criticism; it's information that can be used to help you achieve your goals. If it helps you in your quest then you could call it good; if it doesn't then you could call it bad; but really, it's just information.

It is the same with flops: they shouldn't be viewed as negative. Instead, flops should be thought of as information that can help you answer the three feedback (or learning) questions: what am I trying to achieve; how much progress have I made so far; and what should I do next to improve?

A significant step you could take to help your students adopt this attitude is to ensure that all feedback is preceded by an agreement of goals and success criteria. This will help answer the first question: what am I trying to achieve? With a clear idea of the goals, the second question can be answered more objectively: how much progress have I made so far? Finally, the feedback can give you clues about how to answer the third question: what should I do next to improve?

Chapter 4 in *Challenging Learning Through Feedback* explains this in more detail and gives lots of examples of learning intentions and success criteria.

10.2.3 • Feedback should be timely

In Section 8.1, we asked you to imagine driving in a foreign city where they drive on the other side of the road and have rules and patterns of behaviour that are unfamiliar to you. Now let's ask you to imagine you are going to spend two days doing this, during which you will be offered some feedback by a local driver. You have to choose though: you can either receive that feedback after day one so that you have time to put the advice into practice on day two. Or you can wait until the end of the two days and receive advice for the next time you visit the country, if indeed you ever do.

Which one of these options is likely to lead to improved learning outcomes?

Feedback should be a significant part of any learning environment. However, many schools use feedback in a way that often conflicts with a growth mindset culture.

To effectively support learning, feedback should always answer these three questions.

In keeping with growth mindset, feedback should be thought of as advice rather than criticism.

Now consider when students are most likely to receive feedback from their teachers: part-way through an assignment or at the end, once they've finished? Of course, many teachers will say they give lots of advice ahead of similar assignments in the future but how many students take this advice on board and actually remember to apply it in detail next time? Research evidence suggests not very many!

That is why we recommend that you use the Seven Steps to Feedback Success instead:

1. Agree Learning Goals

2. Draft

3. Self- or Peer-Review

4. Edit

5. Teacher Feedback

6. Complete

7. Grade*

This brings forward teacher feedback so it is given just *before* students finish their assignments. This significantly increases the usability and effect of the feedback.

This approach to feedback is written about in depth in *Challenging Learning Through Feedback*. In brief though, the stages are as follows:

1. **Agree Learning Goals**: Agree the learning intentions and success criteria with your students. If you don't do this step then do not give feedback. Give encouragement and challenge but do not give feedback.

2. **Draft**: Encourage your students to think they are doing their 'first draft' or taking their 'first attempt' rather than 'doing their work'. This terminology supports the idea that there will be subsequent edits and improvements. It also makes the idea of 'flops' less worrisome because drafts are expected to be working documents rather than presentation pieces.

3. **Self- or Peer-Review**: Expect your students to review their own and each other's first drafts. Ask them to compare their progress against the agreed learning goals and success criteria, and to suggest next steps. Do not get involved at this stage, other than to orchestrate the structure and timing.

4. **Edit**: Your students should edit their first drafts based on the feedback they have given themselves or received from a friend. If they are writing something then get them to use a different coloured pen for their edits so that the effect of the feedback is more noticeable.

5. **Teacher Feedback**: Give your feedback in the form of advice, advice, advice. Do not use conventions such as 'three stars and a wish' or the 'feedback burger' in which there are two positives for every one negative. These approaches give credence to the idea that feedback is positive or negative, which is something that should be avoided. Keep your feedback as objective as possible: compare their efforts with the success criteria, then give advice about what to do next to make even more progress towards the agreed learning goals.

6. **Complete**: Your students should now complete their assignments or learning activities by applying the advice you have just given them. If writing is involved then get them to use a colour that hasn't been used so far. As with stage four, this is so that the effect of the feedback is more readily evidenced.

7. **Grade***: We have put an asterisk next to this step because grading is not necessary to improve the quality of feedback; indeed, Black, Harrison, Lee, Marshall and Wiliam (1990) and Ruth Butler (1997) found that giving grades with feedback reduces the effect of feedback dramatically. Of course, many teachers do not have a choice: they are obliged to grade students' assignments. If this is the case for you then here are three ways to improve its effect: 1) do not refer to grading as feedback; call it what it is: grading; 2) keep grading separate from feedback; make sure your students have the opportunity to apply the feedback they've received before grades are given; and 3) if you really want grading to help students then teach your students how to grade their own work. This will help them understand the grading criteria more accurately, and will allow you to keep an eye on how realistic they are in assessing their own levels of performance.

> Grades are problematic in so many ways but following the guidance here can help ease the tensions between grading and growth mindset.

Bizarrely enough, some people complain that students are bound to produce better assignments after teacher feedback; therefore, it would be cheating to give them feedback before they have finished! They don't think it is teaching; they don't think it is learning; they think it is cheating!

In our minds, the only possible excuse for thinking it is cheating is if we view teaching as nothing more than adjudicating and monitoring. A few people might agree with this but thankfully most people know that teachers are there to coach, to challenge, to stretch, to encourage, to help; in other words, a teacher's job is to teach; and feedback can play a significant role in this mission – so long as we get the timing right.

10.2.4 • The proof of the pudding is in the eating

What feedback says or how it is delivered is of much less importance than the *impact* of that feedback. Yet, there are still too many leaders in schools monitoring how much and what kind of feedback their teachers are giving students. That is the wrong thing to look at. It is like looking at the quality of teaching rather than the quality of learning. We should instead be looking for what difference our feedback makes because if it is not helping our students to make much more progress in their learning then what is the point of it?

> The main purpose of feedback in a school ought to be to enhance learning. So, rather than considering how well feedback has been delivered, it would be better to think about the effect it has had. After all, the proof of the pudding is not in the making but in the eating.

That is why we have suggested that written work should be colour-coded, with the first draft in one colour; edits in a second colour; and then final edits in a third colour. It is also why we have shared so many examples in Chapter 6 of how to emphasise progress. It is like the story of two friends in which one says, 'I have taught my dog to whistle'. The second one says, 'That's amazing. Let's hear him then'. So, the dog goes 'Woof!' The second one says, 'I thought you said you'd taught your dog to whistle?' The first one says, 'I did teach him; I didn't say he'd learnt how to whistle'.

So, to judge the quality of feedback on what is taught is just plain silly. It is much better to think about the *effect* of the feedback. For, as the saying goes, the proof of the pudding is in the eating.

All of the recommendations in this section show how feedback can support flopped learning. The same can be said in the opposite direction: that these approaches to feedback will support flopped learning. Both approaches treat mistakes as information that will help to answer the three key questions: what am I trying to achieve; how much progress have I made; and what can I do next to improve?

10.3 • FLOPPED PARENTS

> Although a parent's mindset is important, it is their attitude towards failure that is more likely to influence their child's mindset.

Very many teachers we have worked with say, 'It's all well and good us working on growth mindset but what about our students' parents? They must have a greater impact on their children's mindset than we do!' Indeed they might, and yet, so far, *no clear link* has been established between the mindset of a parent and the mindset of their children. What has been found, however, is that a parent's view of *failure* influences their child's theory of intelligence.

Kyla Haimovitz and Carol Dweck (2016) ran a series of studies that showed that parents who believe failure is 'debilitating' have children who are significantly more likely to be in a fixed mindset than those parents who believe failure is 'enhancing'.

Across the four studies, involving approximately 470 parents and 300 children, Haimovitz and Dweck found the following:

1. All people have a mindset that shapes behaviour and aspirations. Parents' beliefs are most likely to shape children's beliefs only if they lead to practices that children notice.

2. A parent's attitude towards failure is more visible to a child than their mindset is, and therefore more likely to influence their child's attitudes.

3. Parents who believe failure is debilitating have children who are significantly more likely to be in a fixed mindset (Studies 1 and 3b).

4. The more parents believe that failure is debilitating, the more likely they are to worry about their child's ability and the less likely they are to react with support for their child's learning and improvement (Studies 2 and 4).

5. Older parents are more likely to believe that failure is enhancing and less likely to endorse performance-orientated responses (see Sections 3.0 and 3.1 for an explanation of performance-orientation).

6. Children are much more accurate when identifying their parent's attitude towards failure than they are towards identifying their parent's mindset (Study 3a).

> Parents who respond to failure with despondency are more likely to put their children into a fixed mindset; whereas those who respond as if failure is a learning opportunity, are more likely to put their children into a growth mindset.

To find out whether parents believe failure is debilitating or enhancing, those involved in the studies were asked how much they agreed with the following statements (taken from page 861 of Haimovitz and Dweck's report):

- 'The effects of failure are positive and should be utilized'.
- 'Experiencing failure facilitates learning and growth'.
- 'Experiencing failure enhances my performance and productivity'.
- 'Experiencing failure inhibits my learning and growth'.
- 'Experiencing failure debilitates my performance and productivity'.
- 'The effects of failure are negative and should be avoided'.

Those agreeing most with the first three statements were deemed to have a 'failure mindset' that believed failure is 'enhancing'; whereas those who showed more agreement for the last three were thought to believe failure is 'debilitating'.

These answers were then added to the results of a scenario in which parents imagined their child had returned home from school with a failing test grade. The participants were

asked how likely they were to have each of several reactions. These included performance-orientated responses such as:

- 'I might worry (at least for a moment) that my child isn't good at this subject'.
- 'I'd try to comfort my child to tell him it's okay if he isn't the most talented in all subjects'.
- 'I'd probably find myself dwelling on his/her performance'.

And learning-orientated responses such as:

- 'I'd encourage my child to tell me what she learned from doing poorly on the test'.
- 'I'd discuss with my child whether it would be useful to ask the teacher for help'.
- 'I'd let my child know that this is a great opportunity to learn this material well'.

These examples are all shown on page 863 of Haimovitz and Dweck's report. At this point, it would be interesting to consider your own responses to these scenarios.

NOW TRY THIS

We have included some of the questions that Haimovitz and Dweck asked parents so that you can think about your own responses. We recommend that you discuss the following questions with a colleague:

1. How much do you agree with each of the statements that Haimovitz and Dweck asked parents?
2. In what ways do you think failure can be positive?
3. In what ways do you think the effects of failure can be negative?
4. Is 'failure' the same as making a mistake?
5. How do you respond when you hear performance-orientated responses from parents of your students?
6. How could you encourage more learning-orientated responses from your students?

Interestingly, the statements that the children were given so that they could indicate their level of agreement or disagreement included:

- 'My parents would be pleased if I could show that school is easy for me'.
- 'My parents ask me how my work in school compares with the work of other students in my class'.
- 'My parents want me to understand homework problems, not just memorise how to do them'.
- 'My parents think how hard I work in school is more important than the grades I get'.

How much would your own students or children agree with these statements? And what can you do about it if their responses indicate fixed mindset thinking? These studies also beg the question, what attitudes towards failure do you inculcate? As Section 10.0 showed you, mistakes aren't just a normal aspect of learning – they can actually enhance learning.

Is this something that your students already understand or is it something that would be worth emphasising again and again until they see the power of flops?

10.4 • EFFORT IS NOT ENOUGH

> One of the most common mistakes to make when beginning a growth mindset journey is to emphasise effort above everything else. Of course effort is important but only if it is put into the right strategy for the right purpose at the right time.

Endurance; resilience; perseverance; 'Rome wasn't built in a day'; the Finnish term, 'sisu'; grit: all of these terms support the idea that effort is important. And yet, in an article for *EdSource*, Carol Dweck is quoted as saying:

> Prodding students to increase effort alone, telling them they would have done better if they had tried harder, isn't enough, Dweck said. Without suggesting learning strategies when students are stymied and judiciously offering help at the right time, a student may feel more incompetent if more effort doesn't work. Telling students to 'keep trying and you'll get it' does not instil a growth mindset, Dweck said. 'I call it nagging'. (Fensterwald, 2015)

That quote points to one of the most common misinterpretations of a growth mindset: that it is all about praising a child's effort. Of course, it's true that effort is important but it is not the *only* factor in the story of success. Imagine putting more effort into an ineffectual strategy; that is *not* going to help you make progress. In fact, in that circumstance, it would be better to *stop* putting effort into the wrong approach than it would to put *more* effort in.

(Authors): I have been interested in music since my early teens. Thanks to an old inherited guitar, I spent hours trying to improvise and play various guitar solos. At that time, there was no such thing as 'online' videos to learn from and I couldn't afford lessons. So, all my effort went into learning the wrong technique! I thought guitarists should only 'pluck' in one direction: upwards. I didn't know that you could also strike the strings downwards as well. So, all my effort went into 'half' playing the guitar. Since then, I have learned to play 'normally' but back then, the combination of lots of effort with the wrong technique led to bad performances.

In Chapter 9, we showed how much better it is to praise actions rather than the person; to say, 'that is a great thing to do' rather than to say, 'clever child'. Indeed, some of the examples we gave included praise such as 'good effort' or 'great determination'. We are not now contradicting that advice; instead, we are adding an extra nuance to it. It is a good thing to praise effort when that effort is effectual. But when it's not then it would be better to redirect your students in some way. For example, by asking, 'Is there another way you could look at this?' or saying, 'It's great to see you putting so much effort in, so now, focus on finding the right strategy and I think you'll be getting there!'

> A lot of parents or teachers say praise the effort, not the outcome. I say [that's] wrong: Praise the effort that led to the outcome or learning progress; tie the praise to it. It's not just effort, but strategy . . . so support the student in finding another strategy. Effective teachers who actually have classrooms full of children with a growth mindset are always supporting children's learning strategies and showing how strategies created that success.

Students need to know that if they're stuck, they don't need just effort. You don't want them redoubling their efforts with the same ineffective strategies. You want them to know when to ask for help and when to use resources that are available. (Dweck, 2016)

In Chapter 7, we shared the 'Power of Yetis'. That would be a good starting point if you notice your students putting efforts into the wrong thing. For example, an 'Accuracy Yeti' could help redirect effort towards being precise with methods, sources or details; and an 'Organising Yeti' could assist with using the same efforts to rearrange, rationalise or sequence ideas and actions.

10.5 • RESILIENCE AND GRIT

Connected to the idea of effort are the notions of resilience and grit. Often thought of as 'non-academic' (or 'non-cognitive') influences on success and performance, these two notions are also commonly connected with mindset. Indeed, as Angela Duckworth – one of the most well-known advocates of 'grit' – says in her TED.com presentation:

> Grit is passion and perseverance for very long-term goals. Grit is having stamina. Grit is sticking with your future, day in, day out, not just for the week, not just for the month, but for years, and working really hard to make that future a reality. Grit is living life like it's a marathon, not a sprint . . . and . . . so far, the best idea I have heard for building grit in kids is something called 'growth mindset'. (Duckworth, 2013)

And as Carol Dweck and her colleague, David Scott Yeager describe in their article, 'Mindsets that promote resilience':

> Our research also shows that students' mindsets can be changed and that doing so can promote resilience. Students can be taught the science underlying people's potential to change their academically and socially relevant characteristics, and they can be shown how to apply these insights to their own lives. When they are, it can have striking effects on resilience. (Yeager & Dweck, 2012: 303)

Advocates of both qualities – resilience and grit – argue that between-person differences in the levels of one or other of these can help to explain why two individuals with the same level of ability in a particular domain are often observed to perform at substantially different levels. Specifically, individuals with a higher degree of resilience or grit are better able to sustain their efforts, interest and determination such that they are less distracted by short-term goals and less discouraged by the failures and setbacks that are commonly encountered in many performance domains.

There are some subtle differences between resilience and grit. Resilience is often described as the ability to withstand disappointment, setbacks and failure. Grit, on the other hand, tends to be thought of as a more general strength of character, that includes a willingness to persevere and focus.

The following two quotes from studies of each quality might help to distinguish between them:

> Resilience can be defined as . . . any behavioural, attributional, or emotional response to an academic or social challenge that is positive and beneficial for development (such as seeking new strategies, putting forth greater effort, or solving conflicts peacefully), and we refer to any response to a challenge that

Resilience and grit are two concepts connected to mindset. To find out more about them, it would be worth reading the work of Angela Duckworth, particularly her book *Grit: The Power and Passion of Perseverance* (2016).

is negative or not beneficial for development (such as helplessness, giving up, cheating, or aggressive retaliation) as not resilient. (Yeager & Dweck, 2012: 303)

Grit is typically operationalized as a higher-order construct with two lower-order facets: 'perseverance of effort' and 'consistency of interest'. These two facets . . . refer to the tendency to work hard even in the face of setbacks and the tendency to not frequently change goals and interests. Both are thought to contribute to success: persistence because the process of attaining mastery in a field often involves initial failures that the individual must persist through, and consistency because many hours of deliberate practice are normally required to achieve mastery. (Credé, Tynan & Harms, 2016: 493)

Irrespective of the differences, both attributes are important, not least because there are challenges everywhere: in schoolwork, in relationships, in the pursuit of dreams, and in life generally. And what determines whether people continue to move towards success in those areas or to give up prematurely, is in part down to their levels of grit and resilience.

At this point, it would be worth thinking back to Chapter 8 about challenge and considering whether or not your students often find themselves in 'the pit'. If they do, then there is a good chance that they will need resilience and grit to get through it. It would also be true to say that the more they go through the pit, the more likely they are to develop resilience and grit. To be willing to do this though, they would need to be in a growth mindset. They would also need to approach 'flopped learning' in a positive, can-do manner.

Just goes to show how interconnected all these ideas are!

10.6 • FLOPPED PREVIEWS

> Previews can shift the emphasis away from who knows and who doesn't, to everyone making progress in learning.

To return to the idea of 'flopped learning', previews are a great way to engage your students and to enhance their resilience, grit and effort. We also mention the idea in this chapter because *'flipped* learning' (part of the inspiration for our term, 'flopped learning') is a form of previewing.

'Preview' refers to the strategy of giving students a preview of what will be studied in the following days or weeks. It typically involves a short introduction a day or two before the 'main' lesson, thus giving students time to prepare themselves ahead of time. It might also involve setting homework that previews future lessons rather than the more traditional setting of homework of reviewing what has just been studied. So, if you are planning for your students to study a new topic about, say, the water cycle, then you would give them a short introduction the week before and ask them to find out what they can before you start the topic properly. Or, if you are planning a lesson involving throwing and catching then you'd let your students know that some practice ahead of time would give them an advantage. Or, if you were going to ask them to engage in a debate about a particular topic, you would give your students extracts from conflicting opinions to study the week before the debate.

(Authors): I used to hate French lessons at school. I had nothing against the language and, to be honest, I wish I could speak it today. However, it seemed so unfair that the kids who got to spend their summer holidays in France always excelled in class whilst those of us who never ventured that far were always left behind, both literally and metaphorically. In class, whenever teachers asked questions, the hands of those who had holidayed in France shot up; they gave answers, received some feedback, and continued to build their confidence as well as their competence. The rest of us just sat back and practised our Gallic shrugs.

Imagine how much better it could have been if the teachers had given us a preview: 'Next week, we will be thinking about ordering food and drink, so before then, look up a few phrases you could use'. The advanced students could have armed themselves with some advanced phrases; I could have practised, 'un croissant et un café, s'il vous plaît'. Okay, so it would hardly have got me into the Sorbonne but it could have meant that I had at least one phrase to offer, receive feedback on and then add to. In other words, I might have actually made *some* progress rather than just sitting at the back regarding 'la montre' (or whatever the French say when they watch the clock).

Strange though it might seem, some teachers actually worry that previewing a topic will spoil the surprise. Our response to that is, if 'surprise' is the main part of your repertoire then you might want to expand your pedagogy just a little bit! It's not about giving away all the wonderful things you have in store for your students; it is about giving them the opportunity to prepare ahead of time so that they are more ready to learn. Of course, you might need to provide resources and/or opportunities for students who get very little support at home. This can include 'preview clubs', before- or after-school opportunities, giving a similar level of support for 'preview work' as you already do for those who struggle to do 'homework', and so on.

We wouldn't expect every lesson to be previewed; it could just be one or two lessons per week that are prepared ahead of time. Or maybe preview could replace the homework that is already set so that it becomes 'home-preparation' rather than 'home-work'.

(Authors): My son is a relatively quiet little fella; he tends to listen and observe more than take centre stage. However, one breakfast time, he told me that he'd been studying 'dinosaurs' at school and was obviously pretty excited about the whole thing. So I promised him that we would find out even more about them when he got home from school that afternoon; which is what we did. Whilst searching online for interesting facts, we came across the news that there was a dinosaur exhibition on in Newcastle upon Tyne so, as a family, we headed down there the following weekend. You can imagine how thrilled Harry was to show us what he'd learnt already and to find out even more about the creatures.

▶ Figure 52: **Preview Learning to Give Students a Head Start with Their Studies**

On the Monday morning, he could hardly contain his excitement at the prospect of showing his teacher everything he'd discovered at the Centre for Life. As we walked home that afternoon, I was expecting him to tell me how brilliant it had been to share his learning with his classmates but what he told me instead was that his teacher had said, 'That's nice, Harry but we've finished dinosaurs now. We've moved on to studying the weather instead'. Imagine how deflated he was! And imagine what little effort it would have taken to send a message home three weeks prior to that, to say something along the lines of, 'Over the coming weeks, we will be studying dinosaurs. So, if you can chat with your children about dinosaurs, have a look online together, or even take a trip to Newcastle to see the exhibition they're staging, then this could really help your child to connect their learning even more'.

So that is preview: giving students the opportunity to think about, and sometimes research or have a go at, a particular topic or skill ahead of time. But what of 'flopped' previews? They are a combination of previews and flopped learning. Instead of giving your students the opportunity to prepare themselves ahead of time, you could create preview tasks that your students are likely to flop with. Or that share the flops made by other people. You can then begin the following lesson by examining the flops together and identifying what can be learned from them. In our experience, this leads to deeper learning rather than to the unnecessary problems that some teachers fear will be created.

For example, you could:

1. Share a false hypothesis or an incorrect experiment in science and ask your students to identify some of the problems within it.

2. Give your students some poorly written assignments about a topic they have yet to study, and ask them to critique the assignments ahead of time.

3. Show images or a video of a skill being performed particularly badly and ask your students to find contrasting examples that show the correct routine.

4. Give younger students a poorly written letter and ask them to improve it before you teach them how to write letters accurately.

5. Show a set of instructions written out in a muddled up way. For example, for pre-school children, put pictures of how to get dressed into the wrong order (e.g. put on coat, then put on underwear) and ask them to rearrange them into the correct order. *Then* introduce the topic of getting dressed.

10.7 • FLOPPED LEADING

Flopped learning is as relevant to leaders as it is to others. Indeed, the old cliché of 'do as I say, not as I do' would come to mind if we were to expect our colleagues (or our students) to respond positively to flops without responding positively to them ourselves. So, to avoid just such a contradiction, here are some ideas for leading a culture of flopped learning.

First of all, embrace flops yourself. Recognise them. Talk about them. Identify the learning that can come from them. And do whatever you can to avoid being one of those leaders who say, 'I want you to take risks' in such a way as to really mean, 'I want you to take risks so long as you don't make mistakes along the way'!

Create ways to amplify and value the learning opportunities that can come from mistakes and failure. You could, for example, have a 'learning from failure' award to recognise the member of staff or student who has identified, examined, learned from and subsequently corrected a significant flop. Or you could deliberately seek out information from others that relates to the mistakes you or your colleagues are currently making. For example, you could ask students or their parents to identify the things that are going wrong and to suggest possible solutions. The more anonymous you make this, the more likely you are to receive authentic responses.

10.7.1 • Ready – Flop – Aim

You could use a sequence of ready–flop–aim with your colleagues. This would be something along the lines of:

Ready – Identify a goal you would like to aim for; select the appropriate resources, opportunity and team; then take the first few steps towards that goal.

Flop – Roll your sleeves up and have a go; take some bold steps; see how far you can go; and make some fabulous flops along the way.

Aim – Come together as colleagues to examine the flops you have made so far: what went wrong (as well as what went right); what can you learn from those experiences; and what could be done to improve things next time?

WHAT NEXT?

The miracle, or the power, that elevates the few is to be found in their industry, application, and perseverance under the prompting of a brave, determined spirit.

Mark Twain, 1835–1910

GROWTH MINDSET LESSONS

11.0 • LEARNING CHALLENGE LESSONS

The lesson activities in this chapter are designed around the Learning Challenge, the stages and aims of which are outlined in Section 8.3. You can read much more about the model in James's book of the same name published in 2017. You could also read *Challenging Learning Through Dialogue* by Nottingham et al. (2017) as this gives lots of techniques for deepening the learning within activities like the ones described in this chapter.

Each lesson has been designed to engage your students in cognitive conflict about some of the important concepts connected with mindset: influence, self-efficacy, heritability, development, challenge, resilience and talent.

You don't have to follow each lesson as if it were a recipe; feel free to pick and choose elements that will suit your students. The important thing is to use whatever will help to engage your students in exploratory talk, cognitive conflict, reasoning and justification.

We are very grateful to Mark Bollom, Jill Nottingham and Lorna Pringle for creating the main body of these lessons.

11.1 • HOW MUCH CAN EMILY INFLUENCE HER FUTURE?

AGE RANGE

8+

KEY CONCEPT

Self-efficacy.

> The 'lessons' in this book are intended as inspiration for learning. They do not need to be followed to the letter. Instead, we encourage you to pick and choose the elements most suitable for your students.

KEY WORDS

Self-efficacy, effect and affect, actions, strategies, thinking, mindset, positive, resilience, practice, help, teachers, peers, homework, friends, family, planning, dreams, goals, well-being, intrinsic and extrinsic.

ANY PRIOR LEARNING NEEDED

Students should know the difference between 'effect' and 'affect'. Generally, 'affect' is the action of influencing something whereas 'effect' is the outcome of something. However, 'effect' can also be used as a verb to mean 'to create'. Both meanings of 'effect' are used in this set of lesson ideas. It would also be useful for your students to know the meanings of 'intrinsic' and 'extrinsic'.

LEARNING INTENTIONS

To know what 'self-efficacy' is, and to understand how it influences our lives.

SUCCESS CRITERIA

We can:

- Explain what 'self-efficacy' means and how it can influence our lives.

- Describe and analyse the difference between things that have an effect on us and the things that we are able to affect.

- Make judgements about how much influence Emily has over her future and support these judgements with reasoning.

- Identify the things we could do to have an influence on our own future learning and success.

STRATEGIES USED

Sorting and classifying.

Mystery.

1. • IDENTIFY IMPORTANT CONCEPTS

Some of the key areas to investigate within and around the concept of 'self-efficacy' are the following:

- the definition of efficacy

- the things we can do to effect (create) outcomes

- the role of challenge in becoming self-efficacious

- the role of others in the development of our own self-efficacy

- mindsets and self-efficacy

- the belief in potential, possibility and self-efficacy

- goal setting and self-efficacy

- the relationship between the three feedback questions shared in Section 10.2 (What am I trying to achieve? How much progress have I made? What can I do next?) and self-efficacy

- the role and use of feedback in developing self-efficacy

- the link between self-efficacy, self-confidence and self-esteem.

2. • CHALLENGE STUDENTS' UNDERSTANDING OF THE CONCEPT

Figure 53 gives examples of the sorts of cognitive conflict you should try to create in the minds of your students.

▶ **Figure 53: Examples of Cognitive Conflict for Self-Efficacy**

Opinion	Conflicting opinion
In order to master something, we need to have a high sense of self-efficacy.	The experience of mastering something leads to high self-efficacy.
I can do things to influence how much success I have in my life.	I'm stuck with being me and need to accept my limits.
I can get better at almost everything.	There are some things that no matter how much I try, I just never seem to get better at (e.g. algebra).
Being stuck is frustrating but I know that if I keep going, then eventually I will succeed. That success will make me happy.	Being stuck is one way to know my own limits. If I reassure myself that we can't all be good at everything then I feel happier.
I think that challenge is interesting and it helps me to grow and develop.	I like to choose easy things because that way, I'm never feeling uncomfortable.
I can't play a musical instrument but I think I could if I put enough effort into it.	I can't play a musical instrument and I don't think it matters how much effort I put in, I am never going to be able to do it.
I'm perfectly happy that I can't play a musical instrument.	I could never play a musical instrument. I'm just not musical. It's really frustrating.
You either have self-efficacy or you don't! I am just not that type of person.	Self-efficacy is constantly evolving as we get older. I am much more confident that I can achieve a place on the sports team now than I was last year.
Self-efficacy is essential to our success at something.	I have very low self-efficacy with language and yet I always get good grades.
Self-efficacy comes from your 'self'.	Self-efficacy is significantly influenced by the people around your 'self'.

Questions for Challenge

- How much influence can you have on what happens in your life?
- How much influence can other people have on what happens in your life?
- What things stop you having an effect on your life?
- Is it possible to be happy with yourself if you don't believe in yourself?
- What does the term 'self-efficacy' mean?
- How important is self-efficacy in determining our chances for success?
- How important is being successful to developing self-efficacy?
- Is it possible to develop self-efficacy without having an optimistic outlook?

By creating cognitive conflict in the minds of your students, you will encourage them into the learning pit (see Section 8.3) and thereby into deeper reflection about important concepts.

- What impact do role models have on our ability to develop self-efficacy?
- How essential is self-efficacy in knowing when to try and when to stop?
- What role does your intelligence have on how much you can affect what happens in your life?
- What role does your intelligence have on how much other people can affect what happens in your life?
- Who or what would persuade you that you couldn't improve?
- Why might it be important to know how you can improve?
- Can you improve something simply by putting more effort into it?
- When might it be okay to not want to improve?
- What are the similarities and differences between self-efficacy and self-confidence?
- What specific things can you do that will influence your life right now?
- What influence could you have on how much you learn from this lesson?

3. • CONSTRUCT UNDERSTANDING

Activity 1: Sorting and Classifying

Ask your students to work in pairs or small groups to sort through the activity cards shown in Figure 54. They should sort the cards three times.

1st sort: Things that have an effect on students in this school *versus* things that have no effect on students in this school.

2nd sort: Things that have an effect on students' learning *versus* things that have no effect on students' learning.

3rd sort: Things that students in this school can affect *versus* things that students in this school can *not* affect.

▶ Figure 54: Items to Sort and Classify

1. The colour of a teacher's car
2. Blackholes
3. Computers
4. Books
5. Pets
6. The colour of your teeth
7. How rich you are
8. Your teachers
9. Where you live
10. How clever you are
11. The weather
12. Knowing where you want to get to in life
13. Knowing what to learn
14. Knowing how to learn
15. Knowing what success looks like
16. Effort
17. Friends
18. Parents

19. Your pet's name	28. Goldfish
20. Mobile phones	29. Movies
21. Sleep	30. The school you go to
22. The full moon	31. Health
23. The sun	32. How tall you are
24. Aliens	33. How old you are
25. Sports results	34. Your handwriting
26. Exercise	35. Your vocabulary
27. Your beliefs	

Activity 2: Mystery

Divide your students into groups of three to five. Print out the information shown in Figure 56, cut them into individual cards, then give each group a full set of cards.

Introduce the question: How much can Emily influence her future?

Then invite your students to sort through the cards. Do not give any other information at this stage. Part of the activity is for your students to solve the 'mystery' by themselves. If they ask clarification or procedural questions, then reflect those questions back by saying something such as, 'That's a good question. Can anyone think of a solution?'

Once your students have had enough time to read all the cards and to begin sorting them, pause all the groups and get them to report back to the whole class. Ask questions such as:

- What have you found out so far?
- Which pieces of evidence suggest that Emily can influence her future and which ones do not?
- How many irrelevant pieces of information have you found?
- What strategy are you using to sort through the cards?
- Are there any other ways you could sort through them?

Sometimes, it helps to give your students the table shown in Figure 55. This can help them to interpret and handle the information more effectively, and to reconstruct their thinking in order to reach an understanding. Do not give this out too early in the process. Make sure your students have had enough time to read and begin sorting first.

Adaptation

You could give your students half of the cards to begin with, and then the second half later. Or you could omit some of the more complex cards. You could also give the Consider Chart shown in Figure 55 earlier in the proceedings.

▶ Figure 55: Consider Chart for Emily Mystery

How Much Can Emily Influence Her Future?		
Information that supports the idea that Emily **can** influence her future.	Information that supports the idea that Emily **cannot** influence her future.	Information that doesn't help to answer the question.
Our conclusion is . . .		
The key reasons for this are . . .		

Extension

You could ask your students to rank a subset of the cards into those factors that make the most difference at the top of the rank, and those that make the least difference at the bottom of the rank. You could also ask each group to come up with three more 'clues' to pass on to other groups.

▶ Figure 56: Clues for the Emily Mystery

Emily is 10 years old.	Emily's new teacher spends a lot of time talking to her students about how to be successful learners.	Emily doesn't believe she's going to cope with the work when she moves up to secondary school next year.
Emily knows the reasons why she's improved so much at swimming.	Emily has an older sister called Sophie, who is 14.	Emily doesn't believe that she'll ever be successful in mathematics.
Emily saw the grades from a reading comprehension test on her teacher's desk. She hadn't done as well as some of her friends.	Emily is very good at swimming and also plays soccer.	Emily trains very hard at swimming: she listens carefully to her coach and spends time watching YouTube clips for advice and tips on how to improve her technique.

Emily heard her Dad say that Sophie has always been a Grade 'A' student.	Emily's teacher is looking forward to telling Emily how much she's improved since her last reading comprehension test.	At a parents' evening last year, Emily's previous teacher said that she wasn't as academically gifted as her older sister.
Emily knows that she learns best when she has an example to follow or step-by-step instructions.	Emily's friend Henry loves maths. He enjoys exploring problems. Emily can't believe it when he says that he actually enjoys getting stuck.	Emily wants to learn how to windsurf.
Emily is worried that if she isn't as successful as her sister, her parents won't be pleased with her.	Emily's Mum told her Dad that they are lucky to have two wonderful daughters and that it's fantastic that they are so different from one another.	Emily never wants to say an answer out loud in maths lessons in case she's wrong.
Emily's Dad had no sporting success as a child. He's delighted that Emily does so well in swimming competitions.	Sophie has already told the family that she'd like to be a medical doctor when she's older.	Emily doesn't like the fact that she finds herself working in different groups from most of her friends.
There is a maths club after school on Wednesday afternoons.	Emily's mum had to take her maths exam twice when she was at school so that she could do the course she wanted to do.	Emily's mum is a physiotherapist.
Emily's coach asked Emily to practise swimming 3 sets of 4 lengths at 80% of her normal speed.	Emily learned a way of working out percentages by copying down a method from the internet.	Emily doesn't think it's very important that she has developed a real talent for painting and pottery.
Emily's friend Josie writes poems. She asked Emily to draw some pictures so that she could put them with her poems and make a book.	Henry goes to maths club. He enjoys helping some of the younger students.	Emily's class teacher runs maths club. She says that she'd like it if Emily could come along.
To calculate a percentage of time Emily had to convert minutes into seconds.	Emily would like to help the swimming coach work with the very youngest children who come for lessons before her training session.	There are four major strokes in swimming – backstroke, breaststroke, butterfly and front crawl. Front crawl is used in freestyle races.
The other day, Emily explained to her class the process she follows for mixing paint. Henry said he realised where he had been going wrong.	Emily likes helping others but feels like she's being 'a pain' when she asks for help for herself.	Emily wishes she was good at what she believes are the important subjects at school.

4. • CONSIDER THE LEARNING JOURNEY

At the end of the activity, invite your students to think about the learning journey they have been on. This can include reflecting on their thinking, their strategy and what they could have done differently.

Remember to refer back to the learning intentions and success criteria, and to ask your students to consider how much progress they have made towards achieving these goals.

You could also ask some of these follow-up questions:

- In what ways can you affect your own life?
- Is believing that you can influence things important if you want to change?
- Do you want to have more or less effect on your future?
- Is it important to know what you want to improve?
- Can you name something you can do or think today that could have an effect on you in the future?
- How did you have an effect on how much you learned in this lesson?
- What actions could you take that will have an effect on your future as a learner?
- What will you remember from this lesson?
- What skills have you used during this lesson?
- What could you do with these skills and this learning?

Ideas for Transfer

You could ask your students to think about the cards in Figure 55 that would apply to all people, some people, only people in economically developed countries, only adults, only English-speakers, and so on.

11.2 • WAS USAIN BOLT BORN TO BE AN OLYMPIC CHAMPION?

AGE RANGE

10+

KEY CONCEPT

Mindset.

KEY WORDS

Mindset, Olympics, champion, growth, development, perseverance, determination, genes, nature, nurture, mental preparation, gifted, talented, dedication, sacrifice, fixed mindset, growth mindset, improvement, progress.

ANY PRIOR LEARNING NEEDED

It would be valuable for your students to watch some online video or access short biographical details about Usain Bolt. This should provide background information about Usain Bolt's achievements and his journey from childhood to multiple Olympic champion.

LEARNING INTENTIONS

To understand the factors that contribute to sporting success and the role that mindset plays in this.

SUCCESS CRITERIA

- Explore where talent comes from.
- Compare the attitudes and actions of a fixed mindset with those of a growth mindset.
- Identify how mindset influences our own progress and achievements.

STRATEGIES USED

Opinion Line.

Mystery.

1. • IDENTIFY IMPORTANT CONCEPTS

Some of the key areas to investigate within and around the concept of 'mindset' are the following:

- fixed mindset
- growth mindset
- nature versus nurture
- practice
- effort
- dedication
- determination
- resilience
- ambition
- progress and improvement
- limitations
- different starting points
- potential
- achievement
- self-esteem
- intelligence.

Activity 1: Opinion Line

To get your students thinking about the concepts shown, you could use an opinion line such as the one shown in Figure 57.

Ask your students to consider how much they agree or disagree with these statements:

- Olympic champions are *naturally* gifted.
- Olympic champions are *lucky*.
- To be an Olympic champion, athletes *have* to be in a growth mindset.
- Dedication, effort, training and ambition are all *necessary* to become an Olympic champion.

▶ Figure 57: Opinion Line of Olympic Success

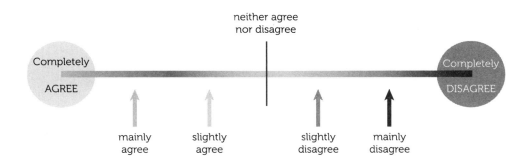

2. • CHALLENGE STUDENTS' UNDERSTANDING OF THE CONCEPT

Figure 58 gives examples of the sorts of cognitive conflict you should try to create in the minds of your students.

Questions for Challenge

- Are some people born destined to be winners?
- Do talented people need to try?
- Do talented people need to learn new things?
- Do talented people have to be coached if they are to become champions?
- Can anyone become talented?
- Could I become men's/women's world 100-metre record holder?
- Could I become a better or more talented 100-metre runner?
- Is the current world record holder for the 100 metres the only person who has ever lived who could run the time he or she ran?
- When should you stop trying to improve?
- Is it wrong to give up on something you can't do?
- Is it ever right to give up on something you can't do?
- Can you give up on something and then return to it at a later date?
- Is failure a sign that you should give up?
- If we are talented at something, should we sit back and enjoy our own brilliance?
- When do you feel clever? Is it when you have mastered something or is it when you are being challenged?
- Is struggling a bad thing or a sign that you are engaged in a challenge?
- Is being challenged a bad thing?
- Are there some challenges you are 'up for' and others that you are not? Is this okay?
- How do you feel when you see someone who is already very talented?
- Is there a talent you would like to have but that you currently don't? What is the evidence that you don't already have it?
- When someone is critical about your performance, do you find it difficult to carry on learning or do you use it as a source of inspiration?

- When you are learning and want to get better at something, should you focus on the improvement you've made or how far you still need or want to go (or both)?

- In terms of our own progress and growth, does it help to know that most 'geniuses' or people that are called 'gifted' have put in (sometimes) thousands of hours of work to get where they are? Or does the knowledge that it takes so long put you off trying?

- Do you like the idea of success without effort? Is that a realistic scenario?

▶ Figure 58: **Examples of Cognitive Conflict for Usain Bolt Mystery**

Opinion	Conflicting opinion
Some people find things easy.	There is no such thing as 'easy'.
Usain Bolt's success comes from his physical superiority.	Usain Bolt's success comes from training, dedication, effort, technique *and* physical superiority.
Everyone can improve if they train hard enough.	I could dedicate my whole life to training and still not beat Usain Bolt.
I'm naturally good at some things and naturally bad at other things.	I am much better than I used to be at some things and much worse at other things.
Being told that I can improve anything I want to is very reassuring.	Being told that I can improve anything I want to stops me from relaxing because it makes me feel I should get on with improving.
Watching Usain Bolt run a race is inspiring.	Watching Usain Bolt run a race makes me feel lazy.
Usain Bolt is so famous because he smashed the 100-metre world record.	Usain Bolt is so famous largely because of his enigmatic personality.
Talent has made Usain Bolt a household name.	The media has made Usain Bolt a household name.
Usain Bolt is lucky.	Usain Bolt has worked hard to be where he is today.

3. • CONSTRUCT UNDERSTANDING

Activity 2: Mystery

Divide your students into groups of three to five. Print out the information shown in Figure 60, cut them into individual cards, then give each group a full set of cards.

Introduce the question: Was Usain Bolt born to be an Olympic champion?

Then invite your students to sort through the cards. Do not give any other information at this stage. Part of the activity is for your students to solve the 'mystery' by themselves. If they ask clarification or procedural questions, then reflect those questions back by saying something such as, 'That's a good question. Can anyone think of a solution?'

Once your students have had enough time to read all the cards and to begin sorting them, pause all the groups and get them to report back to the whole class. Ask questions such as:

- What have you found out so far?
- Which pieces of evidence suggest that Usain Bolt can influence his future and which ones do not?
- How many irrelevant pieces of information have you found?
- What strategy are you using to sort through the cards?
- Are there any other ways you could sort through them?

Sometimes, it helps to give your students the table shown in Figure 58. This can help them to interpret and handle the information more effectively, and to reconstruct their thinking in order to reach an understanding. Do not give this out too early in the process. Make sure your students have had enough time to read and begin sorting first.

Adaptation

You could give your students half of the cards to begin with, and then the second half later. Or you could omit some of the more complex cards. You could also give the Consider Chart shown in Figure 58 earlier in the proceedings.

Extension

You could ask your students to rank a subset of the cards into those factors that make the most difference at the top of the rank, and those that make the least difference at the bottom of the rank. You could also ask each group to come up with three more 'clues' to pass on to other groups.

▶ **Figure 59: Consider Chart for Usain Bolt Mystery**

Was Usain Bolt Born to be an Olympic Champion?		
Information that supports the idea that Bolt was born to be an Olympic champion.	Information that supports the idea that Bolt has had to work hard to become an Olympic champion.	Information that doesn't help to answer the question.

Our conclusion is . . .

The key reasons for this are . . .

'Champions have a strong will to win and are highly competitive – they hate to lose'. Bill Cole, Olympic sports psychologist	'Champions have the courage to risk failure on an international stage'. Bill Cole, Olympic sports psychologist	Less mentally prepared athletes focus on the outcome aspects of their event: 'What will people think if I lose? or 'It would be awful if I let my coach down'.
'You can have all the natural talent in the world but there's no substitute for hard work'. Mo Farah, double Olympic gold medal winner at 5,000 metres and 10,000 metres	'Champions only focus on what they can directly control'. Bill Cole, Olympic sports psychologist	Champions sacrifice more, work harder, control their mind and emotions better, and have a deeper desire for success'. Bill Cole, Olympic sports psychologist
'Champions succeed because they have inner qualities others do not possess and they behave differently.' Bill Cole, Olympic sports psychologist	'Champions are committed to continuously developing their potential'. Bill Cole, Olympic sports psychologist	'Champions have an extreme amount of perseverance and determination to succeed'. Bill Cole, Olympic sports psychologist
In a growth mindset, you believe that abilities are grown.	In a fixed mindset, you believe that abilities are fixed.	In a growth mindset, you seek out challenge.
In a fixed mindset, you avoid challenge.	In a fixed mindset, you try to prove what you can do.	In a growth mindset, you try to improve.
In a fixed mindset, you hide your mistakes and avoid situations that might lead to you making mistakes.	In a growth mindset, you examine and learn from your mistakes.	In a growth mindset, you seek out feedback.
In a fixed mindset, you view feedback as criticism.	Christophe Lemaitre is a French sprinter. He became the first (and only) white man to break the 10-second barrier in an officially timed 100-metre event in 2010.	No African or Caribbean nation has ever hosted the Olympic Games.
'I train for 11 months of the year, six days a week'. Usain Bolt	'It's hard work, sweat and sacrifice. I've sacrificed so much throughout the season, throughout the years. I've been through so much'. Usain Bolt	'World juniors made me who I am today . . . It was one of the toughest races of my life up to this day. I was so nervous running in front of my home crowd'. Usain Bolt
'Training gives you confidence and this helps your state of mind. I know if I'm in good shape it's going to be very hard to beat me, this confidence is very important in performing well'. Usain Bolt	Bolt is a Jamaican-born athletic sprinter, and was born on 21 August 1986 in Trelawny, Jamaica.	Usain Bolt stated, 'there was still room for improvement', even though he won the 100 metres at the Olympic Stadium in 2013.
'You could see this tall young boy – just raw natural talent', remembers Lorna Thorpe, who was then head of sport at the school where Usain Bolt was a student.	Bolt wasn't particularly interested in sprinting. As a child he loved playing football and cricket with his brother.	Jamaica (with a population of just 3 million) has won 14 Olympic gold medals, with many of them in sprinting.

(Continued)

(Continued)

'I've proven that I'm the greatest in this sport and, for me, it's mission accomplished'. Usain Bolt	Bolt made his Olympic debut as a 17-year-old at Athens 2004, where he went out in the opening round of the 200 metres because of a hamstring injury.	Bolt became the first man in history to defend both the 100-metre and 200-metre Olympic sprint titles.
'He has lots of fast twitch muscle fibres that can respond quickly, coupled with his vast stride is what gives him such an extraordinary fast time'. John Barrow, Cambridge University	By the age of 12, Bolt had become the school's fastest runner over the 100 metres distance.	Bolt has raised and donated over $3 million to his hometown of Sherwood Content.
125 sprinters have run the 100 metres in under 10 seconds.	'I'm confident that I'm going to win, but I never think, "No one can beat me"'. Usain Bolt	Bolt received a bronze medal in the 2017 World Athletics Championships.
Bolt paid over £10,000 to adopt an abandoned cheetah cub – named Lightning Bolt – in Nairobi, and continues to pay £2,300 a year to pay for its upkeep at the orphanage.	Bolt owns a restaurant in Jamaica.	'I wouldn't say I'm a phenomenon, just a great athlete'. Usain Bolt
'There you go. I'm the greatest'. Jamaican sprinter Usain Bolt speaking after his 'triple triple' of golds in the 100 metre, 200 metre and 4 × 100 metre relays.	'You have to find that one thing that you know is going to motivate you. You might not enjoy training for example but you have to love competing and winning'. Usain Bolt	Bolt's height is 6 feet 5 inches whereas his competitors tend to be 6ft 2 inches and lower.
'If I start like that in the world championships I will probably finish fifth. I need to work with my coach and figure out how to be more explosive out of the blocks and not so slow'. Usain Bolt reflecting after one of his races in 2013.	He became the youngest gold medallist at the Junior World Championships when he was only 15 years old.	In 2009, Bolt became the world record holder in both the 100 metre (9.58 secs) and the 200 metre (19.19 secs) races.

4. • CONSIDER THE LEARNING JOURNEY

Revisiting the opinion line in Figure 56, and using the same statements recommended in Activity 1, can be a good way for students to reflect on how or if their thinking has changed or evolved.

After that, get your students to refer back to the learning intentions and success criteria, and ask them to consider how much progress they have made towards achieving these goals.

You could also ask some of these follow-up questions:

- What do you understand now about mindsets that you didn't before?

- Has anything you've read or heard in this lesson challenged your thinking, understanding or perspective on the concept of mindsets?

- What are the implications of the understanding you've developed?

- Have the perspectives of others over the course of this lesson been significant?

- What shaped your opinion in relation to the mystery element of this lesson?

- In terms of your life ahead, what does your understanding of and thinking about growth and fixed mindsets mean to you?

Ideas for Transfer

You could ask your students to research biographical details for other high achievers in the world of sport, the arts, business and so on. They could then present their findings to each other, under the heading of: 'Were they born with their talent or did they develop it?'

11.3 • IS CHALLENGE INTERESTING?

AGE RANGE

9+

KEY CONCEPT

Challenge.

KEY WORDS

Challenge, easy, boring, interesting, wobble, difficult, resilience, collaboration, effort, strategy, journey, excitement, risk, reward, progress, physical, physiological, emotional, psychological, curiosity.

ANY PRIOR LEARNING NEEDED

No prior learning is necessary although it would help your students if they are familiar with the concept and language of challenge.

LEARNING INTENTIONS

To understand how challenge is a key component of learning and development.

SUCCESS CRITERIA

- Classify types of challenge.

- Question the value and impact of challenge.

- Evaluate the relationships between things being challenging, interesting, easy or boring.

- Describe the role of challenge in cognitive, physical and emotional development.

- Reflect on how to use and respond to challenge in the future.

STRATEGIES USED

Venn Diagram.

Concept Graph.

1. • IDENTIFY IMPORTANT CONCEPTS

Some of the key areas to investigate within and around the concept of 'challenge' are the following;

- a definition of challenge
- types of challenge
- responses to challenge
- challenge and resilience
- challenge and strategy
- challenge and effort
- challenge and reflection
- challenge versus peril
- challenge and learning
- cognitive conflict
- physical/physiological challenge
- emotional/psychological challenge.

Activity 1: Different Challenges

To get your students thinking about the concepts shown, you could divide everyone into smaller groups (between four and six people per group). Then, using large sheets of paper, each group could draw an outline of a person and add descriptors for every challenge that this person might face in their lives. If your students draw arrows from each descriptor to the relevant part of the body that would be affected by that particular challenge, then this would add another dimension to the task. For example, if they thought of the challenge of running a hard race then they might draw arrows to their heart, lungs and legs.

To get your students started, you might like to give them one or two suggestions from the list below:

- The environment (hot/cold/rain/wind)
- Sensory (smells/sights/tastes/touch/sounds)
- Feelings (fear/sadness/loss/anxiety/excitement/impatience/ambition/enthusiasm)
- Physical activity (running/walking/swimming/cycling/working/fighting/lifting/carrying)
- Health (disease, old age, puberty, illness)
- Disability (various)
- Cognitive activity (ideas/concepts/information/opinions/problem solving/seeking solutions).

For every challenge your students think of, encourage them to think of an associated situation that would make it challenging. For example, if they say 'sound' could be challenging to the ears then they could give the situation of someone screaming close by or the sound of fireworks scaring animals.

Also encourage your students to think about these questions for each of the challenges they think of:

- In what way is this challenging?
- Would this *always* prove challenging?
- When might this not be challenging?

Activity 2: Venn Diagram

Print out the information shown in Figure 61, cut them into individual cards, and give each group a full set of cards. Then continuing to work in the same groups, invite your students to sort the cards shown in Figure 61 into the Venn diagram shown in Figure 62.

▶ Figure 61: Different Forms of Challenge

1. Hot	2. Cold	3. Rain
4. Wind	5. Smell	6. Sights
7. Taste	8. Touch	9. Sound
10. Fear	11. Sadness	12. Loss
13. Anxiety	14. Running	15. Walking
16. Swimming	17. Carrying	18. Disease
19. Old age	20. Illness	21. Puberty
22. Blindness	23. Amputation	24. Sore throat
25. Ideas	26. Information	27. Opinions

▶ Figure 62: Using a Venn Diagram to Sort and Classify Examples of Challenge

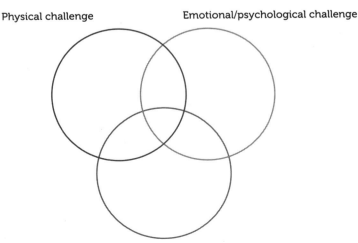

Physical challenge   Emotional/psychological challenge

Cognitive (thinking and understanding) challenge

2. • CHALLENGE STUDENTS' UNDERSTANDING OF THE CONCEPT

Figure 63 gives examples of the sorts of cognitive conflict you should try to create in the minds of your students.

Questions for Challenge

- What does the term 'challenge' mean?
- What does it mean to be challenged?
- What has been the most challenging thing you have done?
- How does challenge make you feel?
- Is challenging the same as difficult?
- What is the difference between something being challenging and something being difficult?
- Does anything good come out of being challenged?
- What are the positive outcomes of being challenged?
- What negative outcomes might there be to being challenged?

► Figure 63: **Examples of Cognitive Conflict When Thinking About Challenge**

Opinion	Conflicting opinion
Why take the challenging option when there's an easy route available?	The challenging route will be much more interesting and rewarding.
The easy route will be better.	The easy route will be boring.
I don't want to have to think. Just tell me what I need to know.	I'll understand something a lot better if I have to think about it.
I'm not very interested in this topic, so I may as well take a short cut.	If it is challenging, then it will make me think and therefore it might become more interesting.
If it's physically challenging, then I'll get fitter and stronger.	If it's physically challenging, then I'll get tired and my body will hurt.
I should avoid challenges that might make me worried.	Emotional challenges will always happen, so I may as well learn to deal with them.
Challenge allows us to see what we are capable of.	Challenge highlights our weaknesses.
We should embrace challenge and use it to our advantage.	Some challenges are beyond our reach and leave us feeling out of control.
With challenge comes reward. I get a great sense of achievement when I complete something that has been particularly challenging.	If I go for the easy option I am more likely to get the reward of a good grade, or the praise and approval of others.
There is nothing wrong with taking short cuts to get to the end point quicker.	If I take the short cut, then I will miss out on an experience and all there is to gain from that.

- Is there a time and a place for things being easy? When might it be preferable for things to be easy?

- What if everything in life was always easy?

- What if everything in life was always challenging?

- Is it ever possible to reach a sense of achievement if no challenge is involved?

- Can people cope with being challenged all the time? What effect might constant challenge have on people?

- What are the benefits of cognitive challenge?

- What might the benefits be to emotional challenge?

- How can we make the cognitive areas of our lives interesting?

- How can we make the emotional areas of our lives easy?

- If challenge is always interesting does that mean that easy is always boring?

- How could something be boring and challenging at the same time?

- How significant is it that things are interesting in the physical areas of our lives?

- What would you judge as being most important and why: physical, emotional or cognitive challenge?

3. • CONSTRUCT UNDERSTANDING

Activity 3: Concept Graph

Now split your students into groups of two or three. Print out the information shown in Figure 64, cut them into individual cards, then give each group a full set of cards. Invite your students to place the cards shown in Figure 64 into the Concept Graph shown in Figure 65. When redrawing the concept graph, make sure it is big enough for your students to place the cards into the relevant section. Encourage your students to justify and explain their decisions to each other.

Questions to Extend the Concept Graph Activity

- To what extent are learning tasks more or less interesting when they are challenging?

- When is challenge most interesting?

- When can easy be interesting?

- When is easy most boring?

Adaptation

You could give your students half of the cards to begin with, and then the second half later. Or you could omit some of the more complex cards.

Extension

You could ask your students to rank a subset of the cards in Figure 61 or 64 into those factors that are most challenging at the top of the rank, and those that are least challenging at the bottom of the rank. You could also ask each group to come up with three more situations that they think are very difficult to classify, and then pass these on to other groups.

► Figure 64: Challenging Situations to Place on a Concept Graph

1. You are going to spend two hours helping a parent with the weekly grocery shopping.	2. You have a maths problem to solve which will enable you to work out how many bottles of lemonade and packets of crisps you need to buy for your birthday party.
3. You've been punished and have to write your name and address out 20 times.	4. You need to get past the dragon on level 3 of the video game so that you can enter the next kingdom and find more treasure.
5. You are having a sleepover that involves camping. You and your friends must put up your own tent and cook your own dinner.	6. You are learning to count in French, Spanish, German and Italian.
7. You score lots of penalty goals past your friend's little brother who is in goal.	8. You score a penalty past your friend's big brother who is a goalie in the school team.
9. You spend a whole topic lesson copying a chapter from a book.	10. You use textbooks and the internet to find answers to difficult questions in a topic.
11. The person who sits next to you in science gives you the answers to everything.	12. You wait at an airport for 6 hours because your flight home is delayed.
13. You hike to the top of a mountain.	14. You watch an exciting match, but your team loses in the last minute of the game.
15. You watch a film documentary about the terrible experiences of a small child during World War II.	16. You've got two great ideas but they contradict each other.
17. You feel ill but you don't want to miss a day of your holiday.	18. You have a test at school next week, you have a very poorly close relative and you have to tell your parents that you've lost your mobile phone.
19. You watch the latest animated film at the cinema.	20. In PE you are practising for a race by running around the field three times.

► Figure 65: Concept Graph for Challenge

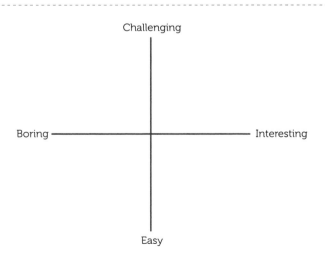

4. • CONSIDER THE LEARNING JOURNEY

At the end of the activity, invite your students to think about the learning journey they have been on. This can include reflecting on their thinking, their strategy and what they could have done differently.

Remember to refer back to the learning intentions and success criteria, and to ask your students to consider how much progress they have made towards achieving these goals.

You could also ask some of these follow-up questions:

- What does challenge mean?
- What are the positive outcomes of being challenged?
- What negative outcomes might there be to being challenged?
- What are the best conditions for challenge?
- Which areas of our lives benefit the most from challenge?
- Which areas of our lives benefit the least from challenge?
- What is the connection between something being interesting and something being challenging?
- How much does the level of interest achieved depend upon the level of challenge?
- When is it a good option to be bored?
- What questions do you still have about the concept of challenge?
- What conclusions have you drawn in this lesson about the concept that you could explain to someone else?
- In what ways might your response to challenge be affected going forward?

Ideas for Transfer

Your students could do a self-audit of all the ways in which they've been challenged in the previous week and consider what sort of challenge it has been (cognitive/emotional/physical).

Your students could explore the structure of Bloom's taxonomy and look at how this describes increasingly complex levels of development in cognitive, psychomotor (physical) and affective (emotional) domains.

REFERENCES

Bandura, A. (1977). Self-efficacy: Toward a unifying theory of behavioral change. *Psychological Review, 84,* 191–215

Barker, G. P., & Graham, S. (1987). Developmental study of praise and blame as attributional cues. *Journal of Educational Psychology, 79,* 62–66.

Beaman, R., & Wheldall, K. (2000). Teachers' use of approval and disapproval in the classroom. *Educational Psychology, 20,* 431–446.

Binet, A., & Simon, T. (1905). Application of the new methods to the diagnosis of the intellectual level among normal and subnormal children in institutions and in the primary schools. *L'Année Psychologique, 12,* 245–336.

Birch, L. L., Marlin, D. W., & Rotter, J. (1984). Eating as the 'means' activity in a contingency: Effects on young children's food preference. *Child Development, 55,* 431–439.

Black, P., Harrison, C., Lee, C., Marshall, B., & Wiliam, D. (1990). Working inside the black box: Assessment for learning in the classroom. *Phi Delta Kappan, 86,* 8–21.

Boggiano, A. K., Main, D. S., Flink, C., Barrett, M., Silvern, L., & Katz, P. (1989). A model of achievement in children: The role of controlling strategies in helplessness and affect. In R. Schwarzer, H. M. van der Ploeg, & C. D. Spielberger (eds), *Advances in Test Anxiety Research.* Lisse, The Netherlands: Swets & Zeitlinger, pp. 13–26.

Brophy, J. (1981). Teacher praise: A functional analysis. *Review of Educational Research, 51,* 5–32.

Burnette, J., Finkle, E., O'Boyle, E., VanEpps, E., & Pollack, J. (2013). Mind-sets matter: A meta-analytic review of implicit theories and self-regulation. *American Psychological Association, 139*(3), 655–701.

Butler, R. (1997). Task-involving and ego-involving properties of evaluation: Effects of different psychology feedback conditions on motivational perceptions, interest and performance. *Journal of Educational Psychology, 79,* 474–482.

Cameron, W. B. (1963). *Informal Sociology: A Casual Introduction to Sociological Thinking.* New York: Random House.

Claro, S., Paunesku, D., & Dweck, C. S. (2016). Growth mindset tempers the effects of poverty on academic achievement. *Proceedings of the National Academy of Sciences of the United States of America, 113*(31), 8664–8668. Retrieved from www.pnas.org/content/113/31/8664 (accessed 12 March 2018).

Coffield, F. (2013). *Learning Styles: Time to Move On.* National College for School Leadership. Retrieved from www.learnersfirst.net/private/wp-content/uploads/Opinion-Piece-Learning-styles-time-to-move-on-Coffield.pdf (accessed 13 March 2018).

Coffield, F., Moseley, D., Hall, E., & Ecclestone, K. (2004). *Learning Styles and Pedagogy in Post 16 Learning: A Systematic and Critical Review.* London: Learning and Skills Research Centre. Retrieved from www.academia.edu/10608972/A_Critical_Analysis_of_Learning_Styles_and_Pedagogy_in_post-16_learning._A_systematic_and_critical_review_published_in_2004_by_Coffield_F._Moseley_D._Hall_E._and_Ecclestone_K (accessed 13 March 2018).

Credé, M., Tynan, M. C., & Harms, P. D. (2016). Much ado about grit: A meta-analytic synthesis of the grit literature. *Journal of Personality and Social Psychology, 113*(3), 492–511.

Deci, E., Koestner, R., & Ryan, R. (1999). A meta-analytic review of experiments examining the effects of extrinsic rewards on intrinsic motivation. *Psychological Bulletin, 125*, 627–626.

Dickens, C. ([1859] 2003). *A Tale of Two Cities*. London: Penguin.

Duckworth, A. (2013). Grit: The power and passion of perseverance. *TED Talks Education*. Retrieved from www.ted.com/talks/angela_lee_duckworth_grit_the_power_of_passion_and_perseverance/transcript (accessed 21 March 2018).

Duckworth, A. (2016). Grit: *The Power and Passion of Perseverance*. London: Vermilion.

Dweck, C. S. (2000). *Self-theories: Their Role in Motivation, Personality and Development*. Philadelphia, PA: Psychology Press.

Dweck, C. (2006a). Is math a gift? Beliefs that put females at risk. In S. J. Ceci, & W. Williams (eds), *Why Aren't More Women in Science? Top Researchers Debate the Evidence*. Washington, DC: American Psychological Association, pp. 47–55.

Dweck, C. (2006b). *Mindset: The New Psychology of Success*. New York: Random House.

Dweck, C. (2012a). *Mindset: How You Can Fulfil Your Potential*. New York: Constable & Robinson.

Dweck, C. S. (2012b). The right mindset for success. *Harvard Business Review*. Retrieved from https://hbr.org/2012/01/the-right-mindset-for-success (accessed 14 March 2018).

Dweck, C. S. (2014). The power of yet. TED.com presentation. Retrieved from www.youtube.com/watch?v=J-swZaKN2lc (accessed 15 December 2017).

Dweck, C. (2015a). Growth mindset, revisited. *Education Week, 35*(5), 20–24. Retrieved from www.edweek.org/ew/articles/2015/09/23/carol-dweck-revisits-the-growth-mindset.html (accessed 16 March 2018).

Dweck, C. S. (2015b). The secret to raising smart kids. ScientificAmerican.com. Retrieved from www.scientificamerican.com/article/the-secret-to-raising-smart-kids1 (accessed 11 February 2018).

Dweck, C. S. (2016). To encourage a mindset, pass it on . . . *Times Educational Supplement*. Retrieved from www.tes.com/news/tes-magazine/tes-magazine/encourage-a-growth-mindset-pass-it (accessed 25 January 2018).

Dweck, C. (2017). Challenging mindset. Challenging Learning Conference. Copenhagen, Denmark.

Eells, R. J. (2011). Meta-analysis of the relationship between collective teacher efficacy and student achievement. *Dissertations*. Paper 133. Retrieved from http://ecommons.luc.edu/luc_diss/133 (accessed 13 March 2018).

Ehrilnger, J., Mitchum, A. L., & Dweck, C. S. (2015). Understanding overconfidence: Theories of intelligence, preferential attention, and distorted self-assessment. *Journal of Experimental Social Psychology, 63*: 94–100.

Fensterwald, J. (2015). There's more to a 'growth mindset' than assuming you have it. EdSource, 23 November. Retrieved from https://edsource.org/2015/theres-more-to-a-growth-mindset-than-assuming-you-have-it/90780 (accessed 21 March 2018).

Gardner, H. (2009). International Conference on Thinking, Kuala Lumpur, Malaysia.

Haimovitz, K., & Dweck, C. S. (2016). Parents' views of failure predict children's fixed and growth intelligence mind-sets. *Psychological Science, 27*(6), 859–869.

Harris, F. R., Wolf, M. M., & Baer, D. M. (1967). Effects of adult social reinforcement on child behavior. In S. W. Bijou, & D. M. Baer (eds), *Child Development: Readings in Experimental Analysis*. New York: Appleton-Century-Crofts, pp. 146–158.

Hattie, J. (2009). *Visible Learning: A Synthesis of Over 800 Meta-Analyses Relating to Achievement*. Abingdon, UK: Routledge.

Hattie, J. (2017). *250+ Influences on Student Achievement*. Retrieved from http://visible learningplus.com/sites/default/files/A0169%20250%20Influences%20010%20DEC%20 2017.pdf (accessed 8 March 2018).

Henderlong Corpus, J., & Lepper, M. R. (2007). The effects of person versus performance praise on children's motivation: Gender and age as moderating factors. *Educational Psychology*, 27(4), 487–508.

Huelser, B. J., & Metcalfe, J. (2012). Making related errors facilitates learning, but learners do not know it. *Memory & Cognition*, 40(4), 514–527.

James, W. (1890). *The Principles of Psychology*. Chapter 1: The Scope of Psychology. Retrieved from https://psychcentral.com/classics/James/Principles/prin1.htm (accessed 25 January 2018).

Kamins, M. L., & Dweck, C. S. (1999). Person versus process praise and criticism: Implications for contingent self-worth and coping. *Developmental Psychology*, 35, 835–847.

Kempner, S. G., McDonald, M. A., & Pomerantz, E. M. (2003). Mothers' responses to children's academic success: The moderating role of children's gender. Poster presented at the biennial meeting of the Society for Research in Child Development, Tampa, FL, April.

Madsen, C. H., Becker, W. C., & Thomas, D. R. (1968). Rules, praise, and ignoring: Elements of elementary classroom control. *Journal of Applied Behavior Analysis*, 1(2), 139–150.

Meyer, W.-U., Bachmann, M., Biermann, U., Hempelmann, M., Ploger, F.-O., & Spiller, H. (1979). The informational value of evaluative behavior: Influences of praise and blame on perceptions of ability. *Journal of Educational Psychology*, 71, 259–268.

Mueller, C. M., & Dweck, C. S. (1998). Intelligence praise can undermine motivation and performance. *Journal of Personality and Social Psychology*, 75, 33–52.

Nottingham, J. A. (2017). *The Learning Challenge: How to Guide Your Students Through the Learning Pit to Achieve Deeper Understanding*. Thousand Oaks, CA: Corwin.

Nottingham, J., & Nottingham, J. (2017). *Challenging Learning Through Feedback*. London: Sage.

Nottingham, J. A., Nottingham J., & Renton, M. (2017). *Challenging Learning Through Dialogue*. Thousand Oaks, CA: Corwin.

Nuthall, G. (2007). *The Hidden Lives of Learners*. Wellington, New Zealand: NZCER Press.

O'Leary, K. D., & O'Leary, S. G. (1977). *Classroom Management: The Successful Use of Behavior Modification* (2nd edn). New York: Pergamon Press.

Pashler, H., McDaniel, M., Rohrer, D., & Bjork, R. (2008). Learning styles: Concepts and evidence. *Psychological Science in the Public Interest*, 9(3): 105–119.

Quinn, D. D. (n.d.). 25 compelling quotes by and for teachers. TeachingDegree.org, blog. Retrieved from www.teachingdegree.org/2012/11/11/25-compelling-quotes-by-and-for-teachers (accessed 25 January 2018).

Schopenhauer, A. (1891, reprinted 2009). *The Art of Literature: A Series of Essays*. Translated by T. Bailey Saunders. Ithaca, NY: Cornell University Library.

Siegler, R. (1992). The other Alfred Binet. *Developmental Psychology*, 28(2): 179–190.

Skinner, B. F. (1948). *Walden Two*. Indianapolis, IN: Hackett Publishing Co. (Reprint edition, 2005).

Smiley, P., Buttitta, K., Chung, S., Dubon, V., & Chang, L. (2016). Mediation models of implicit theories and achievement goals predict planning and withdrawal after failure. *Motivation and Emotion*, 40(6): 878–894.

Terman, L. M. (1916). *The Measurement of Intelligence*. Boston: Houghton Mifflin. Retrieved from www.gutenberg.org/files/20662/20662-h/20662-h.htm (accessed 13 March 2018).

Twain, M. ([1894] 1993). *Tom Sawyer Abroad* (Tom Sawyer & Huckleberry Finn Book 3) [Kindle Edition].

Wiliam, D. (2014). The right questions, the right way. *Educational Leadership*, 71(6): 16–19. Retrieved from www.ascd.org/publications/educational-leadership/mar14/vol71/num06/The-Right-Questions,-The-Right-Way.aspx (accessed 7 December 2018).

Yeager, D. S., & Dweck, C. S. (2012). Mindsets that promote resilience: When students believe that personal characteristics can be developed. *Educational Psychologist*, 47(4), 302–314.

Young, T. (2017). 'Schools are desperate to teach "growth mindset". But it's based on a lie'. *The Spectator*, 21 January. Retrieved from www.spectator.co.uk/2017/01/schools-are-desperate-to-teach-growth-mindset-but-its-based-on-a-lie (accessed 13 March 2018).

Zhao, L., Heyman, G. D., Chen, L., & Lee, K. (2017). Praising young children for being smart promotes cheating. *Psychological Science*, 28(12), 1868–1870.

INDEX

Dulwich Prep, 82, 86, 87fig
Dweck, Carol S., xiv, xv, xvi, 3, 4, 8–10,
    13–15, 16, 25, 26–7, 29, 31, 33, 34–7,
    43, 45fig, 46, 50, 71, 76, 79, 104, 105,
    106, 132, 133, 134, 143, 145, 146, 147,
    148, 150, 154, 158–62

economic inequality, 35
    see also poverty
Edsource, 160
Eells, Rachel, 141
effect, 170
effect size, 23–6, 39–40, 91, 94, 96, 102,
    117–18
effort, 9, 10, 14, 22, 31, 32fig, 33, 34, 76, 77,
    126fig, 130, 142, 151, 160–1, 162
    see also grit; resilience
effort scores, 99–100, 101
Ehrilnger, J., 36
employment, 97
entity theories of intelligence, 8, 14, 24, 25,
    27, 36, 40, 79
errors, 120, 151, 154
    see also mistakes
ethnicity, 33fig
ethos, 40, 71, 72
eugenics, 79
evaluate yeti (younger students), 113fig
evaluation, 107
examples, 70fig
exercise, 33fig, 42–3
expectations, 24, 40, 41–2, 44, 52, 53fig, 54,
    55, 56fig, 57, 72, 73, 93, 97
expert, 19
explore yeti, 112fig
extending yeti, 109fig
extension classes, 56fig, 58fig
extraversion, 15
extrinsic motivators, 56fig, 58fig
extrinsic rewards, 144, 145, 148

failure, 5, 11, 14, 40, 68fig, 120, 123, 130,
    131, 133, 134, 135, 142, 143, 150, 151,
    154, 158–60, 164–5
    see also flopped feedback
failure zones, 126fig
failure-mindset, 68fig, 158
false sense of security, 14, 61
family traits, 53fig, 54, 55
faults, 151
feedback, 6–7, 31, 32fig, 41, 68–9fig, 91,
    129, 130, 131, 144, 151, 152, 154–7
    see also flopped feedback
feedback burger, 156
feed-down, 155
feedforward, 155
feed-up, 155
fictional characters, 44, 47
Finkel, Eli, 23–5, 39–40, 117
fixed mindset, 3–7, 8, 10, 11, 12, 15–16,
    17–19, 23, 27, 36–7, 40, 43, 52, 55, 57,
    60, 62, 80, 126fig, 142, 158

Fixed Mindset Personal (FMP), 43–7
flipped learning, 151, 162
flopped feedback, 154–7
flopped learning, 68fig, 151–2, 154, 162,
    164–5
flopped previews, 68fig, 164
flops, 151, 155, 156, 164–5
Following a Fabulous Flop, 152–3
formative assessment, 68–9fig, 73, 84, 99

Gardner, Howard, 59–60
gender, 54, 141, 143–4
general intelligence, 79, 80
genetics, 4, 34–5, 78, 79
genuineness, 149
gifted, 18–19, 42, 50, 52, 56fig, 57–8fig, 73
girls, 141, 143–4
give reasons yeti, 111fig
goals
    goal achievement, 24, 39, 40
    goal monitoring, 24
    goal operating, 24
    goal setting, 24, 40
Goddard, H.H., 79
Good, Catherine, 37
Google Docs, 91
grades, 11–12, 19, 25, 31, 32fig, 42, 51–2,
    92, 93, 96–9, 100, 144, 157
grammar, 110fig, 114fig
grit, 23, 41, 151, 160, 161–2
    see also determination
*Grit: The Power and Passion of
    Perseverance*, 161
growth mindset
    criticisms of, 33–7
    developing a growth mindset culture,
        65–73
    effect size, 23–6, 39–40, 91, 94, 96, 102,
        117–18
    influences on student achievement, 29–31
    the need for nuanced understanding, 27
    neuroscience, 36–7
    other benefits, 31–3
    over-simplification, 35
    overview of, 3–7, 8, 10, 11, 15–16
    problem of performance-focus, 27–8
    progress, 67fig, 71
    reasons for reduced impact, 26–33
    third hand knowledge, 26–7
    value of, 23

Haimovitz, K., 150, 158–60
handwriting, 90fig
Harrison, C., 157
Hattie, John, 12, 25, 26, 29, 30fig, 31, 33fig,
    34, 59, 91, 94–5, 117–18, 154
helpless strategies, 40, 41
Henderlong Corpus, Jennifer, 129–31, 132
Heyman, G.D., 128, 140, 141
hinge point, 91
home lives, 53–4, 73
houses, 101

Index

talk yeti, 111fig
targets, 107
taxes, 90fig
teacher education, 29, 30fig
teacher subject matter knowledge,
    29, 30fig
teachers, 56–8, 78
TEDx, 105–6
Telford, George, 95–6
Terman, Lewis, 79, 80
testing, 80–5
think yeti, 111fig
thinking journals, 91
Three Before Me, 152
three stars and a wish, 156
time, 28, 29
Times Educational Supplement, 29
timing, 31, 32fig
Tom Sawyer Abroad, 33
trial and error, 67fig
Twain, Mark, 33, 168

VanEpps, Eric, 23–5, 39–40, 117
Visible Learning, 12, 25, 26, 29
Visible Learning Plus, 99
visual learners, 58, 59
Vygotsky, Lev, 124

web-based learning, 30fig
wellbeing, 42, 43
Wiliam, Dylan, 25, 34, 116, 157
Williams, Robbie, 132
wobble, 17
work together yeti, 111fig
writing, 89, 92

Yeager, David Scott, 161–2
yet, 70fig, 105–14
yetis, 106–14, 122
Yinnar School, 95–6

Zhao, L., 128, 140, 141
Zone of Proximal Development, 67fig, 124

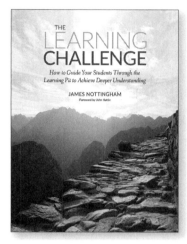
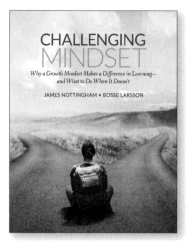
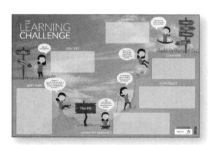
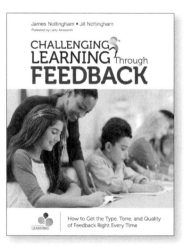

Corwin books represent the latest thinking from some of the most respected experts in PreK–12 education. We are proud of the breadth and depth of the books we publish and the authors we partner with in our mission to better serve educators and students.

Julie Stern, Nathalie Lauriault, Krista Ferraro, and Juliet Mohnkern

Harness natural curiosity for conceptual understanding!

Guy Claxton

Become mind-fit for life!

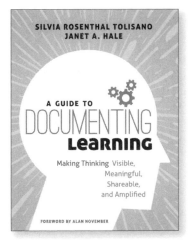

Silvia Rosenthal Tolisano and Janet A. Hale

A new approach to contemporary documentation and learning.

John Antonetti and Terri Stice

The research and strategies educators need to design engaging, powerful learning tasks.

CORWIN
A SAGE Publishing Company

A SAGE Publishing Company

Helping educators make the greatest impact

CORWIN HAS ONE MISSION: to enhance education through intentional professional learning.

We build long-term relationships with our authors, educators, clients, and associations who partner with us to develop and continuously improve the best evidence-based practices that establish and support lifelong learning.